FREDERICK DOUGLASS

Frederick Douglass was born a slave in Talbot County, Maryland, in February, 1818. From these humble beginnings, Douglass went on to become a world-famous orator, newspaper editor, and champion of the rights of women and African Americans. He was the most prominent African American activist of the nineteenth century. He remains important in American history because he moved beyond relief at his own personal freedom to dedicating his life to the progress of his race and his country.

This volume offers a short biographical exploration of Douglass' life in the broader context of the nineteenth century world, and pulls together some of his most important writings on slavery, civil rights, and political issues. *Frederick Douglass: Reformer and Statesman* gives the student of American history a fully-rounded glimpse into the world inhabited by this great figure.

L. Diane Barnes is Professor of History at Youngstown State University.

ROUTLEDGE HISTORICAL AMERICANS

SERIES EDITOR: PAUL FINKELMAN, ALBANY LAW SCHOOL

Routledge Historical Americans is a series of short, vibrant biographies that illuminate the lives of Americans who have had an impact on the world. Each book includes a short overview of the person's life and puts that person into historical context through essential primary documents, written both by the subjects and about them. A series website supports the books, containing extra images and documents, links to further research, and where possible, multi-media sources on the subjects. Perfect for including in any course on American history, the books in the Routledge Historical Americans series show the impact everyday people can have on the course of history.

Woody Guthrie: Writing America's Songs
Ronald D. Cohen

Frederick Douglass: Reformer and Statesman
L. Diane Barnes

Forthcoming:

Harry S. Truman: The Coming of the Cold War
Nicole Anslover

Sojourner Truth: Prophet of Social Justice
Isabelle Kinnard Richman

Joe Louis: Sports and Race in Twentieth Century America
Marcy Sacks

John F. Kennedy: The Burdens of Cold War Liberalism
Jason Duncan

Woodrow Wilson: Progressive President or Moral Crusader?
Kelly A. Woestman

FREDERICK DOUGLASS
REFORMER AND STATESMAN

L. DIANE BARNES

Routledge
Taylor & Francis Group

NEW YORK AND LONDON

www.routledge.com/cw/HistoricalAmericans

First published 2013
by Routledge
711 Third Avenue, New York, NY 10017

Simultaneously published in the UK
by Routledge
2 Park Square, Milton Park, Abingdon, Oxon OX14 4RN

Routledge is an imprint of the Taylor & Francis Group, an informa business

Library of Congress Cataloging in Publication Data
Barnes, L. Diane.
Frederick Douglass : reformer and statesman / by L. Diane Barnes.
p. cm.
1. Douglass, Frederick, 1818–1895. 2. Abolitionists—United States—Biography. 3. Slaves—United States—Biography. 4. Antislavery movements—United States—History—19th century. 5. Douglass, Frederick, 1818–1895—Study and teaching. I. Title.
E449.D75B37 2012
973.8092—dc23
[B]
2012012018

ISBN: 978-0-415-89111-0 (hbk)
ISBN: 978-0-415-89112-7 (pbk)

Typeset in Minion and Scala Sans
by EvS Communication Networx, Inc.

SUSTAINABLE
FORESTRY
INITIATIVE

Certified Sourcing
www.sfiprogram.org
SFI-00555
The SFI label applies to the text stock.

Printed and bound in the United States of America by
Walsworth Publishing Company, Marceline, MO.

For my California girls,
Robin Thomas Dreis and Kim Franklin

CONTENTS

PART II
Documents   103

Acknowledgments

This book was great fun to research and write, allowing me the chance to pull together many years of research into the world-view of Frederick Douglass. That journey began fifteen years ago when I first began working on the Frederick Douglass Papers and I still have much to learn. I owe a great debt to my colleagues there over the years, and especially our project editor, John R. McKivigan, who has been an important mentor and provided me the chance to gain a strong scholarly background in the world of antebellum reform. On several occasions Robin Condon saved the day by looking up facts and sending me additional material only available at the project office in Indianapolis. Thanks also goes to my friend and colleague Paul Finkelman, for inviting me to write this volume for Routledge's Historical Americans series. It's always a pleasure to work with a fine editorial staff, and Rebecca Novack and Kimberly Guinta expertly steered this project toward the finish line. I really appreciate their encouragement, and, on occasion, their patience. Thanks also to Kate Manson for her copyediting prowess and to Gail Newton for steering this book seamlessly through production.

Much of the research and writing time for this volume was provided through a year's sabbatical from Youngstown State University. I thank Shearle Furnish, Dean of the College of Liberal Arts and Social Sciences, for additional time and support for my research. Funding for research travel came through the YSU School of Graduate Studies and Research. Many colleagues in the history department offered advice and encouragement and I especially thank my department chair, Martha Pallante, and colleagues Donna DeBlasio, Mehera Gerardo, and Helene Sinnreich for being there. My capable research assistant Joni Koneval located material and dozens of photographs for the project. Last but certainly not least, my eternal gratitude to Ben Barnes for his patience and, at the end, his proof-reading skills.

INTRODUCTION

FREDERICK DOUGLASS IN AMERICAN HISTORY AND AMERICAN MEMORY

For more than half a century, Frederick Douglass was in the public eye as a reformer, statesman, and public intellectual. He championed the abolition of slavery, women's rights, black suffrage, and was a stalwart adherent to the Republican Party. Yet in his time as in ours, he was most remembered for his youth in slavery. His first autobiography, the *Narrative of the Life of Frederick Douglass, An American Slave Written by Himself* appeared in 1845 and quickly became the most widely read of dozens of similar examples of slave autobiography. Selling more than 30,000 copies by the eve of the Civil War, and appearing in nine British editions, the slim volume brought the horrors of slavery home to readers across the nation and Europe. Today, it is still the most recognizable first-hand account of American slavery and is read in literature and history classes in high schools and universities. Douglass became so closely associated with his slave narrative that he was never able to effectively overcome its popularity. Much to his consternation, his status as America's most famous former slave overshadowed all of his many accomplishments in life; but it also tempered his critics. It also clouds his place in American history and memory.

This biography aims to present a corrective by accentuating Douglass's life in freedom. Escaping slavery at the age of twenty, he lived to the ripe old age of seventy-seven, spending nearly six very productive and meaningful decades in freedom. Within ten years of his self-emancipation, he wrote his first autobiography, edited his own newspaper, and had traveled widely among the British and Irish reform communities. During the Civil

War he recruited troops for the Union Army, advised Lincoln, and in later years several other presidents, on issues of concern to African Americans. In the postwar era Douglass was a bank president, a federal marshal, and eventually served as minister (ambassador) to Haiti. Despite all of these accomplishments, the *New York Times* coverage of his sudden death in 1895 included the sub-headline, "The Slave Who Ran Away."[1] At the end of his long and unusual life, it was still his youth in slavery that captivated audiences and the public.

Although the chapters that follow begin with Douglass's enslavement, his career as a reformer, statesman, and race leader take priority. They trace his accomplishments and challenges as he navigated the world of nineteenth century reform and politics. Beginning his career as an abolitionist lecturer just three years after escaping slavery, Douglass had much to learn from the white and black reformers who tutored him. Within a decade, however, he began to forge his own path, becoming a leader of African American civil rights and an advocate of his own brand of reform. Although he maintained close associations with his early mentors, Douglass often found himself at odds with both white and black reform leaders, including William Lloyd Garrison and Martin R. Delany. In later years his continued espousal of interracial cooperation and loyalty to the Republican Party made his ideas contentious among African Americans. In exploring his activities as a reformer, race leader, and statesman, Douglass emerges here as a complicated man who struggled to forge a unique path through life. His controversial leadership style often found him in conflict with other prominent blacks, but he always stood up against those who oppressed African Americans. At the end of his life, whether they esteemed or detested him, nearly every American knew his name and recognized his face.

The most familiar African American in the nineteenth century, Douglass's place in historical consciousness, even as a fugitive slave, declined during the nadir of American race relations at the turn of the twentieth century, which was well underway even before his death in 1895. A series of setbacks and legal decisions in the 1870s and 1880s pushed back many of the civil rights gains of the Reconstruction Era. The Supreme Court's narrow interpretation of the Fourteenth Amendment in the *Slaughterhouse Cases* (1873) paved the way for southern conservatives to ignore federal guarantees for African American citizenship. A decade later, the Supreme Court dismantled the 1875 Civil Rights Act which, although not always enforced, provided broad protection against discrimination in public accommodations and employment practices. Then in the year following Douglass's death, the Supreme Court's ruling in *Plessy v. Ferguson* (1896) dealt a final death blow to black civil rights by declaring that

Figure 1 Distinguished Colored Men. This widely distributed lithograph from 1883 shows Frederick Douglass as the most prominent leader of his race.
Source: Courtesy of the Library of Congress, LC-DIG-pga-02252

segregation of the races in transportation and other areas of public life was legal so long as facilities were "separate but equal." States and localities across the South followed up with a series of regulations and ordinances, known as Jim Crow laws after a popular black-faced character in minstrel shows. This system of oppression quickly pushed African Americans firmly into second-class citizenship. Throughout the South they lost the right to vote, were educated in inferior schools, and were excluded from restaurants and hotels. From the onset of Jim Crow segregation across the South, through the middle years of the twentieth century, the image of a strong black man like Douglass who had openly challenged the system was hardly popular. More conciliatory leaders, such as Booker T. Washington, emerged to urge American blacks to move slowly on civil rights demands and to pull themselves up through hard work and manual arts education.[2] During the difficult half century that followed, except to a handful of African American scholars working outside the mainstream, Douglass's life and legacy fell dormant.[3]

Following World War II, the consensus historians, who emphasized the unity of an American historical narrative largely devoid of ideological conflict, simply ignored strong African Americans, including Douglass. Headed by the likes of Columbia University's Richard Hofstadter, the University of Chicago's Daniel Borstein, and Stanford's David Potter, their focus was on American political leaders and therefore their writings included little emphasis on women or minorities. Americans schooled before the 1960s were fed a chronological narrative about U.S. presidents and the triumph of American progress. If African Americans appeared in textbooks, it was to emphasize the benevolent nature of slavery and segregation that sheltered an inferior population unable to stand on their own without white guidance. A leading textbook published in the 1930s, and used for the next two decades, began its chapter on slavery with the words "And now for Sambo."[4] Considering the climate and dominant historical interpretation it is not surprising then that one historian recently noted that Douglass's familiarity to the American public is a fairly recent phenomenon. Although perhaps an exaggeration, he contends that most Americans over the age of fifty, including highly educated ones, hardly recognize his name.[5]

Then in the 1960s, shifts in the way historians study history, and in the way students learn it, moved Douglass and other minorities back into the national consciousness. Inspired by the activism of the civil rights and other social movements, scholars sought a more inclusive lens through which to view the nation's past. Examining history from the "bottom up" meant using sources produced by the lower reaches of society. Census records, court documents, and personal letters and diaries were employed to understand the roles of workers, women and slaves, and free blacks. To gain a new perspective on slavery, social historians looked away from the plantation ledgers and journals of slaveholders, turning instead to personal accounts of enslavement contained in dozens of narratives and autobiographies written by former slaves. This social history revolution of the

1960s and 1970s brought the history of African Americans, women, and other minorities to the fore of historical study, and helped restore Frederick Douglass in our collective memory. Although he wrote three autobiographies across his lifetime, his 1845 *Narrative* became a prime source cited in nearly every historical account of slavery since 1970.

Douglass's national revival as a historical figure was strongly debated among late twentieth-century activists and scholars, who sometimes found his leadership disappointing. His willingness to challenge the system and to demand equal rights for his race and for women, but also cooperate across race lines, seemed to beg a comparison between his leadership style and that of modern civil rights leaders, including Martin Luther King, Jr., Malcolm X, and others. Viewed through a twentieth-century lens, Douglass was condemned as a race traitor and a "sell-out" and subsequently celebrated as a "great American." Exploring these reassessments of Douglass, one scholar notes that what confounded many modern activists is a misunderstanding of Douglass's role as an interracial mediator. A determined advocate of a third space between the races, according to Gregory Stephens, Douglass espoused an antiracialism that guided his interactions with both whites and blacks. Although he was able to occupy a "third space," those around him and those reflecting on his life and actions did not fully understand his motives.[6] Douglass was not the only race leader to come under recent scrutiny. The leadership style of Booker T. Washington, whose public persona is described by his recent biographer as a "bargainer, a compromiser, and a conciliator," suited an earlier time and seems weak and ineffectual in the modern United States.[7] So too did some scholars find Douglass's willingness to work across the color line and his deep attachment to the idea of America as the rightful home for blacks a potential weakness. But unlike Washington, whose legacy suffered from his accommodationist philosophy, Douglass emerged from the scholarly debate as an American icon. Both men were included in *Atlantic Monthly*'s list of the top one hundred Americans in 2006, with Douglass placing forty-seventh, and Washington coming in at number ninety-eight.[8]

Although still somewhat controversial, in the post-civil rights era a strong and defiant Douglass was resurrected to reclaim his rightful place as the most well-known African American of the nineteenth century. A leading intellect of his era, the voluminous number of pages he left behind provided a treasure trove for scholars. Modern editions of his three autobiographies were printed, and at least three biographies of his life appeared. Demonstrating that his historical importance stretches far beyond his first slave narrative, a project dedicated to the publication of a modern, scholarly edition of his writings and speeches was begun in 1973, and today continues to produce volumes of his correspondence and autobiographies.

His prolific writings make him the most cited African American. A scholar at a recent conference was overheard to proclaim, "when in doubt, quote Douglass." Indeed, modern Americans, even famous ones, like to do just that. George W. Bush invoked his name during an African visit in 2003, and Supreme Court Justice Clarence Thomas has quoted Douglass in several rulings. More recently, in his own narrative of an exceptional life, President Barack Obama upheld him as a leader "who recognized power would concede nothing without a fight," using an allusion to a line from one of Douglass's most famous orations.[9] The most recent volume on Douglass is a quotation book, ensuring that his phrases will continue to populate literature and popular writings.[10] Scholars, politicians, and students of literature and history read his words, but communities and the public at large also embrace Douglass as an icon of black accomplishment.

Since the 1970s' revival, Douglass has been a dominant figure in both American history and American culture. In fact, modern Americans find constant reminders of his presence and importance. Part of his prominence links to the prolific trail of writings he left or inspired. A search of the card catalog at the Library of Congress, for example, reveals more than 10,000 items related to or written by Douglass. A Google search turns up more than six million references. His image is also spread in the national consciousness through cultural references. Statues to him stand in public places in Harlem, Rochester, and outside the New York Historical Society. Most recently, following an extended controversy, in July 2011 a statue of Douglass was erected before the Easton, Maryland court house, in the very town where as a slave he was jailed following a failed escape attempt. More than two dozen schools, academies, and public buildings bear his name. Streets or boulevards in diverse places such as Harlem, Detroit, and Oklahoma City are named for him, and even a bridge in the nation's capital pays homage to his legacy. Cedar Hill, Douglass's home in Washington, D.C. is a National Park Service site visited by thousands each year, and he has twice been honored on a U.S. postage stamp. He appears as a character in novels by Miriam Grace Monfredo and Jewel Parker Rhodes, in the movie *Glory*, and has been the subject of the poetry of Paul Laurence Dunbar and Robert Hayden. The artist Jacob Lawrence produced a series of thirty-two canvases depicting Douglass's life and celebrating his memory.

What makes Douglass such an enduring symbol in American history and memory? One answer lies in his embodiment of the American dream. If that can be defined as hard work and achievement in the face of adversity, then Douglass's life story resonates. Born enslaved, he effected his own escape and subsequently built an exceptional life. Among the four million men and women who suffered under slavery, attaining freedom was a momentous achievement. Relatively few slaves made it to freedom before the Civil War, but for Douglass his self-emancipation was merely a starting point. It is his life in freedom, not his enslavement, that makes him an important part of American history. Within years of gaining freedom he had published a narrative of his life, and become one of the most widely recognized orators in the United States and Great Britain. In 1848 he stood as the lone male delegate in support of woman suffrage at the Seneca Falls Convention on women's rights. When the Civil War erupted, he sprang into action as an advocate for African Americans, free and enslaved. Moving his family to Washington after the war, he held minor federal appointments, and eventually a diplomatic post. Ending his life in his twenty-one room mansion in 1895, he had traversed a social distance farther than seems humanly possible from the Maryland slave cabin in which he was born.[11]

In recent decades Douglass has become a symbol of black achievement and a cultural icon, but has also come under considerable criticism from both scholars and popular audiences. He made a life-long commitment to biracial cooperation in his reform activities, and continued to adhere to the Republican Party even when it abandoned its push for civil rights and black equality. The exceptional life he built after shaking off the adversity of slavery inspires those reading his words and studying his life even today. His remarkable life story has much to teach us about history, race relations, and human nature. If he could achieve so much after his most humble of beginnings, perhaps it is still possible for the rest of us to realize the American dream. Whether he is beloved for taking a stand against the system, or criticized for compromising and cooperating with white oppressors, Douglass stands as a ubiquitous reminder of the nation's historical past.

PART **I**

FREDERICK DOUGLASS

CHAPTER 1

Twenty Years in Bondage

When he was born in February 1818, Frederick Augustus Washington Bailey could not have known that he was destined to become the most famous African American of the nineteenth century, but the name his mother bestowed upon him suggested he was fated for a life outside of slavery. It took twenty years before Harriet Bailey's son broke the bonds that held him in slavery, first on Maryland's Eastern Shore and later in the shipbuilding city of Baltimore. The fourth of Harriet's six or seven children, Frederick's birth is recorded in his owner's business ledger, but the day was not noted. Not having access to that record, Frederick later adopted February 14 to mark his birthday, but believed all his life that he was born a year earlier in 1817.[1] Uncertainty about early life was common among the enslaved. In his first autobiography Frederick recalled "I do not remember to ever have met a slave who could tell his birthday."[2] Although he shared this ambiguity about his origins with other slaves, his years in bondage were in many ways as exceptional as his life in freedom.

A slave owned by Aaron Anthony, Frederick's mother spent her entire life working as a field hand. She was the daughter of a free black sawyer named Isaac Bailey and his wife Betsey, another Anthony slave. The chief overseer and general manager of thirteen farms owned by the wealthy Lloyd family of Talbot County, Maryland, Anthony amassed three farms and thirty slaves of his own. It is likely that a number of those slaves, including Frederick, were his own children. As was common after labor-intensive tobacco cultivation shifted toward food crops in the early nineteenth century Chesapeake, Harriet spent most of her adult life hired out to smaller farms surrounding the Eastern Shore's large plantations. For 1818 and subsequent years, Anthony hired her to work for Perry Stewart, a tenant farmer on Anthony's Holme Hill Farm, along Tuckahoe Creek. It was there that Frederick was born.

The long hours his mother spent in the field precluded caring for an infant, so Frederick was soon sent to live with his maternal grandmother, Betsey Bailey. Residing in her own cabin with her husband Isaac, Betsey cared for many of Anthony's enslaved children and although enslaved, she received pay for her special services as a midwife to the greater plantation community. Under Betsey's care, Frederick and the other slave children too young to work were temporarily sheltered from the realities of slavery. They played together along the streams and fields that dotted Talbot County and wondered about the mysterious "Old Master" of which their elders spoke. Frederick's earliest family memories are of his grandmother, recalling later seeing his mother only on four or five occasions. Holme Hill Farm was nearly twelve miles from the Bailey cabin and Harriet rarely had the energy to walk the entire distance and back after a full day's work. She died in 1825 after a long illness, leaving seven-year-old Frederick and his siblings with few memories: "Never having enjoyed, to any considerable extent, her soothing presence, her tender and watchful care, I received the tidings of her death with much the same emotions I should have probably felt at the death of a stranger."[3]

Several months before learning of his mother's death, Frederick became acutely aware of his status as a slave and learned firsthand why the other slaves whispered about "Old Master." One morning his grandmother tied a bandana about her hair, packed a little cornbread in her pocket and told Frederick he would accompany her on a long journey. Unbeknownst to the boy, it was time for him to join Anthony's other slaves at his home farm on the Wye River, about a dozen miles from the Bailey cabin on Tuckahoe Creek. Although then in her early fifties, Betsey Bailey was a strong woman, occasionally carrying Frederick on her shoulder when his legs grew tired from the long walk. Passing fields and woods, the pair finally approached the tall ornamental gate marking the half-mile lane leading to the great Wye House plantation, where Aaron Anthony acted as chief overseer and manager. Owned then by Edward Lloyd V, the plantation encompassed nearly 12,000 acres and nearly two hundred slaves toiled in Lloyd's fields. The Lloyd family operated a plantation on the location from at least the 1660s, and the great house Frederick saw for the first time that day was constructed about 1785.[4]

Betsey led Frederick away from the great white mansion and past the main slave quarters, ice house, carpenter shop, and other buildings dotting the lawn known as the Long Green to a plain red-brick house. The home of his master included a separate kitchen building where Anthony's own slaves lived and worked.[5] Soon surrounded by children of all ages and sizes, Betsey introduced Frederick to his brother Perry, sisters Sarah and Eliza, and a number of cousins. Somewhat overwhelmed, he recalled, "Brothers and sisters we were by blood; but *slavery* had made us strangers." Unsure what to do, he stood back while the others played together. Before long Frederick realized that his grandmother was gone and he burst into tears, pushing off his sisters' attempts at comfort. In later writings he recounted the incident in minute detail, remembering clearly what he called his "first introduction to the realities of slavery."[6]

For the next two years Frederick lived on the Wye House plantation with Anthony's other slaves. Old enough to perform only minor tasks, however, he and the other slave children received little care and attention. Although Maryland winters could get quite cold, Frederick had only a coarse linen shirt to cover his body, and no shoes or pants. In warmer months the children ran about nearly naked, especially once the two shirts they were given each year became worn. Sleeping on the floor among the other slaves, Frederick recalled fighting with the group of children to claim his share of the tasteless gruel served up in a trough in the same fashion as pig slop. Subservient to all on the plantation, enslaved children negotiated a careful path through each day. Penalties for minor infractions could make life even more miserable as Frederick soon learned when he somehow offended his master's enslaved cook, who once refused to feed him for a full day.

From his small vantage point in the slave quarters, he learned what it meant to be a slave. He absorbed events that later became fodder for his abolitionist orations and filled the pages of three autobiographies. He gained a special disdain for the series of overseers his old master hired to manage one or more of the Lloyd farms. One overseer, Austin Gore, notoriously shot a slave named Demby for refusing to obey an order. Another, a cruel drunkard named Mr. Plummer, severely beat his Aunt Hester just a short time after Frederick came to Wye House. The aptly named William Sevier stood outside the slave quarters' door each morning with a hickory switch, hitting any slave late for work in the field.[7] The shelter of the Bailey cabin had not prepared Frederick for the cruelty of the plantation and from the moment Betsey left his side he hoped for some way out of the nightmare that was slavery.

Life-altering events in 1826 set Frederick's life on a unique path, taking him away from the plantation before he was old enough for field work. During the two years he spent at Wye House, he had few duties save helping to drive the cows in at night and keeping the farm animals out of the house gardens. Perhaps recognizing something special in the boy's intelligence and demeanor, Aaron Anthony chose him from among the several enslaved children he owned to travel to Baltimore to live in the household of his daughter's brother-in-law. Anthony had two sons and a daughter, Lucretia Planner Anthony Auld. She married Thomas Auld, a shipbuilder and captain of Edward Lloyd's personal sloop. Frederick was sent to live with his brother, Hugh Auld, who worked as shipbuilder in Baltimore. Excited at the prospect of his big adventure, eight-year-old Frederick was cleaned up and given trousers for the first time in his life. Sailing aboard the Lloyd sloop for the city early on a Saturday morning, he reflected later "I left without a regret, and with the highest hopes of future happiness."[8]

Docking at the Fell's Point wharf Sunday morning, Frederick was escorted to his new home on Aliceanna Street, all the way gawking at the sights, sounds, and smells of the city. Everything was new and amazing to a small boy raised in the shelter of the Eastern Shore. Reaching the small and slightly shabby frame house that would be his new home, he was welcomed by Hugh and Sophia Auld, and their two-year-old son, Tommy. He learned that his main duty would be to act as a companion to the toddler, and Frederick found being kind to the sweet, small boy easy for he had "already fallen in love with the dear boy." He later wrote that removal to Baltimore proved to be an important, and perhaps the most critical, turning point in his exceptional life: "but for the mere circumstance of being thus removed before the rigors of slavery had fastened upon me; before my young spirit had been crushed under the iron control of the slave driver, instead of today being a FREEMAN, I might have been wearing the galling chains of slavery."[9]

The Aulds had no previous experience as slave masters and initially treated him as their own child. For the first two of the seven years he spent with the Aulds, Frederick was mostly left in the care of Sophia Auld. He adored his new mistress for her kindness, enjoying the affection she bestowed upon him. Seeing his eagerness to learn, she began teaching Frederick the alphabet and the basics of reading, and for a short time he nearly forgot that he was a slave. When Hugh Auld learned of his wife's transgression, however, the lessons promptly ceased. Maryland law forbade teaching slaves to read and write, he told her, and besides, teaching a slave to read was dangerous: "he should know nothing but the will of his master, and learn to obey it."[10] But the seed of knowledge was already planted in Frederick, and his master's determination to keep him ignorant made him even more eager to learn. In future months he tried a number of schemes to increase his literacy, even tricking or bribing white boys in the neighborhood into helping him in his quest.

The reality of slavery came crashing down on Frederick soon thereafter, following the death of Aaron Anthony. For a brief time it seemed he might be returned to rural Maryland, a very frightening prospect for one already accustomed to city life and kind treatment. At his old master's passing in November 1826, in accordance with Maryland law he and the other Anthony slaves were assessed as property in his considerable estate, valued at more than $8,000. In October of the following year, he was called to Talbot County for appraisal and the official dividing of the estate. When Hugh Auld set off with Frederick for the wharf, Sophia Auld burst into tears, for she knew something her young slave did not. Lucretia Anthony Auld had died following her father, and while her part of the estate would fall to her husband Thomas, there was a chance that Frederick would be assigned to one of Anthony's surviving sons. With no family link to the Aulds, there was little reason to believe that either would have reason to return the nine-year-old boy to them in Baltimore. In one of the cruel certainties of slavery, Frederick watched as his brother, sisters, and cousins were valued and divided along with the others, totaling thirty men, women, and children. Sarah and Perry Bailey were allotted to Andrew Anthony. Sarah and her son were subsequently sold to a slaveholder in Mississippi. After Perry's wife was sold to a Texas planter, he somehow managed to follow her. Frederick saw neither for many years to come. At the end of the day fortune smiled on him again, and he and his sister Eliza fell into the lot awarded to Thomas Auld. By November he was safe back home in Baltimore, where he remained for the next five years.[11]

When little Tommy began attending public school, Frederick was put to work running errands and doing odd jobs at Auld and Harrison's shipyard. Spending considerable time away from the watchful eye of Sophia Auld, he began to investigate the limited freedom many urban slaves enjoyed. Baltimore held more free blacks than slaves, and Frederick began exploring the larger African American community where free men and women mingled with their enslaved counterparts. In this urban setting, working-class whites and blacks intermingled at work and in some social settings. Always eager to learn, he paid attention to his surroundings, and carefully studied the ship carpenters' mathematical scrawls and queried his white friends about their school days. In his spare moments Frederick worked out his letters, found in a worn edition of Webster's spelling book, and surreptitiously borrowed Tommy's copy books. From a group of white boys he learned about a school book called *The Columbian Orator*, and purchased a copy with fifty cents he earned from shining boots and other odd jobs. Compiled in its first edition in 1797 by Caleb Bingham, the book included the texts of famous speeches by the likes of Cato, George Washington, William Pitt, and others. Studying the orations celebrating democracy, freedom, and liberty, the book became immensely important to Frederick's future. Writing of its influence, he recalled, "The reading of these speeches added much to my limited stock of language, and enabled me to give tongue to many interesting thoughts, which had frequently flashed through my soul, and died away for want of utterance. … [From these speeches] I got a bold and powerful denunciation of oppression, and a most brilliant vindication of the rights of man."[12]

As he grew into his early teen years, now literate and experienced in the ways of the city, Frederick's world was about to undergo another upheaval. In the early 1830s, Hugh Auld's fortune waned, and he reportedly turned to the bottle. Facing the pressures of motherhood and of her husband's misfortune Sophia Auld was no longer the kind and gentle mistress he had once adored. Still, Frederick knew that his life in Baltimore placed him in a more advantageous situation than the rural life of his siblings. Although he was still a slave, he enjoyed some free time away from the Aulds' scrutiny and came to know many in the city's black community. He had almost forgotten his legal owner was Thomas, not Hugh Auld. The truth of his situation came crashing home, however, in March 1833. A quarrel between the Auld brothers over another slave ended with Thomas ordering Frederick removed from his brother's custody. With little warning he was placed aboard the Lloyd sloop *Amanda* and returned to his legal master on the Eastern Shore.[13]

Frederick soon longed for the easier life he had enjoyed in Baltimore, finding his real master to be pitiless and unkind. Thomas Auld, now a general store operator in the town of St. Michaels, was a miser in comparison to his brother, providing few provisions so that his slaves were often hungry. He found himself reunited with his sister Eliza, cousin Henny, and aunt Priscilla. The four shared the floor of Auld's small kitchen and less than a bushel of corn meal a week. Accustomed to kind treatment and to spending much time away from his master, he immediately clashed with both Thomas Auld and his wife Rowena. Disparaging Auld in his first autobiography, Frederick proclaimed, "he was mean; and, like most other mean men, he lacked the ability to contain his meanness." Although Auld was a devout Methodist, Frederick found his master used his religion to defend his cruelty as a slaveholder. Following a religious conversion in the early 1830s, Auld became a class leader and exhorter, or lay preacher, in the Methodist Church, but apparently his Christianity did not make him a kinder slave master. Frederick witnessed Auld whip a slave woman until she bled, and then paraphrase scripture to justify the act: "He that knoweth his master's will, and doeth it not, shall be beaten with many stripes."[14] Rooted in these youthful experiences, the hypocrisy of pious slave masters later occupied many of his speeches and writings.

It was soon clear to all that Frederick's years in Baltimore did nothing to prepare him for life on the Eastern Shore, and despite his sister's attempts to help him adjust, he chafed at the closer bonds of rural slavery. He worked half-heartedly and carelessly, purposely allowing Auld's horse to escape to his father-in-law's house, where Frederick knew he would be offered extra food when he came to retrieve it. Ill-suited for and unaccustomed to farm labor, Frederick's insolence was a shock to his master, who proclaimed that city life "had had a pernicious effect" upon him.[15]

Hoping to bring him into full control and use, Auld leased Frederick to Edward Covey, a local small farmer with a reputation for breaking the will of strong-minded slaves. Slave hiring usually meant an annual contract beginning in January, and helped spread the institution of slavery to those outside the planter class. Small farmers who could not afford to purchase many slaves often leased their labor and in many cases worked alongside them in the fields. Originally a poor tenant farmer in Talbot County, Covey's reputation as a slave breaker provided him slave labor at a discount in return for teaching slaves proper discipline. Frederick's year on Covey's farm, which began in January 1834, proved to be perhaps the most remarkable year in the young slave's life, and certainly his harshest. It was the first time in his sixteen years that he toiled at the physical farm labor that characterized most slaves' experiences. The prospect of becoming a field hand was not one that he relished or one that he planned to adapt to despite Covey's concerted effort at breaking his willful spirit.[16]

"I was now, for the first time in my life, a field hand," Frederick wrote of his time at Covey's farm. Walking the seven miles or so from his master's house he arrived at a weather-beaten and unpainted house along the shore. Covey rented a farm of about 150 acres that was hardly impressive. When he arrived, the household included several of Covey's relatives, an enslaved woman named Caroline, and another leased slave, Bill Smith. Frederick worked harder than ever before from his first days on the farm, cutting and hauling wood, and attending to other manual chores about the property. His first beating at the hands of Covey happened a week later. On a bitter January morning, his new master ordered Frederick to take an oxen team and cart into the woods to haul a load of firewood. His urban experiences did nothing to prepare him for handling a team of draft animals, so it is not surprising that a terrified Frederick lost control of the animals, upsetting the cart. Somehow managing to put it right again and eventually return with the wood, an enraged Covey nevertheless ordered him to strip for a beating. With a switch cut from a nearby tree, he flogged the willful teenager. His year with Covey was to be a long one: he later wrote, "during the first six months, of that year, scarce a week passed without his whipping me."[17]

Covey's determination to force Frederick into submission somewhat ironically led Frederick to physically assert himself for the first time. At sixteen, he had nearly reached his full height of just over six feet and was lean and muscular. By summer, he was even stronger from hard work and was growing more insolent by the day. On an especially hot day in August, Covey set Frederick, Bill Smith, and two other laborers to fanning wheat, a physical process separating the usable kernels from the chaff, or waste. Ill from heat or perhaps a virus, Frederick collapsed in the yard in plain view of Covey, who kicked and beat him severely. Bruised and bleeding, he managed to travel to Auld's house, appealing to him for mercy, but was immediately sent back to Covey's farm. However, if his master believed the cruel slave breaker was succeeding in bending Frederick's willful nature, he was mistaken. Realizing that violence was his only defense, the next time Covey tried to whip him, Frederick fought back and was victorious. In an extended wrestling match witnessed by the other household slaves, Frederick and Covey clashed until the slave breaker gave up. That he was not punished for lashing out against a white man was likely due to the damage such a charge might do to Covey's reputation as a slave breaker. Remaining on the farm for the rest of 1834, Frederick was never again beaten or whipped. Recounting his battle with Covey on numerous occasions during his life in freedom, Frederick counted it as "the turning-point in my career as a slave … [H]owever long I might remain a slave in form, the day had passed forever when I could be a slave in fact."[18] Frederick was already planning his life in freedom, although he would not escape slavery for four more years.

For the following two years, Auld leased Frederick to William Freeland, another small farmer in the St. Michaels area. He found his new situation greatly improved, having at least gained familiarity with farm and field work during his year with Covey. Although not a wealthy man, Freeland had a kind nature and Frederick later recalled him as "quite preferable to any master I ever had."[19] While there, Frederick began operating a Sabbath (Sunday) school for other slaves in the area. Held at the home of a free black man on the only day slaves enjoyed off from work each week, the meetings were attended by a growing number of people who desperately wanted to learn to read. Pleased as he was to be helping his fellow slaves, Frederick soon began to plan for his escape from slavery, remarking, "by this time I began to want to live *upon free land* as well as with *Freeland*."[20]

Before long he conceived of a plan to leave the Eastern Shore. Bringing five other slaves from Freeland's and surrounding farms into the plot, the group aimed to appropriate a large canoe that a local farmer used to gather oysters. Although none had a solid sense of navigation, they were determined that following the North Star would lead them eventually to a free state, hopefully Pennsylvania. One of the conspirators, Sandy Jenkins, dropped out, but Frederick and the others prepared to set out at the end of their half work-day on April 2, 1836, the day before Easter. Since slaves would enjoy an extended weekend for the holiday, Frederick hoped that they would be long gone before anyone noticed their absence. It was not to be. In the morning as he rose for work, William Freeland and several constables confronted Frederick about the escape plot. Someone, probably another slave hoping his or her telling would put them in favor with their master, revealed the plan. Although all had been sworn to secrecy, such an ambitious plot could hardly remain a secret in the network of the slave community. Frederick and two other slaves on the Freeland farm, John and Henry Harris, as well as two from a neighboring farm, were arrested and jailed in Easton, Maryland.[21]

During the fifteen-mile journey to town, Frederick managed to communicate with his co-conspirators, convincing them to swallow the forged free passes he had penned for each man. Arriving at the jail, all were terrified, with good reason. Frederick remembered that within minutes of their incarceration, agents for several slave traders came to inquire if they were for sale. In addition to holding those accused of crimes, southern jails acted as holding pens for the regional slave trade. Traders paid jailers room and board to house enslaved men, women and even children so that they could transact additional business unencumbered. Along with the other Chesapeake states, Maryland's agricultural diversification decreased the demand for slave labor, and thousands of slaves were sold to the expanding cotton regions of the Lower South. Regional slave traders, such as Austin Woolfolk, were notoriously and rightly feared within the slave community. Basing his operations in Baltimore, it is estimated that each year Woolfolk transported between 230 and 460 slaves from the Upper South to market in New Orleans. Many came from the Eastern Shore, and recalcitrant slaves who rebelled or ran away were especially liable to sale.[22] Like most slaves in the region, Frederick had experienced the separation of his family through the slave trade. His fear of being sent to the Deep South, where slavery on the cotton plantations was harsh and chances of escape were diminished, was legitimate.

Jailed in Easton with his companions for the weekend, Frederick found himself alone after the holiday when William Freeland and the master of the other two men took them home. Certain that as the chief conspirator he would soon be sold South, he found once again that his life was about to take another unexpected turn. Instead of placing him in the hands of a slave trader's agent, when Thomas Auld came to claim him he sent him back to Baltimore to live again with his brother. Frederick would never be much use as a field hand, he reasoned, and his presence among the rural slave community made him a danger to the fragile control Auld and his fellow masters had over their workforce. Thus, at eighteen, he returned home to the city, where within a week Hugh Auld arranged that he be hired to Fell's Point shipbuilder William Gardiner to learn the trade of a caulker.

Returning to Baltimore after almost three years on the Eastern Shore, Frederick was more determined than ever to gain his freedom. Following his failed escape attempt, Thomas Auld promised to emancipate him when he reached twenty-five if he was patient and behaved himself properly, but Frederick had no patience. Instead, as he became reacquainted with the city, he sought opportunities and collaborations that would help him reach freedom in the North. At Gardiner's shipyard he hoped to learn a skill that would provide a living once he was free, but spent most of his apprenticeship fetching and carrying for the carpenters, and on odd jobs. He also learned that Baltimore's slave society did not well tolerate slaves who asserted themselves. In the mixed workplace of the waterfront, whites, free blacks and slaves all worked together, and although relations were generally smooth, racial tensions sometimes flared. The workplace conflicts that kept blacks out of many skilled jobs in northern cities were less common in the South, but when financial panic or strain struck in Baltimore workers objected to competition from blacks. Nearly eight months into his apprenticeship, the white carpenters at Gardiner's yard walked off the job, refusing to work alongside the black ship carpenters, many of whom were free men. Powerless to confront their employers, the economic tensions and distress experienced by all the skilled carpenters led many whites to lash out at their fellow black workers. Animosity then spread among the white apprentices who refused to work with Frederick. An argument soon turned violent. Vowing to stand on his own after his fight with Covey, Frederick struck back when one of the white boys attacked him. Shocked at such insolence on the part of a slave, the whole group of apprentices fell upon him, armed with stones, bricks, and boards. The severe beating that followed left him bruised and bleeding, nearly losing one eye.

Recalling later that a crowd of white men stood by cheering as he was beaten, the violent attack shook his faith in his ability to navigate the city. Managing to get away and return home, he related the events to his master. Unlike his brother, who had turned a cold shoulder to Frederick's mistreatment at the hands of Covey, Hugh Auld was furious. Sophia once again took pity on him, cleaning his wounds and dressing his head. Auld tried to press charges, but none of the white witnesses corroborated Frederick's account and Maryland law forbade black testimony against whites. The Baltimore of his youth had turned, it seemed, into a virulent and dangerous place for African Americans. No white was willing to testify on a slave's behalf, as he later wrote, because to do so would be to place themselves in peril, "for just at that time, the slightest manifestation of humanity towards a colored person was denounced as abolitionism, and that name subjected its bearer to frightful liabilities. The watchwords of the bloody-minded in that region, and in those days, were 'Damn the abolitionists!' and 'Damn the niggers!'."[23] Another in the amazing series of events that characterized his enslavement, his beating at the hands of the white apprentices provided more fodder for later abolitionist lectures and inflamed his growing desire to break the bonds of slavery.

Removing him from Gardiner's shipyard, Auld found Frederick a place at the Fell's Point shipyard of Walter Price. Having lost his own business several years before, Auld worked as Price's foreman and therefore could keep a watchful eye on him. Under his master's tutelage, Frederick finally gained proficiency at the caulker's trade, learning to skillfully patch a ship's hull so that no water would leak inside. He took pride in his trade, but would have been dismayed to learn that at least three of the Baltimore schooners on which he worked in 1837 were used in the illegal slave trade.[24] Within a year, his skills were in high demand and he was earning six and seven dollars a week, and on occasion as high as nine dollars. However, his earnings were not his own, but all paid to his master. His anger at the unfairness of the slave system that deprived him of the money he had rightfully earned burned ever brighter. In his second narrative of his enslavement he wrote: "it was not long before I began to show signs of disquiet with slavery, and to look around for means to get out of that condition by the shortest route."[25]

In seeking to get the most earnings from Frederick's labor, Hugh Auld's greed may have provided the final factor that made his escape from slavery possible. Realizing that Frederick could earn more if he made his own contracts and collected his earnings, Auld allowed him to find his own lodgings as well. Although technically illegal in Maryland and most of the slave South, many urban slaves "lived out," enjoying the freedom to work and socialize as they saw fit so long as they turned over their weekly wages to their masters. Frederick's own arrangement was to pay Auld three dollars every week and use the remainder for room and board and caulking tools. This quasi-freedom gave Frederick control of his free time and he used it wisely to make important connections in the city's African American community, but it also drove him to work hard to earn enough for both his board and his master's share so that he could continue to arrange his own time.

Mingling with mostly free blacks, he joined a church and a debating society, where he spent hours reading and discussing contemporary issues, including the abolition of slavery. He continued to improve his literacy under the guidance of his more educated friends, and honed his public speaking ability. Several years before being removed to the Eastern Shore he had attended the Bethel African Methodist Church, but in the year before his escape he abandoned it for the Sharp Street African Methodist Episcopal Church because the former did not endorse abolition. He took up music, somehow learning to play the violin in his spare time. He also began to study escape routes, eyeing the newly connected northbound railroad, on which a calculating slave might simply ride toward freedom.

One week he stretched his quasi-freedom a bit too far, badly miscalculating his master's leniency, and making escape even more necessary. Determined to join some friends at a weekend religious camp meeting some twelve miles from the city, he put off paying Auld until his return to Baltimore. Working late at the shipyard on Saturday, and not wanting to delay his friends, Frederick headed off to the camp meeting, staying the entire weekend. Finally appearing at Auld's door with his three dollars on Monday night, he found his master in a rage. "Now, you scoundrel!" Auld shouted, "You have done for yourself; you shall hire your time no longer. The next thing I shall hear of, will be your running away. Bring home your tools and your clothes, at once."[26] He was immediately ordered into the house, where an irate Frederick considered striking out at him. Instead he sulked about the house, refusing to work and weighing his master's threats of a beating or worse. Realizing "resistance to him could not have ended so happily," and that his conduct was "more folly than wisdom," he finally relented and returned to work. For the next few weeks Auld demanded all of Frederick's wages. At the end of the second week he brought his master nine dollars and was rewarded with twenty-five cents and the admonition to spend it wisely. He later recalled, "I told him I would, for one of the uses to which I meant to put it, was to pay my fare on the underground railroad."[27] While outwardly appearing submissive and remorseful, Frederick was making definite plans to escape.

CHAPTER 2

BUILDING A FREE LIFE

Implementing a well-organized plan, on September 3, 1838 Frederick Bailey began his life as a free man. In order to protect those who aided his escape from slavery, he did not reveal the details until late in life, describing it fully only in his final autobiography. On that Monday morning, disguised as one of the many sailors mingling on Baltimore's wharves, he boarded a train bound for Wilmington, Delaware. In case he was stopped, he carried free papers borrowed from an African American sailor. In the South, blacks were required to carry proof of their free status, and sailors, who often traveled between states and at sea, were issued special documentation that permitted travel across state lines. Because the papers described a man physically very different from himself, Bailey was transported directly to the segregated "negro car" by black cart driver Isaac Rolls. He hoped that with the jostle and business of the departing train purchasing a ticket from the conductor would bring less scrutiny than approaching a ticket window in the station. He was right: only the most cursory attention was given to his documentation. Still, it was a harrowing journey involving changing to a ferry and then a Philadelphia-bound steamboat once he reached Wilmington. He began to breathe a little easier when he reached Philadelphia, where he boarded a train at the Willow Street station for New York City. Arriving Tuesday morning, less than twenty-four hours after leaving Baltimore, Frederick Bailey had navigated his own way across the Underground Railroad.

Arrangements for his successful escape took some three weeks to prepare. Central to the plot was Bailey's fiancée, Anna Murray. Born free about 1813 in Caroline County on Maryland's Eastern Shore, Murray worked as a domestic housekeeper in Baltimore. She and Bailey likely became acquainted at a social gathering of the East Baltimore Mental Improvement Society, an educational and debating institution popular among the city's growing free African American population. It was she who helped to finance his journey northward, reportedly selling a feather bed to help pay for the train fare, and altering Bailey's clothilng so that he appeared to be a sailor.[1] Murray followed Bailey to New York a few days later and there the two were married. The union would last forty-four years, and produce children, but Anna, who remained illiterate, existed mostly in the shadows of her husband who gained national and international recognition within a few years of their marriage. Because he wrote little about his domestic life, it is difficult to gain a clear picture of their relationship.

The insecurity and trepidation Bailey felt during his first days as a free man were eased to some degree by connections within New York's black community. There Bailey came into contact with and was mentored by several individuals who would become colleagues in his quest for the abolition of slavery and the advancement of black rights. Spending his first few nights of freedom "wandering about the streets of New York, and lodging at least one night among the barrels on one of the wharves," he surprisingly encountered William Dixon, a man whom he had known in Baltimore as "Allender's Jake." Himself self-emancipated, Dixon warned Bailey about kidnappers and urged him to be cautious.[2] After several days of hesitation and living rough, he approached a black sailor named Stuart for assistance. Housing the tired and anxious fugitive in his home for a night, the next day the man brought Bailey to 36 Lispenard Street, the home of David Ruggles, the twenty-eight-year-old head of the New York Vigilance Committee. It was Bailey's first meeting with a black abolitionist in the North, and Ruggles provided important advice on securing employment and on how to maintain his safety, with many necessary precautions to be taken even far above Mason and Dixon's line. The pair spent a number of evenings discussing abolitionism and the struggle for black advancement, forging a friendship that would last until Ruggles's untimely death in 1849 at the age of thirty-nine.[3]

Among the tasks facing the self-emancipated Bailey was the choice of a new name, and at first he settled on Frederick Johnson. He wrote to Anna in Baltimore and in a few days' time she followed his route to New York. Although there was no question about her free status or papers, it must have been a distressing journey to make alone for a woman who could not read or write. On Saturday September 15, with him less than two weeks removed from slavery, Frederick and Anna were married by newly ordained Congregational minister James W.C. Pennington. Himself a former slave, along with Ruggles, Pennington was active in antislavery organizations and in the New York Vigilance Committee that strove to protect the rights of African Americans within the city. Contact with these two strong and willful black activists must have been a unique and gratifying experience for twenty-year-old Frederick Johnson, né Bailey. Eager to act as mentors for one so soon out of the bonds of slavery, both Ruggles and Pennington demonstrated that there was much to be gained in freedom, but first Frederick and Anna needed to establish a home and find a living. Ruggles suggested the couple locate in New Bedford, Massachusetts, where a vibrant African American community existed, and where Frederick might find work in his trade as a ship's caulker. He arranged for them to be assisted there by Nathan Johnson, a caterer and confectionary shop owner, and one of the most prominent African Americans in New Bedford.

Journeying first to Newport, Rhode Island, the newlyweds continued aboard a public coach, but upon arrival in New Bedford, they had no money to pay the fare. They were assisted and encouraged by two fellow travelers, Joseph Ricketson and William C. Taber, both well-known New Bedford businessmen and Quakers sympathetic to the antislavery movement, who directed them to the home of Nathan and Mary Johnson on Seventh Street. Johnson provided the two dollars needed to retrieve their luggage from the depot, and soon suggested that the couple adopt a different family name as Johnsons were already too numerous in New Bedford. His fear was that the name might mark the pair as fugitives. He suggested Douglas, after a character in Sir Walter Scott's *Lady of the Lake*, and may have pointed out that the name was spelled with a double "s" by prominent African Americans in Philadelphia and other areas of the northeast.[4] Agreeing, Frederick Augustus Washington Bailey began his free life in this new town as Frederick Douglass.

Hailed by scholar Kathryn Grover as the "fugitive's Gibraltar," New Bedford was a vibrant and growing maritime city. Known for whaling and shipbuilding, Douglass had high hopes that he could secure employment in the caulker's trade. A small city of just over 12,000, New Bedford was also home to more than a thousand African Americans when Douglass first arrived. Although there were numerous self-emancipated blacks among the townsfolk, New Bedford contained a growing number of African American businessmen, such as Nathan Johnson, who formed the core of a black middle class. Douglass was amazed at the wealth and refinement of New Bedford's African Americans, noting that Johnson had a "nicer house, dined at more ample board, and was the owner of more books" than most of the slaveholders of Talbot County, Maryland.[5] The cultivation of relationships with these individuals and involvement with local black churches exposed Douglass to a range of intellectual and social experiences that had a lasting impact on the direction in which he sought to take his new-found freedom. However, before he could think about intellectual expansion, economic considerations were at hand. He sought work to support his household, for soon after arriving in New Bedford, it became apparent that Anna was expecting their first child.

Setting out to find work on the wharves of New Bedford on his fifth day in the city, Douglass was impressed with the industrious activity at the port and was struck by how different it appeared from Baltimore. Instead of the noisy shouts and singing slaves, ship workers and laborers toiled side by side and "everything went on as smoothly as the works of a well adjusted machine."[6] He accepted whatever odd jobs he could find, first earning two dollars for shoveling coal into a basement for the Unitarian minister, then unloading a ship's cargo, and sawing wood with a saw and buck borrowed from Nathan Johnson. Learning that men in his trade earned two dollars per day, Douglass eagerly applied and was hired as a caulker at the shipyard of Rodney French. It proved to be one of his first lessons in the racist and intolerant nature of the antebellum North. In Baltimore's harbor it was not unusual for enslaved and free black men to work side by side with whites, but this was not true of New Bedford. When he appeared on the ship's float-stage for work, Douglass learned that the remainder of the crew—all white men—threatened to strike in protest. Apparently, not all residents of New Bedford welcomed their African American neighbors.

The first winter in freedom proved to be particularly lean, but Douglass toiled eagerly at whatever common labor came his way. Concern over his economic uncertainty eased a bit when he was hired as a laborer at the candleworks of Joseph Ricketson, one of the businessmen he had encountered on the coach to New Bedford. When that job ended, through the winter he worked at any odd job on the wharves, and as a bellows operator at a brass foundry. Even lacking steady employment, Douglass recalled the "consciousness that I was free—no longer a slave—kept me cheerful" under the many proscriptions he faced.[7] By the spring he was settling well into the city's black community, and adjusting to his growing family, as Anna gave birth to their first daughter, Rosetta, on June 24, 1839. Son Lewis Henry was born the following year on October 9, 1840. While Anna strove to create a home for Douglass and the children, her husband began to explore the intellectual and reform opportunities freedom offered.

Shifting between jobs provided Douglass the opportunity to come into contact with many individuals in New Bedford's white and black communities. The city had a reputation for abolitionism and for harboring many who, like Douglass, had chosen to escape from southern bondage. It stood to reason that New Bedford also had a strong coalition of individuals opposed to slavery. Douglass first encountered black abolitionists David Ruggles and James W.C. Pennington during his brief stay in New York, but in New Bedford he learned firsthand that whites were also involved in the antislavery movement. Douglass's one-time employer, Joseph Ricketson, was one of the founding members of the Anti-Slavery Society of New Bedford, which formed in 1834. Numerous prominent businessmen and clergy were also active members of the society. In the winter of 1838–1839 someone in the city, possibly a member of this integrated antislavery organization, offered Douglass a copy of William Lloyd Garrison's antislavery weekly, the *Liberator*. Impressed with what he read, he initiated his own subscription despite his protestation of poverty. The antislavery weekly became as essential to his life and survival as the food he put on the table for his family. The paper proved a major influence on Douglass's decision to become a reformer; he later recalled that the "paper took its place with me next to the Bible."[8]

Reading the *Liberator* religiously every week, Douglass also began to attend local antislavery meetings. His first recorded public participation came at an anticolonization meeting held March 12, 1839. There he was among those speaking out in favor of resolutions condemning the colonization of blacks in Africa and supporting the work of Garrison and of New York black activist Samuel Cornish.[9] A few weeks later he had the chance to hear Garrison in person when he lectured at New Bedford's Liberty Hall, on April 16. "I sat away back in the hall and listened to his mighty words, mighty in truth, mighty in their simple earnestness. I had not long been a reader of the *Liberator*, and a listener to its editor, before I got a clear comprehension of the principles of the antislavery movement."[10] By the summer of 1839, Douglass was increasingly interested in the cause of abolition and eager to learn more. He scoured the *Liberator* every week and attended all antislavery meetings held in New Bedford. There he learned that the antislavery movement spread throughout New England and the northeast. He read about the lecturing tours of Garrison and other abolitionists, and gained a sense of how the national political system supported southern slaveholders. Although his heart was committed to abolition, priorities closer to home occupied Douglass's first three years as a free man. In that time he also began to build ties within New Bedford's black community and its houses of worship.

In his first autobiography, *Narrative of the Life of Frederick Douglass* (1845), Douglass wrote disparagingly of the religion of slaveholders and of his master in particular, who seemed to become more cruel once he converted to evangelical Christianity. Douglass was so concerned that his portrayal of Christianity would be misunderstood that he added a special statement at the end of the *Narrative* explaining that his criticism only "applied to the *slaveholding religion* of this land."[11] Douglass's participation in organized religion has been hard for scholars to firmly grasp. It is known that he operated a forbidden Sabbath school for a short time in Maryland,

and he was certainly well read in the Scriptures. There is evidence that in New Bedford, likely for the first time in his life, he became committed to the black church. In Baltimore he had somewhat regularly attended an African Methodist Episcopal church, but in New Bedford Douglass soon learned that most northern churches were as segregated as those in the South. Church attendance was an important activity in the nineteenth century community, marking African American families as respectable and serving as training grounds for community leaders. Many of the leading black abolitionists, including J.W.C. Pennington and Henry Highland Garnet, were also ministers in various Protestant denominations. Belonging to an established house of worship allowed Douglass to socialize with and make connections among many of the prominent African American businessmen and clergy in New Bedford.

Douglass wrote most extensively of his involvement in church life in his second autobiography *My Bondage and My Freedom* (1855), noting that "among my first concerns on reaching New Bedford, was to become united with the church, for I had never given up, in reality, my religious faith."[12] Although he would soon begin to regularly scorn the religious hypocrisy of slaveholders, in 1838 he was not yet aware of the connection between organized Protestant denominations in the North and southern slavery. Because he had attended a Methodist church in Maryland, he felt it was his "duty to join the Methodist church."[13] This compulsion did not last long as his first experience in the Elm Street Methodist Church pastored by Isaac Bonney soon taught him a lesson on the segregated nature of American religion, even in more accepting communities such as New Bedford. When the dozen or so African Americans in the church were forced to take communion separately and after the white parishioners, Douglass remembered "the colored members—poor, slavish souls—went forward, as invited. I went *out*," never to return to that church.[14] He tried several other houses of worship, finally settling on the small African Methodist Episcopal Zion Church. This small denomination formally broke from the white-dominated Methodist Church in 1796, but was distinct from the larger African Methodist Episcopal Church. In the early nineteenth century the AME Zion Church opposed racism, but did not openly embrace abolitionist religious principles.[15]

The small size and itinerant nature of the clergy at the New Bedford Zion Church, which met at a schoolhouse on Second Street, meant numerous roles were open to lay leaders. Douglass detailed in an 1894 letter that he served in many capacities within the church including as sexton, steward, class leader, and clerk. He was soon granted a license from the denomination's Quarterly Conference to act as a local preacher. A common position borrowed from the Methodists, local preachers often filled in for ordained ministers when they were out of the pulpit, leading services or making pastoral visits.[16] It is not clear how long Douglass continued his association with the church once he became active as an abolitionist, but the AME Zion Church's refusal to prohibit the membership of slaveholders suggests that his affiliation was fleeting, and certainly over once he became committed to Garrisonian principles. Quickly becoming a strong influence on Douglass's thinking, Garrison rejected organized religion as corrupt for its connection to the slaveholding South.

Whatever his later thoughts on organized denominations, it is likely that Douglass made his first forays as a public orator as a licensed preacher at the AME Zion Church, putting into practice the techniques learned from his well-worn copy of the *Columbian Orator*. Less than a year out of slavery, he was quickly moving into more community and civic participation. By mid-1839 he had joined the Wilberforce Debating Society, early on defending his position against William Henry Johnson that slavery was a greater societal ill than intemperance. Massachusetts granted universal suffrage rights without regard to race and Douglass also registered to vote.[17] He moved in both integrated and African American institutions and reform-oriented organizations from his first months in New Bedford. A number of the antislavery meetings he attended brought blacks and whites together, but Douglass also made important connections with African American reformers and leaders.

In March 1839 he attended a meeting of African Americans at the African Christian Church aimed at protesting the colonization of freed blacks by the American Colonization Society. Led by prominent local activists William P. Powell, who kept a temperance boarding house for black sailors, and Nathaniel A. Borden, a restaurant and grocery owner, the meeting opened Douglass's eyes to the parallel movement for African American civil rights. That same year, African Americans in New Bedford nominated Borden for the Massachusetts senate, so it is likely that Douglass cast his first ballot in concert with other black abolitionists for a black representative. Borden served as secretary for the March anticolonization meeting. At the meeting, Douglass stood and vocally supported a series of resolutions condemning colonization and supporting the rights of African American men.[18] When reflecting on his early days of freedom in his third autobiography, Douglass fondly remembered Nathan Johnson and Powell as important influences on his career as a reformer. He counted Borden among those who saw merit in his abilities and encouraged him to step into the public arena as a reformer and advocate for his race. With the venerable examples of these individuals, Douglass's activist spirit was beginning to grow, but at this stage in his free life he "had not then dreamed of the possibility of becoming a public advocate of the cause so deeply imbedded in [his] heart."[19]

Instead, Douglass spent his first year in Massachusetts striving to maintain steady employment in support of his family, but he nevertheless made numerous connections within the broader community as well. His nonworking hours were spent reading about the abolition movement in the *Liberator* and other publications, taking an increasingly public and responsible role within the AME Zion Church and debating society, establishing a pattern of outward focus that characterized the remainder of his life. In contrast, the life of Anna Murray Douglass was establishing an insularity that served to make the domestic sphere the focal point of her life. Douglass wrote little about the woman with whom he shared forty-four years of his life, and because she was illiterate Anna Douglass left no written evidence of her own. An account written by her daughter Rosetta Douglass Sprague offers the best glimpse of the contrasting lives of husband and wife.

It was Anna who made a home for the Douglass family in New Bedford. When leaving Baltimore, she arrived in the North with bedding, linens, cutlery, and other items needed to establish a household. Upon leaving their refuge at the home of Nathan and Mary Johnson, Anna and Frederick took up residence in a small house at 157 Elm Street, moving to a larger house on Ray Street in 1841 with knowledge that another child, Frederick Jr., was on the way. With his birth on March 3, 1842, Anna had three children under the age of four and a household to supervise. Her daughter recalled that her mother always prepared a solid evening meal and presented a "neatly set table with its snowy white cloth—coarse tho' it was." She took care of all the domestic responsibilities, and kept a kitchen garden to supplement her husband's meager earnings. Later, when Douglass began traveling frequently, she took in work as a shoe binder.[20] With a full range of household work and child rearing to occupy her time, in the early years of their marriage Anna Douglass had little time to explore the larger world that was increasingly engaging her husband's attention.

In 1841 Douglass's role in the antislavery movement shifted from that of an observer to that of an energetic participant. By that time he was well aware of the activities of abolitionists outside New Bedford. In addition to reading the weekly *Liberator*, discussions with his friend Nathan Johnson, who participated in a broad range of state-level abolitionist activities, taught Douglass much about the interconnectedness of black and white reformers in opposition to slavery. In 1837, just before Douglass's escape from slavery, Johnson represented black abolitionists on a committee that screened and endorsed state legislature candidates based on their adherence to antislavery principles. In October 1840, Johnson was among two hundred attending the annual meeting of the Massachusetts Anti-Slavery Society (MASS) held at Worcester.[21] Other members of the statewide society soon took notice of Douglass's interest in abolition and of his unique ability to communicate. Douglass's involvement with the Zion Church, including his preaching, gained the attention of New Bedford white abolitionist William C. Coffin. An accountant for the Mechanic's Bank, Coffin was recorder for the Bristol County Anti-Slavery Society, and a close friend of William Lloyd Garrison. He invited Douglass to speak at a special meeting of the MASS to be held at Nantucket on August 10–12, 1841.[22]

Taking leave of his family and his work, Douglass boarded a steam packet to Nantucket for the three-day convention, which was certainly the largest gathering of abolitionists he had yet encountered. Not quite three years out of slavery, he would share the stage with Garrison and other luminaries of the abolition movement. Looking closely at the Nantucket convention reveals the world of reform to which Douglass was poised to commit his life and work. The abolitionists debated and unanimously passed three resolutions, all of which were central to Douglass's recent experiences both in slavery and in his short three years of freedom. The roots of his commitment to William Lloyd Garrison and the civil rights of black northerners were both reflected. Although Douglass was still intimately involved with the Zion Church, the Garrisonian brand of abolition espoused by members of the MASS condemned established Protestant denominations for their refusal to openly oppose slavery and urged abolitionists to "come out" of these churches.[23] Offering the first declaration of the convention, Garrison himself resolved that commitment to antislavery principles "imperatively demands of all those who profess to be its friends" that they "shake off the dust from their feet against those church organizations which countenance or in any wise connive at the enslavement of two millions and a half of our fellow-creatures."[24] Garrison's powerful statement deeply affected Douglass, leading him to soon break his affiliation with New Bedford's Zion Church in particular, and organized religion in general. In *My Bondage and My Freedom* he wrote, "many seasons of peace and joy I experienced among them, … although I could not see it to be my duty to remain with that body, when I found that it consented to the same spirit which held my brethren in chains."[25]

Douglass himself was among the advocates for the second resolution condemning the prejudice of northerners against African Americans. Recalling his recent experience at Rodney French's shipyard, when the white workers threatened to strike if he were employed, Douglass must have cheered Garrison's resolution that held that through their prejudice, northerners were "putting arguments into the mouths of southern taskmasters, and acting as the body-guard of slavery."[26] Before long, Douglass would become one of the most outspoken challengers to segregated facilities and accommodations that were common in New England. The final resolution linked southern slavery with northern commerce and manufacturing, arguing that no change in national policies or laws could bring prosperity to the U.S. so long as slavery existed. Douglass watched the convention-goers, white and black, thrash out the language of their convictions in total concert and learned the value of cooperation between the races. It was a model he would follow throughout his career.

All the while absorbing the heated discussion over these resolutions, Douglass's task during the convention was to offer the crowd a detailed account of his personal experience in slavery, and he was terrified. He was not the first to deliver a firsthand account of slavery, but he would quickly gain a reputation as a powerful and persuasive speaker. However, in his first outing before such a prestigious audience, Douglass felt insecure and humbled to be sharing the platform with men much more experienced. He haltingly began his speech at the end of the evening session on Wednesday, August 11, and resumed during the morning of August 12. Douglass's audience was sympathetic to his nervous demeanor, but he later recalled: "It was with the utmost difficulty that I could stand erect, or that I could command and articulate two words without hesitation and stammering. I trembled in every limb. I am not sure that my embarrassment was not the most effective part of my speech, if speech it could be called."[27] Garrison followed him on the platform, using Douglass's example as his text, although he could not recall his first name when reporting on the meeting in the *Liberator*. At the end of the meeting John A. Collins, then the MASS general agent, offered Douglass a temporary three-month position as an agent for the society. This meant he would travel and tell his story of enslavement to audiences around the state, seeking converts to the cause of abolition, and subscriptions for Garrison's *Liberator*. Douglass hesitated, for although he was gaining confidence, the public nature of the agent's role could expose his status as a fugitive, potentially alerting his slave master to his location.[28] In the end the offer of a steady salary and a break from common labor, and above all the desire to act on his convictions as an abolitionist, led him to accept.

CHAPTER **3**

THE LECTURING FIELD

Five days after the Nantucket meeting, Frederick Douglass made his first appearance as an agent of the Massachusetts Anti-Slavery Society (MASS) at the organization's quarterly meeting. The Millbury, Massachusetts convention was one of more than two dozen public forums where Douglass spoke in the last quarter of 1841. If he had flirted with a religious attachment to the Zion Church, in the antislavery movement he found his true spiritual calling. "My whole heart went with the holy cause," he recalled, "and my most fervent prayer to the Almighty Disposer of the hearts of men, were continually offered for its early triumph. 'Who or what,' thought I, 'can withstand a cause so good, so holy, so indescribably glorious. The God of Israel is with us.'"[1] Douglass's movement into the realm of abolitionism marked a new chapter in his life as he stepped onto the public stage of antebellum reform. He soon learned that his new-found faith was a complicated one, and that even within the confines of the abolition movement he would need to navigate carefully to realize his heartfelt desire for racial equality.

Douglass's new employer, MASS, evolved from the New England Anti-Slavery Society, which William Lloyd Garrison formed in 1831, soon after the inception of his antislavery weekly the *Liberator*. After the 1833 formation of the more broadly focused American Anti-Slavery Society (AASS), also a largely Garrison-led venture, MASS centered its attention on reform within the commonwealth. Like other antislavery societies influenced by Garrison, through the use of a tactic called "moral suasion," MASS aimed to sway public opinion about the sinfulness of slavery. Antislavery society members brought their message to all who would listen through public lectures, the publication of abolition-focused newspapers and pamphlets, and petitions to state legislatures and Congress. Always a minority in antebellum America, even among abolitionists, the Garrisonians whom Douglass joined in 1841 were the most radical or "ultra" abolitionists in the northeast. Born in 1805 and trained as a printer, Garrison was the most recognized and outspoken critic of slavery in the nation. He demanded that his followers adopt his positions opposing organized Protestant denominations because they refused to condemn slavery, and eschew political participation or other affiliation with the federal government which he considered corrupt and proslavery. Declaring the U.S. Constitution a proslavery document, by the late 1830s Garrison called for disunion, eventually printing his motto, "no union with slaveholders" on the masthead of his weekly newspaper.[2] Looking to Garrison for mentoring in his new calling as a reformer, Douglass soon became an ardent adherent to Garrisonian principles. In ensuing years, the two became close associates, often traveling together on the lecture circuit and sharing lodgings as well as the speaking platform.

On the lecture circuit around the counties of Massachusetts and adjoining New England states, Douglass's task was to secure subscribers for Garrison's *Liberator* and for the *National Anti-Slavery Standard*, the official organ of AASS. For safety and companionship agents usually traveled together in pairs or small, often integrated, groups. George Foster, a Quaker activist from Amherst was Douglass's companion for his first foray into the lecture field. Another occasional companion that fall was John A. Collins, the MASS general agent who initially urged Douglass onto the public stage. In settings ranging from local courthouses to churches, Douglass's mentors directed him to tell the story of his life in bondage to crowds of New Englanders, most of whom had never encountered a former slave. He recalled, "I was generally introduced as a '*chattel*'—a '*thing*'— a piece of southern '*property*'—the chairman assuring the audience that *it* could speak."[3] His ability to recount his personal experiences provided invaluable propaganda at once more rich and revealing than any pamphlet or newspaper could convey.

The speech Douglass gave on these occasions offered a personal and in-depth narrative of his life, leaving out his former name, his master's name, and the location of his enslavement. His confidence grew as he held sway with audiences and his renowned oratory skill evolved. He also became increasingly frustrated and bored with repeating the same story meeting after meeting. The tension that would eventually lead him to step away from the Garrisonians was evident from his first months as an agent. Foster and Collins urged him to stick with "the facts," but Douglass sought to expand the subject of his orations. Although he saw the need to gain converts to abolition, he also wanted to make New Englanders aware of the aggravation African Americans faced daily. A dual concern with abolishing slavery, winning civil rights for blacks in the North was of particular concern to black abolitionists, including Douglass. He began to infuse his narrative with commentary on the wretched state of race relations in the North and other issues capturing the attention of his growing intellect. He was angered with the suggestion, espoused by opponents of abolition, that emancipation would bring a flood of indigent African Americans into the northern states. At a meeting just more than a month after entering the lecture field, Douglass told a Lynn, Massachusetts audience, "prejudice against color is stronger north than south; it hangs around my neck like a heavy weight. It presses me out from among my fellow men, and, although I have met it at every step the three years I have been out of southern slavery, I have been able, in spite of its influence, 'to take good care of myself.'"[4]

Although his Garrisonian companions continued to urge him to keep his speeches tied to his personal narrative in slavery, Douglass's orations were informed as much by his current situation and experiences in freedom as by his recent past in slavery. In November 1841, Douglass again took up the complaint of northern prejudice. At a meeting of the Plymouth County Anti-Slavery Society, Douglass testified not to his experience as slave, but to the effects of northern prejudice. He told of being forced to work at common labor despite the fact that jobs in his trade were readily available. He condemned, as any solid Garrisonian would, segregation and prejudice within northern churches with their "*Jim Crow pews.*" He detailed the segregation of blacks in the Methodist Church in New Bedford, linking his experience with the impiety of his slave master, whom he described as even more cruel once he became a class leader in the church.[5]

These experiences and other more recent ones were uppermost in Douglass's mind. The extensive travel of the lecture circuit meant he frequently faced and challenged the regulations and policies that segregated northern travelers by race. Particularly in areas with a significant African American population, public conveyances, including coaches and railroads, restricted or separated black and white travelers. Hotels and restaurants regularly denied him service. On September 8, 1841, Douglass had been traveling along with John A. Collins aboard the Boston to Portsmouth Eastern Railroad to an antislavery meeting in Dover, New Hampshire, when the conductor and several others forcibly removed him from the first-class car and placed him in the segregated "Negro car," despite the fact that he had paid the full first-class fare.[6] He recalled, "I was dragged out of my seat, beaten, and severely bruised, by conductors and brakemen."[7] In coming to his defense, Collins was roughed up as well. Douglass was outraged and humiliated.

After this first incident, Douglass determined to challenge the railroad policies by always beginning his excursions in the first-class car. Although it was not codified as later Jim Crow laws in southern states would be, racial segregation was common throughout Massachusetts. Douglass was only one of several black passengers who chose to openly defy the regulations, and in joining fellow African Americans in opposing these policies he engaged in one of his first acts aimed at fighting prejudice against his race. Three weeks after the first incident, Douglass boarded the first-class car at Lynn, Massachusetts en route to Newburyport, but was accosted by the conductor who admitted he was denying Douglass a seat because he was black. When Douglass denied that he *was* black, the conductor sought a number of volunteers to forcibly remove him. The act resulted in significant physical damage to the seats, to which Douglass had affixed his rather large frame. The Eastern Railroad superintendent, Stephen A. Chase, was reportedly so outraged that he ordered the train to bypass the Lynn station for several days. Pressure from Douglass and other activists paid off in 1842 when the Massachusetts legislature appointed a committee to look into the segregation policies of public conveyances. Although the committee's bill banning the practice failed to pass, the pressure from abolitionists and African Americans led most rail lines to abandon segregation in the early 1840s.[8]

For the remainder of 1841, Douglass traveled almost constantly in the company of white MASS agent John A. Collins, appearing at local and regional antislavery meetings where he shared the platform with Garrison and came to know other important abolitionists, including Parker Pillsbury, Stephen S. Foster, and Abby Kelley. Perhaps already convinced that his time as a manual laborer was in the past, although his association with MASS was temporary, he moved his family from New Bedford to Lynn, which was only ten miles from the abolitionist offices in Boston. The fall of 1841 must have been a difficult time for Anna Douglass, who, in the midst of her third pregnancy, had to pack up her household and move with two small children to a new city. She also had to adjust to her husband's frequent absences, a pattern that characterized the remainder of their married life.

Douglass's attachment to MASS gained permanence when he was hired as a regular lecturer in January 1842, providing some financial stability for his family, which increased by one with the birth of Frederick Jr. on March 3. With the help of his fellow abolitionists Douglass made a down payment on a small house, providing a real home for his wife and growing family, although Anna and the children might have preferred to have his company. She did have for a time the company of Ruth Cox, who resided with the Douglasses for an unspecified period in 1843.[9] An escaped slave from Talbot County, Maryland, Douglass had mistakenly identified Cox as his sister Harriet. Since leaving the Eastern Shore as a teen, Douglass had had no contact with his siblings, making his initial confusion over Cox's identity understandable. The ruse seemed to work in her favor: taking the name Harriet Bailey to protect her identity, Cox assisted Anna in running the household while Douglass was away. Keeping the household running required much coordination and it is likely that in Lynn Anna and Cox supplemented the family earnings by taking in piecework from the region's numerous local shoemakers.[10] A resourceful woman, Anna Douglass did what she needed to support her family while her husband was traveling, including asking the antislavery office to remind him to send money. After receiving such a plea from home, Douglass wrote to Maria Weston Chapman, business manager for MASS, asking that $25 or $30 be sent to his home as "I have none to send hir."[11]

Douglass certainly earned his agent's salary—reportedly $300.36 for 1842—however sporadically it arrived, for in the first six months of 1842 he was almost continually away from home, save for a brief respite during the month of Frederick Jr.'s birth.[12] Slightly more than three weeks after his son's arrival, Douglass embarked on a grueling travel schedule, speaking almost daily at county antislavery meetings across Massachusetts in April and early May. He traveled to New York City to attend the ninth annual meeting of the American Anti-Slavery Society at the city's Broadway Tabernacle. There he stood shoulder to shoulder with the most active and outspoken abolitionists in the North, although reports indicated that the hall was only half filled. According to one observer, "the acting portion of the assembly were made up of religious abolitionists, quakers, deists, transcendentalists, agrarians, Garrisonians, dissolve-the-Unionites, female lecturers, blacks, whites, and seemingly all the 'odds and ends' of creation."[13]

Speaking at a host of rural antislavery meetings across Massachusetts in the summer of 1842, Douglass marked his one-year anniversary as a lecturing agent at the annual Nantucket meeting of MASS. Emphasizing the proslavery connections of organized Protestant churches, Douglass and other speakers at the Athenaeum Hall came under attack by an antiabolition mob, which flung bits of brick through the windows, striking and injuring one woman severely. It was one of many violent incidents Douglass and other abolitionists faced, reminding them that abolitionists were a small and often detested minority even among the northern populace. Douglass was gaining a solid sense of the integrated and diverse abolition movement led by the Garrisonians, but also of the difficulties of publicly espousing antislavery sentiments. Later in 1842 Douglass's circle of associates expanded when he became embroiled in a controversial fugitive slave case centered in Boston.[14]

The abolitionists of Boston and the city's African American community were outraged with the October 20, 1842 arrest of George Latimer, a fugitive slave claimed by Norfolk, Virginia slave owner James B. Gray. The protests surrounding Latimer's case served to connect Douglass intimately with Boston's black activists and reinforced his commitment to achieving full rights for African American men in the North. White and black activists protested the impending return of Latimer to slavery, and formed committees that clamored for his release. Douglass joined with fellow black abolitionist Charles Lenox Remond in raising funds to purchase Latimer's freedom. Remond, a free-born barber from Salem, had acted as an agent for the *Liberator* since 1832, and was the first African American lecturing agent appointed by AASS in 1838.[15] The pair spoke at a host of pro-Latimer meetings, in and around Boston. Douglass felt a special kinship with Latimer, writing to Garrison, "I sympathize with George Latimer, having myself been cast into a miserable jail on suspicion of my intending to do what he is said to have done, viz. appropriating my own body to my use."[16] Although many of the pro-Latimer meetings were integrated, some were exclusively African American gatherings, especially a large meeting held November 30 at Boston's Baptist Church on Belknap Street. There Douglass and fellow black activists protested not only Latimer's arrest and detainment, but the implied threat to the rights and freedoms of African Americans in the commonwealth. If Massachusetts authorities were to make a policy of aiding slaveholders in reclaiming self-emancipated slaves, all blacks faced potential danger. Even after Latimer's freedom was secured, therefore, the committees continued, gathering more than 64,000 signatures on a petition presented to the Massachusetts legislature. The lawmakers responded by passing the 1843 Personal Liberty Act forbidding the involvement of Massachusetts officials or use of state facilities in the apprehension or return of fugitive slaves. It was a major victory for abolitionists and set the stage for the passage of similar laws in other northern states.[17] Once Latimer's freedom was secured, Douglass and Remond returned to the lecture field, accompanied by Latimer, who gratefully shared his story with sympathetic audiences across Massachusetts.[18]

The year 1843 proved to be one of the most active for Douglass and his fellow agents, as the American Anti-Slavery Society and its affiliates such as MASS determined to link New England abolitionists with their coadjutors in the western states, including New York, Pennsylvania, Ohio, and Indiana. The organizations declared the intention to hold one hundred antislavery conventions within the year in the West and in New England. After spending the late spring and early summer traveling with Remond and Latimer, in July Douglass embarked on the "Hundred Conventions" circuit with an expanded group of reformers. In addition to Remond, he was accompanied by several Garrisonians, including his old companion John A. Collins. George Bradburn, a Whig politician who led a successful effort to repeal the Massachusetts antimiscegenation law, as well as Jacob Ferris, James Monroe, William A. White, and Sydney Howard Gay, were also part of the tour. Holding its first meeting in Middlebury, Vermont, the Hundred Conventions tour proceeded next to western New York where Douglass shared the platform with Bradburn, Gay, and Collins. Several memorable and important developments that came to shape Douglass's career as a reformer occurred at points along this lengthy tour. In Rochester, New York, he became acquainted with Quaker activists Amy and Isaac Post, with whom he became lifelong friends; but much of Douglass's tour was marked by conflict.

Although in the lecturing field for less than two years, Douglass began to assert his own opinions, much to the chagrin of his mentors. His few years out of slavery found him already chafing at his sometimes paternal treatment by some white abolitionists. In August, Douglass openly challenged the leadership and actions of John A. Collins, one of his first mentors and frequent travel companions, for sidetracking the important antislavery message the conventions meant to convey with an alternative agenda. Collins had recently returned from Great Britain and was becoming increasingly influenced by the utopian ideas of anticapitalists such as Charles Fourier and Robert Owen, who opposed individually owned property and supported communal living. Tensions between Douglass and Collins escalated when Collins announced he would hold an antiproperty meeting in conjunction with a two-day antislavery convention held at Syracuse, New York at the end of July. Douglass vocally objected, arguing that such a meeting would detract from the message that he and the other agents were being paid to convey. Additionally, he pointed out that abolition was already an unpopular idea, and adding the even more unpopular antiproperty message would dilute the influence of their intended message. Douglass wrote angrily to Maria Weston Chapman of the AASS board of managers, "It was not that Mr. Collins had not a right to be a nonproperty man, nor was it that he had not the right to devote one half of his time to the one, and the other half to the antislavery cause. No, this was the question whether it was just or honorable for Mr. Collins to labor in the one for the distruction of the other."[19] Instead of agreeing, Chapman chastised Douglass for insubordination to his superiors. Experiencing the sting of paternalism that came to cloud his relationship with many white abolitionists, Douglass later reflected, "this was a strange and distressing revelation to me, and one of which I was not soon relieved."[20]

His disagreement with Collins and Chapman's reaction were likely still stinging when Douglass and Remond broke briefly from the integrated group to attend the Buffalo meeting of the National Convention of Colored Men in mid-August.[21] Although Douglass had attended meetings called by local black activists in New Bedford and Boston, this was his first experience with the larger issues that concerned those who gathered regularly as a part of the national convention movements. Beginning in 1830, African American social leaders and reformers came together at national conventions to discuss and enact a platform of actions and resolutions on issues of concern to blacks in America. Concerned with issues facing African Americans in the North as well as the abolition of slavery, they debated colonization, how best to secure universal suffrage, and how to enhance educational and economic opportunities for their race. At the Buffalo convention, though, the forty to fifty men assembled also debated resolutions relating to established churches and political involvement in the abolition of slavery. Some argued strongly that both religious and political means could help achieve an end to slavery. It may have been Douglass's first exposure to abolitionists who opposed Garrison's rigid dismissal of organized religion and the Constitution. One report of the meeting observed, "During the debate, Wm. L. Garrison was brought in for his share of abuse."[22]

Remond, Douglass, and fellow Garrisonian William Wells Brown were among a small minority opposing the convention's endorsement of the antislavery Liberty Party, which had formed in 1840 to bring a political challenge to slavery. Douglass also toed the Garrisonian line when he led the vocal opposition to Henry Highland Garnet's insistence that militant slave resistance was not only appropriate but necessary to end slavery.[23] Only five years out of slavery, Douglass had yet to express an independent opinion on the use of violence or political means in the antislavery cause, but in succeeding years he would come to endorse both. Although in 1843 he remained firmly in the Garrisonian camp, as evidenced by his position on these resolutions, the convention did have a lingering influence on Douglass, including the resolution calling for the institution of a newspaper aimed at expressing the opinions of African Americans.[24] Indeed, attendance at this and succeeding conventions, where northern black activists gathered to ponder the condition of their place in American society, had a profound effect on Douglass. At the Buffalo Convention in 1843, Douglass came to understand the need to broaden his reform agenda. Although the men gathered did not all agree on the proper direction to take, all were deeply committed to racial uplift and black civil rights in addition to the abolition of slavery.[25]

After traveling to Buffalo, Douglass and Remond rejoined the Hundred Conventions lecturing tour on its way to Ohio. There, he and Remond parted company as Douglass headed on to meet up with George Bradburn and William A. White in Indiana. The western field, and particularly Indiana, was known for virulent racism and opposition to abolitionism.

Although lecturers were used to facing hostile audiences, the Hoosier crowds were especially challenging. Crossing from Ohio to Richmond, Indiana Douglass recalled, "at our first meeting we were mobbed, and some of us had our good clothes spoiled by evil-smelling eggs."[26] This initial hostility was a harbinger of incidents to come.

The most violent meeting of the Hundred Conventions occurred in Pendleton, Indiana, a few miles northeast of the state capital, Indianapolis. On September 14–16, Douglass, White, and Bradburn were scheduled to appear there together. The first meeting, held in the Baptist church, was uneventful, although a large number of unruly and possibly intoxicated men appeared around the edges of the crowd. Concerned with preserving their property, church officials denied the abolitionists access to the sanctuary for their subsequent meetings, one of which they held on the church steps, but Bradburn's address was ended anyway by a rain shower. On September 16, the meeting moved to a wooded area with a makeshift platform, but the "mobocratic spirit was even more pronounced," and the abolitionists were attacked by a gang of some sixty men. The stage was dismantled, and William White was wounded on his head, knocking out several teeth and badly cutting his scalp. Abandoning any Garrisonian commitment to nonviolence in the wake of this attack on their physical safety, Douglass took up a club and lashed out at the crowd, but was soon relieved of his weapon. Describing the events in a letter to Garrison, White noted, "I hope never to look upon so fearful a sight, as poor Frederick flying before these hell-hounds, panting for his blood."[27] In the ensuing fight Douglass's right hand was badly broken, leaving him partially disabled for the remainder of his life.[28] Aided after the attack by local Quaker Neal Hardy, his injured hand was nevertheless not correctly set, leaving him with lingering pain and mobility problems. Despite their injuries, the tour resumed and in a few days' time Douglass was back on the platform with a renewed sense of commitment.

Within a week of the Pendleton incident, the Hundred Conventions lecturers spoke at the annual meeting of the Indiana Anti-Slavery Society at Jonesboro. By then a veteran of the abolitionist platform, Douglass was becoming increasingly comfortable expressing his own opinion and disagreeing with his coadjutors when necessary. Perhaps inspired by the Buffalo convention, and certainly by his discussions with Remond, Douglass was no longer willing to stand silent in the face of white abolitionists' paternal treatment. Joined again by Remond, the meeting at Jonesboro was marked by another dispute, this time between Remond, Douglass, and George Bradburn. When Douglass and then Remond interrupted Bradburn's speech, which they felt was getting too far off the subject of abolition, the meeting's chair silenced them. A witness wrote to Maria

Weston Chapman that "Remond and Douglass choose to be the lions of the party and are unwilling to be directed by others."[29] Douglass and Remond subsequently broke away from the Hundred Conventions agents and proceeded to hold meetings on their own in rural Indiana and Ohio. In Clinton County, Ohio, Douglass sparred verbally with Henry B. Stanton, husband of Elizabeth Cady Stanton, and another abolitionist, sparking another rebuke from Chapman, but he and Remond continued to draw large crowds.

Reconciled with the group by December, Douglass was present in Philadelphia for the American Anti-Slavery Society convention at the end of the Hundred Conventions. Marking the tenth anniversary of the society's founding, the meeting's chair was Robert Purvis, reputed to be the wealthiest African American in the U.S., and president of the Vigilant Committee of Philadelphia.[30] Although Douglass and Purvis occasionally clashed in future years, seeing a prominent African American chair the celebratory meeting further demonstrated to Douglass that there was little need for him to be subservient to the white-dominated board of managers of the antislavery society.

Douglass returned home to his family in Lynn by Christmas, and remained nearby through mid-February 1844. Perhaps already anticipating that his family was about to expand yet again, he responded to Wendell Phillips's invitation to undertake another extended convention tour with a request for a more stable salary. An elite Boston native and Harvard graduate, Phillips was one of the most prominent reformers and orators of the nineteenth century. Abandoning the practice of law because he came to agree with Garrison on the proslavery nature of the U.S. Constitution, Phillips became active in the business operations of MASS. For the preceding year's Hundred Conventions tour, Douglass had been paid $142, but as his letter to Chapman requesting that money be sent to his family suggests, payment may have been irregular in arriving. Douglass asked Phillips to settle on a definite payment of $7 to $8 per week and was also concerned that white and black agents receive equal pay. Understanding the value of his oratory in the lecturing field, Douglass had little compunction about demanding pay equity. He wrote, "I would not consent to work side by side with a Br[other] agent paying the same for the necesisaries [of] life—laboring as hard as myself and yet for his labor getting less than myself. Nor could I on the other hand be satisfied—with a reversed arrangement by which I should have less than an equal fellow laborer."[31] His concerns about pay inequality were unfounded, as records indicate he was the highest-paid agent, black or white, on the preceding year's tour.

It was to be an eventful year. Douglass embarked in late February for a new series of "hundred conventions," this time closer to home in

Massachusetts. His fourth child, Charles Remond Douglass was born October 21, 1844, named for Douglass's most constant friend and traveling companion. While Anna was managing their expanded household, Doulass undertook a new project that would alter their lives forever. One result of his growing intellect and confidence was that audiences became skeptical that he was an imposter. By all accounts Douglass had a commanding stage presence, and was taking on subjects far afield from Garrison's original intention that he provide a flesh and blood example of the evils of the slave system. He later wrote in his third autobiography, "People doubted if I had ever been a slave. They said I did not talk like a slave, look like a slave, or act like a slave, and that they believed I had never been south of Mason and Dixon's line."[32] To counter this line of criticism Douglass was encouraged and determined to write his own narrative.

Encouraged particularly by Wendell Phillips and Garrison, who each offered endorsement and testimony at the beginning of the autobiography, the *Narrative of the Life of Frederick Douglass, An American Slave Written by Himself*, was published in the spring of 1845 by the Anti-Slavery Office in Boston. Having read many autobiographies and particularly the two dozen or so narratives written by former slaves, the twenty-seven-year-old Douglass penned a masterful piece of antislavery propaganda. The slim book sold five thousand copies within four months of its publication and by 1860, thirty thousand copies. In Great Britain the *Narrative* appeared in nine editions between 1845 and 1847. The unprecedented success of the book made him a celebrity, cementing his standing as America's most famous former slave. Although he reveled in the initial attention, for the remainder of his life Douglass struggled to transcend that reputation.[33]

Douglass's *Narrative* followed the usual format of slave autobiographies, which, by 1845, were a standard propaganda tool of abolitionists. His audience was northern whites, especially those individuals who had to be convinced of the need to bring an immediate end to slavery.[34] Aiming for the broadest popular readership, Douglass's *Narrative* followed the convention of relying on whites to establish credibility. His text was prefaced by introductory letters penned by William Lloyd Garrison and Wendell Phillips, the two most prominent abolitionists in the United States. Garrison and Phillips dutifully attested to Douglass's credibility and authenticity as a fugitive slave.[35] But for Douglass there was a secondary and possibly more important motive. The autobiography offered validity at a time when Douglass's credibility was under question. Beginning his career as an antislavery lecturer in 1841, Douglass quickly gained a reputation as a polished and thoughtful orator. In fact, with every eloquent performance on the lecture platform more audience members came to doubt that he was ever a slave. In publishing the *Narrative*, Douglass quieted his doubters, but put himself substantially at risk. Unlike other slave narratives, Douglass fully revealed all details of his enslavement, including the name of his master, and extensive details of the cruel treatment he and other slaves endured. According to the laws of Maryland, in fact, he remained the fugitive property of his owner Thomas Auld. Once his new name was revealed, his prominent presence in New England antislavery circles made him an easy target for slave catchers who might hope for a handsome reward for capturing such an outspoken and brazen fugitive slave. Friends and associates warned Douglass that he was in danger. He recalled, "it was felt that I had committed the double offense of running away, and exposing the secrets and crimes of slavery and slaveholders ... . I was constantly in danger of being spirited away, at a moment when my friends could render me no assistance."[36] In order to protect his freedom and shield his family, Douglass agreed to embark on an extended lecture tour of Ireland and Great Britain. On August 16, 1845, he boarded the Cunard steam liner *Cambria* along with James N. Buffum, a fellow resident of Lynn and champion of Garrisonian abolitionism. Douglass would not see his family or his home for the next eighteen months.

CHAPTER 4

The World of Transatlantic Reform

Departing Boston on August 16, 1845, Douglass headed toward an unknown world where he would be welcomed as a reformer and not merely as a former slave. The eighteen months he spent abroad boosted his self-confidence, exposing him to a place and culture unlike America, and served to loosen his ties with William Lloyd Garrison. Slavery no longer existed in the British empire, following the 1834 emancipation of slaves in the British Caribbean, and, unlike the U.S., support for abolition there was widespread. Douglass was not the first African American to travel across the Atlantic, but he would become the most celebrated. The path had been paved most recently in 1841, by his friend and frequent companion on the lecture circuit, Charles Lenox Remond. Like Douglass, Remond's tour of Britain began in Ireland and drew large audiences wanting to hear and see a black abolitionist from America.[1] Arriving on the heels of the American publication of his *Narrative*, Douglass was welcomed into British and Irish reform circles, where he was the frequent companion of wealthy and influential men and women. Aboard the Cunard line's *Cambria*, however, Douglass was still subjected to the racial conventions and prejudices of his home country.

Preparing to board the *Cambria* at Boston, Cunard officials informed Douglass and his traveling companion, the white Garrisonian James Buffum, that Douglass was expected to travel in steerage, below deck, and that he could not purchase a first-class cabin. The apartment-like cabins were generally reserved for the wealthiest passengers, and most travelers bought steerage or second-class passage, where they occupied bunks in shared rooms. Accustomed to facing down segregation in public accommodations, Douglass was nevertheless stung by this particular denial. When he challenged the use of Jim Crow cars on the Massachusetts railroads, or slept out of doors when denied room at an inn or hotel while on the lecture circuit, Douglass understood the rebuff as part of the larger system of racial discrimination that permeated nineteenth-century America. The society that supported southern slavery was intimately linked to northern facilities through political and financial ties. On board the British-owned *Cambria*, Douglass had expected more equitable treatment, but it was not to be.

Writing of the experience Douglass later noted, "The insult was keenly felt by my white friends, but to me, it was common, expected, and therefore, a thing of no great consequence, whether I went in the cabin or in the steerage."[2] During the voyage a number of first-class passengers descended into the second-class cabin to visit with Douglass, including the Hutchinsons, a family of abolitionist singers from New Hampshire. Much to the chagrin of several American passengers, shortly before landing at Liverpool, Captain Charles Judkins invited Douglass to lecture on slavery. It was his first appearance before a largely British audience, although the captain's invitation may have been born of personal motives rather than a desire to appease Douglass's affront over having a steerage berth. The previous year a number of outraged passengers had signed a remonstrance against Judkins after he denied a Haitian first-class passenger a seat in the common dining saloon. Published in the *Glasgow Argus*, the rebuke placed both the Cunard line and Judkins in the awkward position of trying to satisfy their passengers who regularly stood on opposite sides of the slavery debate as well as on opposite shores of the Atlantic. Perhaps even more ironically, one of those signing the remonstrance was the Scottish Presbyterian minister George Lewis, whom Douglass would soon denounce for his fundraising activities among proslavery churches in the American South.[3]

Regardless of his motives, according to various witness accounts Judkins defended Douglass against the threats of fellow passengers who objected to being subjected to an abolitionist lecture. As Douglass and others later described, some passengers from the U.S. considered throwing him overboard, but Judkins subdued them by threatening to "put the salt water mobocrats in irons."[4] Soon after the *Cambria* docked at Liverpool on August 28, accounts of the events during the passage spread through British newspaper and personal accounts. Reprints of these articles and letters appeared at home soon after, in Garrison's *Liberator* and other U.S. newspapers.[5] The British and Irish reform communities were outraged by his mistreatment and Douglass capitalized on the incident by incorporating it into his personal narrative during Irish and British speaking engagements. Addressing a Cork audience two months later, Douglass dramatically recounted the events, including Judkins coming to his defense in what nearly resulted in a duel. "Now came the Captain—he was met by one of the other party, who put out his fist at him—the Captain knocked him down—instead of his bowie, the fallen man drew out his card crying 'I'll meet you in Liverpool.' 'Well,' said the Captain, 'and I'll meet you.'"[6] The incident provided the perfect introduction into Irish and British society, for when he appeared, the learned crowds were already eager to hear from the former slave.

Douglass and Buffum dove into the world of transatlantic reform almost immediately. Douglass soon discovered that activists held a number of causes near and dear to their hearts in addition to the abolition of slavery. Two days after landing at Liverpool, the pair embarked on a tour of Ireland that took them first to a local temperance society meeting and then to Dublin, where they spent several weeks lecturing for the Hibernian Anti-Slavery Society.[7] In Dublin, Douglass housed with printer and Garrisonian abolitionist, Richard Webb, and met Webb's brother-in-law, Richard Allen. Webb was a leading Garrisonian who maintained close ties across the Atlantic with Garrison and American Anti-Slavery Society (AASS) business manager Maria Weston Chapman. Heading the Hibernian Anti-Slavery Society, these men introduced Douglass to the world of Irish reform. In addition to the abolition of slavery, these activists were interested in a host of reform causes, especially temperance. Already opposing strong liquor, Douglass came to closely associate with temperance activists in the transnational community. In Ireland, Webb introduced him to James Haughton, and his mentor the famous Irish temperance champion Father Theobald Mathew, with whom Douglass formed a lasting friendship.[8]

While in Dublin, Douglass negotiated the publication of an Irish edition of his *Narrative*. As a printer and publisher of the Garrisonian weekly *Anti-Slavery Advocate*, and numerous pamphlets, Richard Webb was the logical choice, and the pair began negotiations for producing the volume and developing a marketing plan, although their personal relationship soon became strained. Never shy to express his opinions, Webb wrote to Maria Weston Chapman that he found Douglass to be irreverent and scornful toward his traveling companion, James Buffum. Douglass's impatience with Buffum may have sprung from his irritation with the paternalistic treatment emanating from the antislavery office in Boston. Although Douglass was the stronger orator and, following the publication of his recent book, more of a celebrity in reform circles, Chapman had ordered Buffum to take charge of their travel arrangements, including money management.[9] By his own accounts, Douglass was feeling the pressure from the Garrisonians, who wanted to control his words and to limit his orations to abolition and his own experience in slavery. Already straining out of that mold before boarding the *Cambria*, his time abroad was quickly eroding both Douglass's patience and his willingness to toe the Garrisonian line. The British tour introduced Douglass to countless reformers who operated outside of, or were critical of, the Garrisonian circle. The trip spurred and reinforced his independence. Webb's charge of Douglass's insolence may also have been a reflection of Webb's own racial intolerance, demonstrating that even the most liberal of reformers struggled with social boundaries of their own.[10]

After a somewhat tense month in Webb's home, the Irish lecture tour took Douglass and Buffum to Cork, Limerick, and finally Belfast, in a circuit occupying the last four months of 1845. They received warm welcomes from reformers, and especially from Unitarians and Quaker activists. In Cork, Douglass housed for a month with Thomas and Ann Jennings and their numerous children, finding the experience more amicable than his previous arrangement with Webb. Several of the Jennings daughters were active in the Cork Ladies' Anti-Slavery Society, and Douglass would retain a corresponding relationship with one daughter, Isabel Jennings, following his return to the U.S. It was during his tour of Ireland and Britain that Douglass gained a reputation for befriending women. Standing over six feet tall, well-dressed and well-read, he was an attractive and interesting man. Flattered by the attention paid to him by white women, Douglass cultivated relationships with numerous female activists. While engaged there for the month of December, Douglass inspired female reformers in Belfast to form their own antislavery society.[11] The Cork Ladies' Anti-Slavery Society held bazaars to raise money for his expenses long after he returned to America.

Douglass's affinity for women also attracted the negative attention of men such as Webb, whose letters to Chapman reflected concern. He wrote, "I wonder how he will bear the site of his wife, after all the petting he gets from beautiful, elegant, and accomplished women."[12] As Alan J. Rice and Martin Crawford have acknowledged, some of the criticism may tie to the uneasiness middle class reformers felt when confronted with "an actual black man" in their parlors. In Britain as in America, white abolitionists' struggle to practice the full equality that they preached often fell short of the mark and they sometimes slipped into the same paternalistic stereotypes which they professed to abhor. Another transatlantic reformer wrote of Douglass's alarming attraction and attention to white women. "You can hardly imagine how he is noticed,—*petted* I may say by *ladies*." It is entirely likely that this reformer, as well as Webb, did not realize that their use of "petting" compared Douglass to a domestic animal, or perhaps as a southern planter might, to his favorite slave.[13] Although male reformers may have been unaware of the implications of their words, Douglass was not. The women who found him so attractive also saw in him a kinship of oppression. The following year, a coalition of non-Garrisonian abolitionists, many of them women, spearheaded a fundraising drive to buy Doulass's freedom from his master Thomas Auld.

The time in Britain drew Douglass into the reform issues that concerned his transatlantic audiences in addition to the abolition of American slavery. He almost immediately became central to a controversy within the recently formed Free Church of Scotland. As Richard Blackett has shown, the connection between British churches and their counterparts in the U.S., particularly in those denominations prominent in the South, was a precarious one. Debate over an international approach to the problem of slaveholding denominations expanded in earnest after the London 1840 World Anti-Slavery Conference where the issue took center stage. When Douglass arrived in 1845, espousing the anticlerical Garrisonian agenda, he dove directly into center of an ongoing controversy.[14] He learned from British abolitionists that, following an internal conflict within the Church of Scotland, in 1843 breakaway congregations formed the independent Free Church of Scotland, and immediately began to raise funds from American Presbyterian churches, including those in the southern states. Despite the objections of abolitionists, the Free Church refused to sever ties with churches that permitted slaveholding members. Prominent clergy traveled to the U.S. where they raised substantial sums of money for their common ministries from southern churches. Begun by British abolitionists and other American Garrisonians, including Henry C. Wright who had been in Scotland since 1843, Douglass eagerly joined in a campaign urging Scottish Presbyterians to "send back the money."[15]

In December 1845, Douglass gave a series of seven lectures for the Belfast Anti-Slavery Society in which he attacked the Free Church of Scotland. He told the crowds that the unanimous cry of the people should be, "Have no communion with slaveholders," and that the only safe course was to send back the money. As Alasdair Pettinger has shown, it was Douglass's unique ability to link his personal narrative of enslavement in America to the Free Church controversy that made his message so powerful. He built a credible case study linking Free Church minister George Lewis, his former slave master Thomas Auld, a slave auctioneer, and himself. In this often-repeated hypothetical situation, Lewis solicited Auld for a donation to aid the Free Church of Scotland, obtaining the money by selling his slave.[16] The clear message that the donations were linked to the sale and enslavement of men, women, and children, had a powerful effect on British audiences, bringing home the link between slavery and the Free Church fund drive. Not surprisingly, some Free Church ministers tried to discredit Douglass with a rumor that he had been seen leaving a brothel, but his reputation and popularity continued to grow, and he became the most recognized leader of the campaign against the Free Church. He continued his lectures in Scotland, drawing huge crowds and adding opposition to a transnational Evangelical Alliance that refused to exclude slaveholders.[17] By the time William Lloyd Garrison joined him in July 1846, Douglass was no longer the fugitive slave telling his story, but the most sought-after orator on the British reform circuit. Although Garrison received top billing on their lecture tour across Scotland and England, it was now often Douglass who attracted the most applause and the largest crowds. In Britain, at least, he had managed to transcend his reputation as America's most famous former slave, and to be taken seriously as a reformer.

Douglass was also making important connections with British reformers outside Garrison's circle. He attended and spoke at several meetings sponsored by the rival British and Foreign Anti-Slavery Society, which was openly critical of the Garrisonians. To continue his attacks on the Free Church, Douglass agreed to a limited agency for the Scottish Anti-Slavery Society, with his lecture tour dipping slightly south of the border to Newcastle upon Tyne, where he spoke before crowds of a thousand or more.[18] Soon after, Garrison must have been surprised to learn that Douglass was scheduled to attend the World Temperance Convention with the delegates from Newcastle. Known as a strong teetotaler, Douglass's advocacy of the cause had so impressed leading Irish temperance campaigner Father Theobald Mathew that he held a party in his honor, further enhancing his credentials among British reformers.[19] On August 7, Douglass told those assembled at the London gathering that he could not formally join the American delegation because their organizations prohibited African Americans. Claiming he did not want to "wound the feelings of the American delegates," he nevertheless used the opportunity to encourage them, "on their return home, to enlarge the field of their Temperance operations, and embrace within the scope of their influence, my long neglected race."[20] Knowing full well that the British delegations condemned such discrimination based on race, Douglass used this very public venue far from American shores to condemn and challenge U.S. temperance advocates to expand their racial sensibilities.

Douglass's increasing independence, shown through these public displays, although drawing the ire of some Garrisonians, did not lead to a full-blown schism during the British tour. He spent the fall of 1846 touring Britain with Garrison, Henry C. Wright, and George Thompson, the leading British Garrisonian. A member of Parliament and one of the chief advocates of the 1833 British abolition bill, Thompson had toured in the U.S. in 1834 and 1835. Douglass spent part of his time in Thompson's home in London, and in hopes of moving Douglass to Britain permanently,

Thompson proposed a fund drive to bring Anna and the children to the U.K.[21] Shortly following the temperance convention the group formed the Anti-Slavery League, with Thompson as president, to act as a solidifying organization for British Garrisonians and their agenda. Once Garrison left for home in November, Douglass's self-determination once again surfaced.

Instead of moving his family to England, Douglass indicated his intent to return to the United States. Although he was at risk of capture in the excitement surrounding the publication of his autobiography, Douglass resented implications that he had abandoned his family to enter hiding abroad. Responding to a published account appearing in a U.S. newspaper accusing him of just that, Douglass told the editor of the Belfast *Protestant Journal,* "Whether a slave or a freeman, America is my home, and there I mean to spend and be spent in the cause of my outraged fellow-countrymen."[22] During his time in Britain the stakes on his return grew, when in the wake of the publication of the *Narrative,* Douglass's slave master, Thomas Auld, announced his determination to capture and reenslave Douglass as soon as he set foot on American soil. Upon learning of this threat to his personal safety, British abolitionists immediately began a campaign to purchase Douglass's freedom, so that he could return to his family.

If Douglass's ties with Garrison were eased during his first months abroad, the drive to secure his emancipation served to further assert his independence, literally granting him his freedom. Fundraising efforts were led by Anna Richardson, a Quaker activist from Newcastle upon Tyne. A strong critic of Garrisonian abolitionism, Richardson, her husband Henry, and sister-in-law Ellen Richardson were committed abolitionists and peace reformers. Emphasizing the practical over the ideological, Anna Richardson wrote to Auld to negotiate the financial transaction that would exchange £150 for a deed of manumission declaring Douglass a free man.[23] Although Garrison did not publicly address the issue with Douglass, abolitionists in his circle, including Richard Webb and Henry C. Wright, openly condemned the purchase scheme, claiming that any exchange of money validated the slave system. Wright wrote to Douglass in December begging him to reconsider. "I cannot think of the transaction without vexation. I would see you free—you *are* free—you always *were* free, and the man is a villain who claims you as a slave. ... I would see your right to freedom, and to a standing on the platform of humanity, openly acknowledged by every human being—not on the testimony of a bit of paper, signed and sealed by an acknowledged thief."[24] Webb urged Douglass to stop the transaction, arguing, "it was worth running some risk for the sake of the conflict, and the certain result" of uncompensated freedom for it required a "self-emancipated captive" to call to order "that piratical Republic before the world."[25]

Such advice was well and good coming from free white men who had never known the bonds of slavery or had to look over a shoulder for the slave catcher, but Douglass needed to be more practical. He appreciated and agreed with Wright's philosophical point, but replied that "I am in England, my family are in the United States. Thomas Auld, *aided by the American Government*, can seize, bind and fetter, and drag me from my family, feed his cruel revenge upon me, and doom me to unending slavery."[26] By the time Webb and Wright wrote to Douglass, it was already too late to change his mind. While the Garrisonians continued to debate the moral dilemma of paying to secure his freedom, Douglass was grateful to his British friends for their practical and swift assistance. In November, to effect the transaction Anna Richardson secured the services of Boston abolitionists, including Garrisonian Ellis Gray Loring, and Walter Lowrie of New York City. Hugh Auld, with whom Douglass had lived in Baltimore, negotiated for his brother Thomas. Upon proving legal ownership, funds were transmitted for the final transaction. Thomas Auld legally transferred ownership to Hugh Auld, and then on December 5, 1846 manumission papers were filed in Baltimore County. A week later the receipts and paperwork proving his freedom were on the way to Douglass across the Atlantic.[27]

British reformers such as the Richardsons tended to be much more practical in their approach to reform and were often impatient with the militant radical positions taken by Garrisonians such as Wright and Webb. Correspondence between the reformers remained cordial as Douglass navigated between the practicality of British reformers such as Anna and Ellen Richardson and his Garrisonian mentors. Nevertheless, as Richard Blackett has shown, the public debate over Douglass's purchase increased the distance between Douglass and the Garrisonians. As would become apparent once he returned to the U.S., his time abroad and his new-found freedom pushed Douglass to think in new and independent directions.[28] The openness with which he was accepted among British reformers demonstrated their willingness to accept him as an equal, and was quite unlike the Garrisonians' attempts to channel his career as an abolitionist lecturer. In effect the Garrisonians viewed his ability to provide firsthand testimony about the evils of slavery to be of most value to the movement. Although his years in slavery would always assert a significant influence on his life and actions, Douglass wanted to expand his sphere as a reformer. He shared with his British friends his aspiration to edit a newspaper of his own, one that would approach issues of reform from the perspective of African Americans, but said nothing to Garrison about his plans. Douglass had attended a meeting of the National Convention of Colored Men at Buffalo in 1843 at which one of the calls was for an independent black voice in the newspaper world.[29] The idea had been in the back of his mind ever since, and the confidence and experiences gained during his time in Britain led Douglass to believe his was the proper voice to express the position of African Americans in U.S. reform circles. His British colleagues agreed, and led by Jonathan D. Carr, the baker responsible for Carr's water biscuits, they raised funds equivalent to more than $2,000 as a "testimony" to help him establish a newspaper.[30]

Contact with these reformers also led some, such as Webb, to further speculate about Douglass's associations with female reformers. Whether those relationships were inappropriate has long been a source of speculation among historians as well as Douglass's contemporaries. It is true that although Carr coordinated the financial transaction in transferring the testimony for Douglass's newspaper venture, those prominent among the fundraisers were Isabel Jennings of Cork, Ireland, Anna Richardson, and Julia and Eliza Griffiths of London.[31] Clearly, he enjoyed a special kinship with women, who in Britain as in the U.S. did not enjoy voting rights and were often subservient to men in many aspects of public and legal life. Douglass recognized that women's place in society was not altogether different from that of the slave, but he also clearly liked the company of intelligent women. Those he chose as his close companions tended to be strong, independent, well educated, and white. All were very unlike his wife, who remained illiterate, and shunned the public arena for the domestic sphere. In 1846 Douglass formed a lasting friendship with Julia Griffiths. The daughter of prominent barrister and British and Foreign Anti-Slavery Society member Thomas Powis Griffiths, she became a veritable money-raising machine for Douglass's newspaper venture. Eventually Griffiths and her sister Eliza traveled to the U.S., where she lived in Douglass's home with his family for some time, raising the eyebrows of his friends and critics alike.[32]

Equipped with his free papers and emboldened by a year and a half's absence of open racial prejudice, Douglass prepared to return to the U.S. in the spring of 1847. Booking passage in London on Cunard's *Cambria*, paying the full first-class fare for a voyage embarking April 4, Douglass tried to ascertain whether his color would form a barrier denying him access as had happened in 1845. He was told that he would have full access. When he arrived at the Liverpool dock, however, Douglass learned that he had been misinformed by the London agent, and that his cabin had been assigned to someone else. Cunard officials did not fully acquiesce in the matter, but resolution of the situation was much different than his previous experience, when he passed the whole voyage in steerage. In 1845 Douglass had been a little-known escaped slave, but after eighteen months in Britain he was recognized as an international orator and man of letters. This time Captain Charles Judkins accompanied him to the Cunard Line's Liverpool office to negotiate a compromise. In exchange for agreeing to dine alone and avoid company in the saloon, Douglass was given a plush cabin recently occupied by the Canadian governor general. Cunard officials thus sought both to appease Douglass, and to prevent a repeat of the excitement caused by his speech on board in 1845. The crossing went without incident, and Douglass returned home to his family in Lynn upon landing in Boston on April 20; but the episode received much attention in both Britain and America.[33]

Before leaving for the U.S. Douglass wrote to the editor of the London *Times*, a leading national newspaper, arguing that he "felt it due to my own rights as a man, as well as to the honour and dignity of the British public, to lay these facts before them, sincerely believing that the British public will pronounce a just verdict on such proceedings."[34] He was right. The letter appeared in the *Times* as well as other London and Bristol newspapers, and was widely reprinted in the U.S. *Times* editor John Thadeus Delane sided with Douglass, condemning the Cunard Line for pandering to the prejudices of their American travelers. Public pressure led Samuel Cunard to formally denounce the practice of segregating black passengers, noting "*nothing of the kind will again take place in steamships with which I am connected.*"[35] Douglass's first transatlantic journey, then, made a lasting impact beyond his personal experience and on the experience of all African Americans traveling on Cunard ships thereafter. Returning to Massachusetts, he turned his attention toward expanding his influence at home in the United States.

CHAPTER 5

BECOMING HIS OWN MAN

As many as seven hundred turned out for a farewell reception at the London Tavern on the city's Bishopsgate Street. George Thompson and other reformers wished Douglass well, and even Charles Dickens sent a letter expressing his regret at being unable to attend. Addressing this, his final London audience, Douglass delivered a fiery Garrisonian attack on American slavery and the Constitution that protected it. Despite calls to move his family to the U.K., Douglass chose to return to the United States. He told those gathered, "I prefer living a life of activity in the service of my brethren. I choose rather to go home; to return to America. I glory in the conflict, that I may hereafter exult in victory."[1] Turning toward America, Douglass was confronted with the reality of holding loyalty to a nation that gave African Americans few advancements and fewer opportunities to exercise citizenship rights. In Britain, despite a few racist overtones, he had enjoyed a freedom unknown to all but a small handful of black Americans. Moving his family to England would certainly mean better educational and career opportunities for his four children. But he was not a Brit, and although he struggled almost his entire life for a rightful place within the social and political structure of America, Douglass returned because it was his home and birthright. Later, he would turn away from a brief flirtation with colonization for the same reasons. The United States, despite all its many flaws, was home, and Douglass felt compelled to strive to make it a better place for himself, his family, and his race. When he reached Massachusetts on April 20, 1847, he began in earnest on a new path. He remained committed to William Lloyd Garrison and his principles of radical abolition, but Douglass was deeply affected and emboldened by his time abroad. Unbeknownst to Garrison, the British tour inspired Douglass to embark on a new and independent path, developing his own brand of reform that coupled the priorities and needs of free blacks in the North with the over-arching goal of abolishing slavery in the South. In addition to being an abolitionist, he was becoming a race man.

At home, Douglass found his happy family eagerly waiting. In his excite-ment to see his wife and children, he had left his bags on the wharf and ignored a group gathered there to welcome him, jumping aboard the first available train from Boston to Lynn. He recalled that Lewis and Frederick Jr. "ran with sparkling eyes, dancing with very joy to meet me. Frederick I caught up into my arms, and taking Lewis by the hand, I ran with them into the house, and relieved all anxious expectation."[2] In a rare glimpse into his married life, he wrote to Anna Richardson, "my dear Anna is not well, but much better than I expected to find her, as she seldom enjoys good health." He marveled at how much all three boys had grown, and it is likely that Charles Remond had little memory of this father who had been away more than half his three years. As the Douglasses became reac-quainted, plans were made for Douglass and Anna to travel to Albany, New York, where eight-year-old Rosetta was attending school and living in the home of Abigail and Lydia Mott. Cousins of prominent abolition-ists Lucretia Coffin and James Mott, the pair operated a formal school near their home.[3]

But even while Douglass declared that "for once all cares of a public nature were cast aside," he was still seething inside from the compromise he had agreed to during his passage on the *Cambria*. During the sixteen days on board, Douglass had been "confined like a criminal to a certain part of the ship because of my color." He had reflected in those long hours of solitude on the path that lay before him once he reached Massachusetts and determined which way to go forward. Within days of returning home, a letter to British abolitionists William and Robert Smeal declared, "I will not be silent. I am still strongly determined to devote myself to *printing* as well as *speaking* for my race."[4] Douglass intended to put the funds raised by his British friends to use, operating his own newspaper that would give a voice to a uniquely African American brand of reform. He was willing to proudly declare his intention to the Smeals, but in reality he had no experi-ence or knowledge of editing or business operations. He also hesitated to tell Garrison of his plans, suspecting correctly that his decision would not be popular with his longtime friend and mentor.

The idea of editing his own antislavery newspaper was alluring to Douglass, but convincing the Garrisonians was a daunting prospect. Gar-rison and others, including Wendell Phillips, who had endorsed Doulass's *Narrative*, likely learned from the British reformers who had raised funds that their protégé was contemplating starting a newspaper. In the late spring and early summer speculation raged in private correspondence and the reform press. British abolitionist Joseph Lupton admitted as much in a letter to Garrison's *Liberator*, claiming he was willing to accept funds from reformers in Leeds, finding "it would do great service to the cause of humanity to enable him [Douglass] to become the proprietor and editor of an Anti-Slavery newspaper." Lupton spoke for other Douglass supporters, noting it would be "an appropriate testimonial," to his "character and talents."[5] Campaigns, including one specifically to purchase a printing press, managed to raise as much as $4,000, sufficient to establish a small business. Garrison and Phillips were nevertheless opposed to the idea, pointing out that at least four other weeklies already spoke for the black voice of reform, including Thomas Van Rensellaer's *Ram's Horn* published in New York, and Martin Delany's *Mystery*, published sporadically in Pittsburgh.

The complexity of the relationship between Douglass and his Garrisonian colleagues made it difficult for him to assert his independence and desire to make his own voice heard. Garrison's objection was partly rooted in the reality of editorship. No antislavery newspaper, including the *Liberator*, was financially solvent, requiring a constant diligence in gaining subscriptions and outside fundraising to keep it afloat. Garrison knew that even if his friend possessed a strong head for business (which Douglass did not), his newspaper was unlikely to succeed. Douglass was inexperienced in business matters, but evidence suggests he did believe that he could make it as an editor. If Garrison could successfully balance running a newspaper with extended lecturing tours, why could Douglass not follow his mentor's example? In the postscript of a letter to Anna Richardson he remarked, "I still look forward to some connection with the press as a means of promoting the cause, and securing a living."[6]

Whatever his fears for his friend's financial solvency, Garrison also struggled to accept Douglass's autonomy and likely detested the introduction of another reform paper with which the *Liberator* would have to compete. A large number of *Liberator* subscribers were African American, and Douglass's growing reputation as a black leader had the potential to draw these supporters away. His protégé's popularity complicated matters, too. Garrison biographer Henry Mayer observes that Douglass was unique among former fugitive slaves involved in the abolition movement. He possessed a talent and presence that catapulted him from the shadows of white abolitionists to stand as an equal and in some senses to eclipse both Garrison and Phillips in popularity and influence. He embodied and embraced the vision of equality immediate abolitionists claimed they strove for, becoming a symbol that none wanted to antagonize or repress.[7] Douglass as a newspaper editor might prove to be too equal and slip outside their sphere of influence. A combination of these factors swirled in the confines of their relationship, making it difficult for each man to accurately express his feelings. The contradiction also made it hard for Garrison to argue against the prospect of Douglass's newspaper, but he persisted in his opposition.

Even as Douglass and Garrison prepared to embark together on a lengthy lecture tour in late summer, Douglass became increasingly aloof from his white colleagues, all the while contemplating his own future. Officially, he announced that he was putting plans for his newspaper on hold. He owed a considerable debt to Garrison, who first recognized Douglass's abilities and urged him into the lecture field. He was his tutor in the abolition movement, and the pair had a lengthy history of companionship, as they spent much time traveling together and in conversation about their cause and lives. Garrison had also supported and facilitated the publication of Douglass's *Narrative* and joined him on the British tour that followed. Douglass's hesitation to begin his newspaper may have sprung as much from a reluctance to harm his relationship with Garrison as from uncertainty about his own ability to succeed. He needed help from somewhere, for although he often corresponded with the reform press, he had little knowledge of the daily operation of a newspaper. If his friend Garrison, an experienced editor and printer, was unwilling to support and advise him in establishing his own press, Douglass had to look elsewhere or abandon the prospect.

Garrison seemed to put the matter out of his mind after printing an announcement in the *Liberator* indicating Douglass was no longer pursuing the idea of an independent press, but the matter did not die so easily among Douglass's supporters. An anonymous enthusiast suggested that abandoning the venture was an act "in which Mr. Douglass's inclinations have been less consulted than those of some of the leading abolitionists."[8] Others speculated that his action was influenced "by a few leading abolitionists in whom he put confidence, contrary to his own feelings," because his press might harm the circulation of other antislavery newspapers, including those edited by black men.[9] Douglass patiently denied claims that his decision was influenced by the paternalistic guidance of the Garrisonians. In a letter clearly written for publication, Douglass apologized to Garrison for the attack on his character made by his eager supporters who had urged him to go forward with the venture. "This is absolutely grievous; and I feel it due to yourself and friends, and all concerned, to say at once, distinctly and publicly, that, in this matter I have acted independently, and wholly on my own responsibility."[10] Less than three weeks later, Douglass and Garrison left together for a western tour which took them to Pennsylvania and Ohio. So far as his friend and companion knew, Douglass had given up the idea of his own newspaper.

On his first lengthy lecture tour since returning to America, Douglass soon had no doubt that he was no longer in England. Acting as a correspondent for the American Anti-Slavery Society's weekly *National Anti-Slavery Standard*, he wrote letters to editor Sydney Howard Gay describing their daily travels and events along the way. At a meeting in Harrisburg, Pennsylvania Douglass and Garrison were pelted with rotten eggs and greeted with cries of *"throw out the nigger."* Soon after, a ticketing error separated the pair, forcing Douglass to endure "a series of brutal insults and outrages" during his lone two-day train journey from Chambersburg to Pittsburgh.[11] Reunited with Garrison and warmly welcomed by Pittsburgh's black community, Douglass encountered for the first time Martin R. Delany, a physician and editor of the *Mystery*, one of the four existing weeklies published by an African American. A prominent intellectual, Delany eventually became the highest-ranking black commissioned officer during the Civil War. Later, Douglass and Delany were often at odds on important currents concerning African Americans, but in 1847 meeting Delany was a fateful moment in Douglass's career. If plans for his own press had been put aside, connecting with Delany at Pittsburgh certainly rekindled the flame of desire.

Douglass was already exploring other ways to take up the editor's pen, including a partnership or alliance with an existing black-owned newspaper. While in Pittsburgh, he wrote asking Sydney Howard Gay, himself an experienced newspaper man, to examine the solvency of Thomas Van Rensellaer's *Ram's Horn*, to determine the feasibility of becoming a partner. During the western lecture tour, Douglass also acted as a corresponding contributor for that journal.[12] He was clearly eager for a more substantial role in the field of reform. Similar discussions likely passed between Doulass and Delany, ending in a fruitful newspaper partnership in the months to come, but if they had already stuck a deal in August and September, he made no mention of it to Garrison. The pair continued into Ohio where they lectured extensively with agents of the Western Anti-Slavery Society and enjoyed an affirmative reception in the abolitionist-friendly Western Reserve. In mid-September, Garrison fell seriously ill at Cleveland with brain fever, an ailment akin to meningitis, and was forced to remain in the home of antislavery friends for a lengthy recuperation.

Douglass continued on the schedule, in the company of Garrisonian Stephen S. Foster, to Buffalo, where he met up with his old lecturing companions, Charles Lenox Remond and Joseph Hathaway. While Garrison lay in Cleveland slowly recovering, Douglass lectured across New York's "burned-over district," so-called because the western region of the state was awash with evangelical revivals and a hotbed for reform movements. Learning that Garrison's condition was very serious, Douglass regretted having left his side, but he could not turn back. With Remond and Hatha-way he proceeded through Rochester, Seneca Falls, Syracuse, and Albany. Of the meetings in Rochester he was particularly impressed, writing to Gay that they "were all that we could desire."[13] Although he had telegraphed Cleveland to inquire about his friend's health, he made no attempt to write or contact Garrison directly. He could not bring himself to tell his mentor, now grievously ill and far from home, that he had decided to defy all odds and establish his own newspaper. "I had not decided against the publica-tion of a paper one month, before I became satisfied that I had made a mistake, and each subsequent month's experience has confirmed in me the conviction," he recalled.[14] His time spent in western New York helped to cement another stone in the wall he was constructing between himself and Garrison, and opened his eyes to new possibilities.

Home at Lynn again in late October, he wrote his friend Amy Post, "I have finally decided on publishing the *North Star* in Rochester, and to make that city my future home."[15] If looking for a place to cut his ties from the Garrisonian circles emanating from Boston, Rochester was a likely choice. One of the last stops on the Underground Railroad before Canada, the city boasted a strong and vibrant community of reformers and particularly of political abolitionists. Welcomed there by Amy and Isaac Post, Samuel D. Porter, and others, Douglass arrived in November 1847, publishing the first issue of the *North Star* on December 3. He began the venture in part-nership with Martin Delany, who spent much of his time traveling across the northeast securing subscriptions for the new weekly.

Traveling ahead of his family, who came to Rochester the following February, Douglass was too busy to worry about the consequences of Gar-rison's annoyance at his betrayal. He moved from the relative security of employment by the American Anti-Slavery Society (AASS) to being edi-tor in chief of his own newspaper and master of his own fortune. In the weekly's first issue he proclaimed, "THE object of the NORTH STAR will be to attack SLAVERY in all its forms and aspects; advocate UNIVERSAL EMANCIPATION; exalt the standard of PUBLIC MORALITY; promote the moral and intellectual improvement of the COLORED PEOPLE."[16] The advancement of his race was a growing concern that Douglass fully embraced soon after locating in Rochester, but first he had to secure the stable operation of his business.

Using a large portion of the money his British supporters provided, Douglass bought a printing press, but knowing little about such equip-ment, the press was apparently inadequate for the job. He soon had to con-tract out the printing of the newspaper, employing John Dick as printer. Although Delany's name appeared on the masthead of the *North Star* as coeditor until the middle of 1849, his actual involvement in the newspaper is not fully clear. More ready assistance came from William Cooper Nell, a black Garrisonian who previously worked for the *Liberator*. He moved to Rochester, lived as a guest of Amy and Isaac Post, and took the reins as the *North Star*'s publisher with its first issue in December 1847. Nell acted as editor when Douglass was on the lecture circuit, working closely with him until 1851 when Douglass broke with the Garrisonians and adopted a new view on the use of politics in the abolition of slavery.

Even after beginning publication of the *North Star*, Douglass remained ideologically loyal to Garrison and continued to lecture on behalf of the AASS, but he was exercising an independent voice through his newspaper and his removal from the center of Garrisonian activity in Boston found him regularly interacting with reformers who shared a number of perspectives. Amy and Isaac Post, whom Douglass befriended on an earlier lecture tour, became close friends and associates. These Hicksite Quaker activists were key planners in the Rochester antislavery movement. Amy Post, along with Abby Kelley Foster, was one of the founders of the Western New York Anti-Slavery Society, and had actively encouraged Douglass to move to the city. Along with her husband, Post was an active spiritualist, apparently temporarily drawing Douglass's publisher Nell into their "rapping" meetings, at which spirits were said to reveal themselves by rapping on the table.[17]

Lasting connections with other western New York activists also had significant influence on Douglass's new career and reform path. Soon after commencing the *North Star*, Douglass found a new circle of abolitionists reaching out to him. He received a congratulatory note from Garrisonian abolitionist Samuel J. May, who was also a lecturing agent for AASS. A Unitarian minister from Boston, May had moved to Syracuse in 1845. He and Douglass had much in common: in 1848 May was committed to the principles of nonresistance and rejected political means to end slavery, but along with Douglass he would find that position untenable following the passage of the 1850 Fugitive Slave Law. The pair cemented their friendship in 1849 when Douglass attended an antislavery lecture May delivered at Rochester's Unitarian church. When Douglass undertook a western New York lecture tour that spring, he stayed in May's home while in Syracuse. In the years to come May and Douglass worked closely together with other black abolitionists including Samuel Ringgold Ward and Rev. James Wesley Loguen, on an agenda very different from their Garrisonian roots.[18]

The most significant relationship formed in New York, however, was between Douglass and philanthropist Gerrit Smith. Historian John R. McKivigan has marked the onset of their friendship as a turning point in Douglass's career.[19] In what was probably their first contact, in December 1847, Smith wrote subscribing to the *North Star*, but also enclosing deeds to parcels of land he granted to both Douglass and Nell. "Inasmuch as you and Mr. Nell have become inhabitants of this State," a surprised Douglass read, "I feel at liberty to convey a parcel of land to each of you."[20] Smith, who lived in the small village of Peterboro, in Madison County, was heir to a large fortune and as much as a quarter million acres of land in upstate New York. His great wealth provided ample time to support a host of reform causes such as temperance, women's rights, and prison reform, but he was most devoted to the abolition of slavery. Through his philanthropy, Smith purchased the freedom of numerous slaves and encouraged them to settle in Peterboro and the surrounding area. At the time of Douglass's arrival in Rochester, Smith was in the midst of a great land giveaway, parceling out some 140,000 acres of land in upstate New York to three thousand African Americans.[21] Although the land was not very useful for cultivation, the grants did make the deed holders property owners and thereby more likely to be in a position to demonstrate the necessary $250 holding required for black men to vote in New York.

Douglass's horizon was also stretched by his increasing involvement and leadership in the Negro Convention Movement. One impetus for starting his own newspaper was his growing desire to give voice to African Americans' roles and priorities in achieving the abolition of slavery as well as making a case for black citizenship rights. Although many blacks, including Douglass, adopted the established Garrisonian tactics of moral suasion and nonresistance, employed petitions and took to the lecture circuit, African Americans had a bigger and more personal stake in achieving equal rights for blacks in the North. Blacks rarely enjoyed full citizenship, even in the free states. Most northern states denied blacks any voting rights, while in New York they were required to own property, which was not a requirement for white voters. In the 1830s Jacksonian Democracy led to the elimination of many voting restrictions for whites, but at the same time three states, Tennessee, North Carolina, and Pennsylvania, took the vote away from free blacks. As they entered the Union, three western states, Ohio, Indiana, and Illinois, adopted restrictive Black Laws aimed at deterring African Americans from sullying their vision for a "free white West." Ohio would repeal its black laws in 1849 but Indiana and Illinois would maintain them until after the Civil War ended, and Iowa would have them for a few years in the 1850s. In Indiana, Illinois, Ohio (until 1849), and California (until 1862), African Americans were forbidden to testify against whites. Throughout the North blacks were forced to endure Jim Crow segregation on public accommodations, as Douglass well knew from his extensive travels. His white traveling companions were generally sympathetic, but as Nathan Huggins pointed out, African Americans could hardly expect white reformers or their organizations to fully press the issues of equality.[22]

Advocating the cause of black civil rights in systematic fashion was the force behind the black convention movement that began in 1830, and lasted somewhat sporadically well into the Civil War. Initially a national movement that met annually until 1835, the conventions gathered prominent black leaders as needed between 1843 and 1864. Sometimes mirrored by conventions of black men on the state level, the movement was spawned in the wake of a vicious antiblack riot in Cincinnati in 1829. After that race riot as many as a thousand blacks chose to emigrate to Canada rather than remain in the so-called free state of Ohio, although many later returned.[23] The conventions brought black leaders together to collectively consider issues of concern to their race. In a format closely mirroring antislavery gatherings, convention attendees debated issues of supreme importance to African Americans, including the colonization of freed blacks in the African colony of Liberia, voting rights, and educational and economic opportunities. The early conventions had been controlled by elite blacks in cities such as Philadelphia, but by the time Douglass attended his first national convention at Buffalo in 1843 a new generation of black leaders was emerging to lead a call for the improvement of their race. At that meeting, the impatience of the new leadership was apparent in Henry Highland Garnet's resolution calling for a violent overthrow of the slave system. Then firmly in the Garrisonian camp, Douglass led the opposition to Garnet's radicalism, claiming then that moral suasion was the only effective way to abolish slavery.[24] Although still ideologically linked with his Boston mentor, after Douglass moved to Rochester he openly sought a leadership role in the conventions, and was both influenced by the connections he made there and beginning to sway and shape the convention movement with his editorial pen.

In Douglass's evolving view, black elevation was intimately tied to the abolition movement and he sought to expand his involvement with his race peers. Two months before initiating the *North Star,* he attended a black convention held at Troy, New York. His speech on this occasion also reflected his attachment to the Garrisonians, as he urged convention-goers to reject their proslavery churches because their altars were stained with the blood of slaves. Reports of the convention noted that Douglass's words "created some excitement—for colored men, like others, don't care to be reminded of their inconsistencies."[25] But the convention also raised Douglass's awareness of the most pressing issues of debate among black intellectuals, including the establishment of independent colleges for blacks, fostering business and commerce, black suffrage, and a prominent presence for the black press.²⁶ In a report entered by a committee headed by black physician James McCune Smith, the convention called for a national press that would promote the interests of African Americans in the North as well as advocate for the abolition of slavery. Considering Douglass was in the midst of plans for the *North Star*, he must have been pleased with this discussion. Perhaps he entertained thoughts that his paper would become the national organ McCune Smith called for at the convention.²⁷ In the first issue of his paper, Douglass expressed a similar desire for the African American reform voice to be heard: "it is evident we must be our own representatives and advocates, not exclusively, but peculiarly—not distinct from, but in connection with our white friends."²⁸

The following year Douglass's increasing involvement in the movement for black elevation was reflected in the pages of the *North Star*. His editorials calling for suffrage, opposing colonization, and supporting equal rights established Douglass as a leader among African Americans. Quoting his favorite line from Lord Byron's *Childe Harold*, "Hereditary bondmen! know ye not/Who would be free, themselves must strike the first blow?"²⁹ Douglass urged African Americans to work actively on behalf of their race. Although Douglass has sometimes been criticized for his commitment to assimilation and integration, his editorials began warning against relying on white reformers to advance the cause of African Americans:³⁰

> If there is one evil spirit among us, for the casting out of which we pray more earnestly than another, it is the lazy, mean and cowardly spirit, that robs us of all manly self-reliance, and teaches us to depend upon others for the accomplishment of that which we should achieve with our own hands.³¹

Perhaps Douglass was thinking of his own dependence on the Garrisonians during the first seven years of his abolitionist career. Whatever he had in mind when he penned this critique, it became clear in 1848 that he was emerging as his own man.

Probably due to the tone of his recent editorials, in September 1848 he was elected president of the National Negro Convention held at Cleveland. The meeting opened his eyes to the needs of African Americans and cemented his commitment to fight for civil rights. He came to see his fellow black activists in a new light, remarking, "We return from this Convention with a higher sense of the excellence of character and mental ability of our people, than we have ever entertained before." The newly independent-minded Douglass regretted that his longtime ties to the Garrisonians kept him from knowing the hearts and minds of northern black activists:

> Cut off from them for seven years past by the duties of our vocation as a lecturer, and seldom meeting them when their characters and sentiments could

be well determined, we had almost come to think that they cared very little about the fettered bondman, and less about their own elevation and improvement. No man with such impressions could have gone to a better place than the Colored National Convention at Cleveland, during last week, to have such impressions entirely removed.[32]

Douglass's leadership at the convention cemented his reputation as an important race leader. He drafted much of the memorable "Address to the Colored People of the United States," which asserted the position of the convention's leaders. In it, Douglass connected the movement for race elevation with the plight of southern slaves, telling convention-goers, "Every one of us should be ashamed to consider himself free, while his brother is a slave." He also argued for blacks to make their way into manual labor, skilled trades, and to take up farming, noting "Every blow of the sledge hammer, wielded by a sable arm, is a powerful blow, in support of our cause." However, after seven years of working closely with white reformers, Douglass knew that black elevation could not be achieved through the actions of African Americans alone. He urged African Americans to "act with white Abolition societies wherever you can, and where you cannot, get up societies among yourselves, but without exclusiveness."[33]

Controlling the content of his newspaper and involvement in the convention movement helped Douglass to deepen his relationships with other black reformers. Many reached out to him to commend him on undertaking the North Star. David Ruggles, chair of the New York City Vigilance Committee, who had aided Douglass in his initial days of freedom, declared that "since yours is a permanent press, and the STAR shines for all, the necessity of the 'National Press,' called for by the Troy Convention, is superseded."[34] Initiating what would become a cherished and long-lasting friendship, black educator and businessman Henry O. Wagoner told Douglass, "I must confess that I have felt a secret joy ever since I first heard your name spoken of in connection with the 'North Star'."[35] The connection sparked between these two men was enduring, eventually leading Wagoner to host Douglass's sons Lewis and Frederick Douglass, Jr. in his Denver, Colorado home, where the pair learned typography. Later Douglass reciprocated, using his influence to help Wagoner's son secure a clerk's position in the consulate at Paris, France.[36]

Others urged Douglass and Delany to push further for reform and racial advocacy. The leading spokesman for the American Moral Reform Society, Pennsylvania black abolitionist William Whipper, defended Douglass's paper against charges that black newspapers served to further separate the races in America. In an early issue, Douglass had editorialized that wielding the editor's pen, regardless of racial designation, helped promote equality between blacks and whites in the same way that black lawyers, artisans, and farmers did. Whipper urged Douglass to go even further. "I have looked carefully over the columns of the 'North Star,' and I am unable to discover any just reason why it should be termed a 'colored newspaper,' any more than the Liberator, Standard, Freeman, or many other Anti-Slavery periodical[s]." Whipper charged that the view that separate "black" newspapers served to further artificially and unnecessarily divide blacks and whites was an old notion that had outlived its usefulness. He saw the *North Star* as the vehicle that could open a new chapter in racial advocacy, provided Douglass was willing to make it truly representative of the African American position. "It is a question of duty," he wrote, "and if it lies entombed in darkness, let us disencumber it of the rubbish of the past, so its luminous rays may light up our pathway to future action."[37]

The early months of 1848 were a busy time, as Douglass struggled to put his newspaper on a solid footing, continued to lecture in and around western New York for the AASS, and made plans to move his family to Rochester. Too busy to reflect too heavily on Whipper's suggestions, he was more immediately concerned with sheltering his family. Following his own unsuccessful hunt for housing, Isaac Post helped Douglass locate and purchase a house at 4 Alexander Street in preparation for his family's move. Anna and the three boys, Lewis, Charles, and Frederick Jr., arrived in late winter, and Rosetta joined the family after the end of her school term. Anna was forced to start over for the third time in their ten-year marriage, but must have been pleased to have the whole family reunited in Rochester. At her husband's insistence, nine-year-old Rosetta had spent more than a year at the home of the Mott sisters, attending their school in Albany. The narrow house on Alexander Street, which had a small yard with room for Anna's beloved garden, became the family's home for more than twenty years, offering Anna and the children stability and the opportunity to settle into the community. According to Rosetta's later reflection on her mother's life, Anna skillfully managed the household with only the aid of a laundress. As the Douglasses saw fit to open their home to fugitive slaves fleeing northward to Canada on the Underground Railroad, it is likely that Anna often entertained unexpected house guests in addition to her own growing family. Other semi-permanent lodgers included Doulass's printer, John Dick, and visitors from abroad. As in Lynn, she continued her antislavery activities with the women of the Rochester community, but, never particularly comfortable in her husband's world, Anna limited her work to the fundraising bazaars that provided aid to the *North Star* and other abolition causes.[38]

By the spring of 1848, Douglass's newspaper was struggling and he was forced to take a mortgage on their new home to keep it afloat. Never a particularly good businessman, he needed help coping with the complexities of running a business while working as an antislavery lecturer. Support came in the controversial extended visit of British abolitionist Julia Griffiths, who arrived in Rochester along with her sister Eliza. Douglass befriended Griffiths during his British tour and maintained a correspondence with her following his return home. Both Griffiths sisters initially lodged with the Douglasses, and then Eliza Griffiths married *North Star* printer John Dick in 1850 and the pair subsequently moved to Toronto. Julia Griffiths remained in Rochester and for a significant part of the next five years resided in Douglass's home. She helped Douglass manage the *North Star*, keeping the books, raising funds and vigorously pursuing subscriptions, putting the weekly on a more solid footing.[39]

Griffiths became active in Rochester abolitionist activities, helping to broaden the reach of the Western New York Anti-Slavery Society by organizing antislavery sewing circles around Rochester. Spending time with her created another influence that helped to pull Douglass farther away from the Garrisonians. Griffiths criticized the Garrisonians' complete rejection of organized Protestant religion as a tool in the fight against slavery. Although she rejected proslavery churches, she argued that abolitionists should work within antislavery churches to reach more converts to the cause. Waldo Martin has shown that Douglass's connection with Griffiths served to soften his view of organized religion and eventually to reject Garrison's antisabbatarian doctrine.[40] Later, after she returned to England, Garrison's resentment of Griffiths surfaced in a letter to Samuel J. May, Jr., in which he suggested Douglass and Griffiths had plotted to discredit the AASS abroad: "Through the machinations of that double-and-twisted worker of iniquity, Julia Griffiths, the hue-and-cry of 'infidelity' is raised afresh in England and Scotland, by various religious cliques, against the American Anti-Slavery Society."[41]

As Douglass's almost constant public companion, speculation raged that theirs was more than a business relationship. Just as had happened in Britain, many began to whisper about Douglass's affinity for white women. With Griffiths living in the Douglass home, and working closely beside him every day, strain must have shown in his relationship with Anna. When Griffiths arrived in Rochester, Anna was once again pregnant. Griffiths returned from a fundraising trip to England shortly after the Douglasses' fifth child, daughter Annie, was born in March 1849. As Anna's duties became increasingly tied to home and family, her husband worked privately and appeared publicly with Griffiths. It is hard to imagine Anna did not resent this cultured, well-educated white woman on whom her husband doted.

Although there is no evidence that definitively points to a romantic relationship or Anna Douglass's reaction, it is clear that many of Douglass's critics (and even some supporters) took notice. As in Britain, many American women reformers found Douglass attractive and personable, and were not ashamed to publicly comment that they found him appealing. Often seen walking arm in arm with white women, Douglass challenged nineteenth-century conventions on numerous occasions. In the restrained circles of British reform, his behavior had prompted John Estlin, Richard Webb, and others to take notice of how women "petted" him and to wonder how his wife would respond had she known. In the U.S. the reaction was occasionally more pronounced. There racial prejudice intertwined with Victorian sexual conventions, making interracial relationships taboo. Seen as an affront to white masculinity, relationships between black men and white women suggested that white men were unsatisfactory sexual companions and simultaneously exacerbated images of black male hypersexuality or virility. Not surprisingly, those who violated societal norms, as Douglass did, often suffered consequences. While walking in New York City with Julia and Eliza Griffiths, a group of hooligans attacked him with a cane, causing physical injury. In Boston images of the Griffith sisters attending to a crass likeness of the "Nigger Douglass" were widely circulated.[42]

Even the Garrisonians, who liberally proclaimed a commitment to racial equality, were critical of Douglass's relationship with Griffiths. Although he was already out of their grasp by 1852, the Garrisonians made a concerted effort to create a scandal that portrayed Griffiths as a home-wrecker, with Douglass and his family as victims of her wiles. They publicized their displeasure in Garrison's *Liberator* and in the *National Anti-Slavery Standard*. Pressure from Garrison and perhaps from within Douglass's own household led Griffiths to eventually move out of Douglass's home and take up residence in a Rochester boarding house. Douglass defended his relationship with Griffiths to fellow local abolitionist Samuel D. Porter. "When she was in my family—I was necessarily much in her society—our walking and riding together was natural. Now we are separate and only meet at my office at business hours and for business purposes—where we are open to the observation of my printers and to the public."[43] Finally, the public and likely private pressure proved too much. In 1855, Griffiths returned to England on a fundraising trip, but did not return to Rochester. In 1859 she married Methodist minister Henry O. Crofts, but maintained her friendship with Douglass through a lively correspondence.[44]

Whatever Douglass's personal relationship with Griffiths and other women whose company he kept, it is evident from his early days in freedom that Douglass earned a respect from female reformers largely because he accepted them as equals and felt a kinship with the subservient place they held in society. Although he would later move away from Garrison's position on slavery and in some respect on rejecting religion, Douglass remained committed to women's rights. In Rochester he met many advocates of the rights of women and was already friends with Lucretia Mott and other women involved in the emerging movement. Douglass was among those invited to speak at the Seneca Falls Convention, the first annual national meeting for women's rights, held in Seneca Falls, New York on July 18 and 19, 1848. In his address on the second day of the convention he endorsed the controversial Declaration of Sentiments put forth by the women, and chided participants into adopting the entire set of resolutions, including one that called for woman suffrage. In a *North Star* editorial describing the convention he reiterated his support:

> We go farther, and express our conviction that all political rights which it is expedient for man to exercise, it is equally so for woman. All that distinguishes man as an intelligent and accountable being, is equally true of woman; and if that government is only just which governs by the free consent of the governed, there can be no reason in the world for denying to woman the exercise of the elective franchise.[45]

After the Seneca Falls meeting, Douglass regularly attended conventions and spoke out in favor of rights for women. Douglass always supported women's voting rights, although his relationship with women's rights activists was strained in the post-Civil War fight for the Fifteenth Amendment which granted black men suffrage. But, even when being attacked by his former allies like Elizabeth Cady Stanton as the Fifteenth Amendment was being considered, he always argued that men deserved no special privileges that women did not have.[46]

The connections Douglass formed in Rochester in 1848 with reformers outside Boston were also important influences on his emerging independence from his initial mentor on issues of disunion and the role of politics in reform. In 1848 he attended his first political convention, probably at the urging of Gerrit Smith and other western New York political abolitionists. The Liberty Party formed in 1840, at about the same time that divisions developed within the AASS, leading those who refused to denounce the U.S. Constitution as a proslavery document to back away from the radicalism of the Garrisonians. Campaigning on a rigorous antislavery platform, the Liberty Party nominated former slaveholder James G. Birney for president in 1840 and 1844. By August 1848 the party was struggling for survival, and at its convention held at Buffalo that month contemplated merging with the newly evolving Free Soil Party. Formed with support of those who hoped to keep slavery from extending into western territories acquired at the end of the Mexican War (1846–1848), the Free Soil Party espoused a more moderate form of political antislavery, and not all members were abolitionists. Although still officially claiming to believe in disunion and to reject politics, attendance at this convention brought Douglass closer to Smith and to other political abolitionists, including Salmon P. Chase of Ohio, and African American Samuel Ringgold Ward.

For the first four years following his move to Rochester, Douglass's writings reflected the Garrisonian position opposing a union with slaveholders and proclaiming the Constitution to be a proslavery document, but he was beginning to explore and reconsider both ideas. In March 1849 he was publicly in Garrison's camp, but there may have been speculation about his loyalty. The editors of the *Anti-Slavery Bugle*, the Garrisonian weekly organ of the Western Anti-Slavery Society, called on Douglass to "show that the American Constitution is not 'a covenant with death.'" He responded curiously: "Why it should call upon us for such an explanation we are at a loss to know, especially as the editor knows that we hold to that *construction* of the instrument which makes it a pro-slavery compact."[47] But before too long, Douglass did radically change his position. He came to believe that disunion was unnecessary and that the Constitution could be used in the abolition of slavery. Much to the chagrin of the Garrisonians, in 1851 Douglass became an ardent political abolitionist. Reflecting on this "radical change in my opinions," he broke with his old friend Garrison and those of his Boston circle, proclaiming, "What they held to be a great and important truth, I now looked upon as a dangerous error."[48]

CHAPTER **6**

THE TUMULTUOUS YEARS

The 1850s saw Douglass mature as a reformer, as he explored the political ideology of his abolitionist colleagues in western New York, became an established leader in the African American intellectual community, and temporarily flirted with ideas such as colonization and the violent overthrow of slavery. The ever-changing political climate of the decade forced many abolitionists to rethink the efficacy of moral suasion and related tactics. The passage of the Fugitive Slave Law of 1850 spurred a new level of antislavery activity that brought many northerners moderately opposed to the institution into political awareness. The new law was part of the Compromise of 1850, which brought California into the union as a free state, allowed residents in the remaining territories gained from the Mexican War to determine if slavery would be permitted, abolished the slave trade in the District of Columbia, and absorbed Texas's pre-statehood debt. Among all the compromise's provisions, the Fugitive Slave Act proved the most controversial. Although both the U.S. Constitution and the Fugitive Slave Act of 1793 provided for the return of self-emancipated slaves, the 1850 law was more onerous, designating government support for the return of slaves who escaped their owners. The law provided for the appointment of commissioners in each county to enforce the law. These commissioners could call on assistance of federal marshals, the military, the state militias, and local citizens to aid in enforcement. The law commanded "all good citizens" to help capture runaways, but had no mechanism for implementing this provision. However, anyone interfering with the law could face six months in prison and thousand-dollar fines. Those arrested under the Act were tried before these commissioners, but were not permitted to testify in their own defense and no jury was present. Even more alarming to many, commissioners received a higher fee when they found in the slaveholder's favor and returned the fugitive to slavery.

Douglass's personal safety was not challenged by this new law, but living in Rochester, which was often considered one of the last stops on the Underground Railroad, he saw the disastrous effects of the Fugitive Slave Act. Although Rochester blacks were rarely arrested, the vigorous enforcement of the law elsewhere instilled fear in the city's fugitive community. He later recalled that self-emancipated slaves, many of whom had lived peacefully in western New York for years, began to flee across the border to Canada in the wake of the law's passage.[1] Abolitionists who had once vehemently rejected the use of violence, including Douglass, began to take bold steps to help fugitives avoid reenslavement. Formerly pacifist abolitionists made several daring rescues during the law's first full year of enforcement. In late September 1851, Douglass received a visit from William Parker, a fugitive slave who had been living in Christiana, Pennsylvania. Parker had resisted the capture of two fellow fugitives in a shootout that left a Maryland slaveholder dead. Parker and two others involved in the rescue stopped at Douglass's house in Rochester, where they received hospitality and offered a firsthand account of events before fleeing to Canada.[2] By that time Douglass had stepped up his own activities on the Underground Railroad, frequently sheltering three or more self-emancipated men and women at a time and helping them reach safety across the border, so his house was a logical stop for Parker. Douglass personally saw Parker and his companions aboard a Toronto-bound steamer, where Parker handed him the very gun that had felled the slave catcher Edward Gorsuch, as a "token of gratitude and a memento of the battle for liberty at Christiana."[3]

The following month, New York abolitionists Gerrit Smith, Samuel J. May, Jermain Wesley Loguen, and Samuel Ringgold Ward were among those who made a daring rescue of Jerry McHenry from the police station in Syracuse. A carpenter who had lived as a free man in Syracuse for a number of years, McHenry's position was not much different than Douglass's before his British friends financed his purchase. Highlighting the strength of antislavery sentiment in western New York, the Jerry Rescue case resulted in a local grand jury indictment against U.S. marshal Henry Allen for kidnapping McHenry. Although the case against the marshal was thrown out and federal charges were brought against several of the rescuers, most cases ended in acquittals or hung juries.[4] In the "burned-over district" of western New York, there was little sympathy for slaveholders or the new law. The incident pushed Douglass farther from Garrisonian nonresistance and into closer cooperation with this circle of New York abolitionists who were willing to put themselves in legal and personal jeopardy to defend the liberty of their fellow men. Douglass's militancy on resistance to this unjust law swelled in succeeding months, until he was willing to openly boast before the 1852 Free Soil Convention at Pittsburgh, "The only way to make the Fugitive Slave Act a dead letter is to make half a dozen or more dead kidnappers."[5] He was also coming to reevaluate Garrison's staunch opposition to the U.S. Constitution as a proslavery document and to openly discuss the efficacy of political action against slavery.

By the time of the Jerry Rescue, Douglass was refashioning himself as a political abolitionist, with his transition aided considerably both intellectually and financially by Gerrit Smith. Their correspondence, which began soon after Douglass located in Rochester, flourished in the wake of the Fugitive Slave Act's passage, and Douglass firmly assured his new friend in early 1851 that he had changed his views on the Constitution and political action. Douglass was decisively changing his allegiance and in the process did not hesitate to alienate his former mentor and others from the Boston Circle of reformers. Tension had been building between Douglass and William Lloyd Garrison since the inception of the *North Star* in 1847, but the men had remained at least formally cordial in their public contacts and through their editorials. Still it must have been a shock when Douglass publicly announced before the seventeenth annual meeting of the American Anti-Slavery Society (AASS) that he refuted Garrison's position on the Constitution.[6] His statement came in the form of an objection to a resolution under the terms of which antislavery newspapers would receive endorsement by the AASS, with Douglass understanding that only those rejecting a proslavery Constitution would get the nod. Recapping the meeting's events in the *North Star*, he told his readers that his change of opinion came after much careful study and affiliation with political abolitionists including Smith, Lysander Spooner, and William Goodell. Examining the facts led him to believe slavery "to be a system of lawless violence; that it never was lawful, and never can be made so; and that it is the first duty of every American citizen, whose conscience permits him so to do, to use his *political* as well as his *moral* power for its overthrow."[7]

If Douglass had hoped that the physical distance between Rochester and Boston would help to buffer his break with Garrison, he was wrong. Garrison and many of his followers openly criticized every facet of Douglass's public and private life, and especially his relationship with Julia Griffiths. The bitterness he felt in the wake of their estrangement and the attacks that followed similarly made Douglass question the Garrisonians' intent and commitment to racial equality. He wrote to Massachusetts senator Charles Sumner that the Garrisonian brand of reform was "*too* narrow in its philosophy and too bigoted in spirit to do justice to any who venture to differ from it." He soon found that strengthening his alliances with other

African American reformers and with the political abolitionists in western New York resulted in deep personal relationships that expanded his abolitionist activities in the political realm and his involvement in a movement to secure more civil and political rights for black Americans.[8]

Douglass's break with Garrison represented an important turning point in his career and in his personal relationship to his fellow reformers, white and black. Garrison's recent biographer argues that Douglass's shift to political abolition was a "pragmatic change of views" undertaken to protect his newspaper from financial collapse.[9] However, since Julia Griffiths began financial management, the *North Star* was in less financial trouble and for a short time may actually have been supporting Douglass's family. Gerrit Smith had other plans when he proposed a merger between the *North Star* and the *Liberty Party Paper,* a flailing political weekly. Edited from Syracuse by John Thomas, the *Liberty Party Paper* was sustained mostly through Smith's subsidy. Maintaining a small subscriber base of around 1,100, the paper offered a political outlet for those Liberty Party adherents who refused to compromise their abolitionist principles, as required for a merger with the Free Soil Party. Formed in 1840, the Liberty Party attracted immediate abolitionists who wanted to use politics to overthrow slavery. The more moderate Free Soil Party included large contingents who opposed only slavery's extension, with a mind to maintaining a free white West. Believing Douglass to be the better editor, and certainly the more prominent abolitionist, Smith hoped that the merger would breathe life into the Liberty Party, and cement Douglass's adherence to his brand of political abolition. Seeing a chance for real financial stability as an editor, Douglass agreed to undertake the merger and to ensure that his would be the dominant editorial voice, he debuted the new paper on June 26, 1851 under the name *Frederick Douglass' Paper.*[10] Thomas's affiliation lasted about a year before the pair fell out over the issue of land reform, so that by 1852 the venture truly was Douglass's own.

Smith placed his financial support firmly behind Douglass's paper and also frequently funded the publication of his prominent speeches in pamphlet form so that they might receive a wider readership. The editor took his new-found political abolitionism to heart, but his pragmatic side soon led him to support cooperation with the Free Soilers. In 1852 the staunchly abolitionist Liberty Party struggled to survive as the more moderately antislavery Free Soil Party moved forward under the banner of Free Democrats. In 1851 the Liberty Party had met at Buffalo and nominated Gerrit Smith for president, but he had not responded to the call, instead opting to seek a seat in the U.S. House of Representatives.[11] Attending the Free Democrat meeting held at Cincinnati in May 1852, Douglass was elected as a convention secretary and felt he was warmly welcomed, but he was more reticent in endorsing either the Free Democrats or the Liberty Party in that year's presidential election. Instead, throughout the fall Douglass campaigned heartily for his friend, giving more than eighty speeches on his behalf. Perhaps to everyone's surprise, Smith was elected as an independent and served part of a single term during the thirty-third Congress, before resigning in August 1854, disgusted over the internal wrangling of Washington politics.[12]

Douglass's relationship with other activists, especially African Americans, also matured following his break with the Garrisonians. Waldo Martin has argued that, following their falling out, he was "more conscious than ever before of the psychological fact that reliance upon a surrogate white father necessarily stifled black masculine identity and independence."[13] Although Douglass's evolving relationship with Smith suggests perhaps that he transferred his alliance from one white father figure to another, the 1850s brought him into closer contact with the champions of black reform and into alliance with many of the era's leading African American intellectuals. *Frederick Douglass' Paper* hosted a continuing dialog on issues important to black northerners, including colonization, the place of African Americans in northern society, and the debate over racial injustice. Among those to whom Douglass became particularly close was James McCune Smith. Educated at the University of Glasgow in Scotland because no American medical school would admit him, McCune Smith was a civil rights leader and probably the most intellectual African American of his generation. Operating a successful pharmacy and medical practice in New York City and acting as chief physician for the city's Colored Orphan Asylum, McCune Smith found time to write essays and engage in abolitionist activities.[14] He became acquainted with Douglass through the Negro Convention Movement and quickly became both the New York correspondent for *Frederick Douglass' Paper* and a close friend.

While Gerrit Smith looked to the weekly as a vehicle for the Liberty Party and political abolition, McCune Smith saw its importance for black activism: "an organ of *our own*." He recognized that his friend was emerging as easily the most prominent and recognizable leader for their race. In October 1851, he urged Douglass to consider issuing the paper twice weekly, even proposing a financial plan. "We need an organ, not only to battle against our foes, but also, to cheer each other on in the struggle."[15] A sense of urgency fueled African Americans in the wake of the Fugitive Slave Act's passage, and men like McCune Smith and Douglass quickly came to reevaluate nonresistance as idealistic and ineffective. They urged political action when possible, but did not reject violence if it was deemed necessary. In this decade of change and escalating sectional tensions, Douglass came to represent the black voice on major political developments, but he never lost his belief in the importance of interracial cooperation.

Friendships with Gerrit Smith and James McCune Smith influenced Douglass's political and racial activism, but his abandonment of non-resistance was most shaped by his interactions with radical abolitionist John Brown. The lives of all four men came together in Gerrit Smith's land giveaway in the 1840s. Douglass and McCune Smith were advocates of Smith's plan and among the 3,000 black recipients of land in New York's Adirondack mountains. Aimed to provide African Americans with enough freehold property to make them eligible to vote, the settlement of Timbucto was an interracial community and buffer against racial prejudice. White abolitionist John Brown moved his family there in 1848, after failing at several business ventures in Massachusetts, Pennsylvania, and Ohio. Together the four men formed the Radical Abolition Party in 1855, and it was from Timbucto that Brown would plan his insurrection and attack on the federal arsenal at Harpers Ferry, Virginia.

Douglass and Brown met for the first time in late 1847 or early 1848, at Brown's home in Springfield, Massachusetts. An active but unusual abolitionist, John Brown had tried his hand as a tanner, land developer, canal builder, wool dealer, and farmer, but was unsuccessful at each undertaking. During their first visit, Brown told Douglass of his plan to draw southern slaves off into the Allegheny Mountains. Still attached to the Garrisonian principles of nonresistance and moral suasion at that first meeting, Douglass later recalled he had tried to convince Brown of the illogical nature of these ideas and that instead effort should concentrate on converting the slaveholder to the cause of abolition. Following published accounts of Douglass's travels in Britain and the U.S., Brown recognized him as an emerging race leader and tried to convince him of the rightness of his plan. Unsuccessful at winning Douglass's heart and mind at this first meeting, he nevertheless made a lasting impression. Douglass recalled, "He denounced slavery in look and language fierce and bitter, thought that slaveholders had forfeited their right to live, that the slaves had the right to gain their liberty in any way they could, did not believe that moral suasion would ever liberate the slave, or that political action would abolish the system."[16] Despite having differing philosophies, Douglass was impressed with Brown's absolute lack of antiblack prejudice and his fiery commitment to the overthrow of slavery. The friendship begun at their first meeting lasted through Brown's conviction and execution for treason in 1859. The pair corresponded and met occasionally, and not long after the Fugitive Slave Act Douglass found his views on the use of violence shifting in Brown's favor.

Even while editing his weekly, Douglass continued to lecture widely on the antislavery circuit. Often leaving his family and his business for weeks at a time, he broadened his audiences by speaking on issues of importance including women's property rights, colonization, political antislavery, and black civil rights. In 1852 he delivered his most well-known speech before a packed room at Rochester's Corinthian Hall. Invited by the Rochester Ladies Anti-Slavery Society to offer the annual address at the city's Independence Day celebration, Douglass instead delivered a scathing attack on racial inequality and condemned slavery, on July 5. He asked the more than five hundred people who came to hear him, "What, to the American slave, is your Fourth of July? I answer: a day that reveals to him, more than all other days in the year, the gross injustice and cruelty to which he is the constant victim."[17] Issued soon after in pamphlet form with Gerrit Smith's funding, the oration became a master text in the condemnation of the slave system, and brought Douglass even more attention as the nation's leading black spokesman.

The intellectual journey Douglass made in his first two decades of freedom put much distance between his life in slavery and his reality in the mid-1850s. By that time he was the editor of the nation's longest-lived black newspaper, an accomplished orator, and author of pamphlets and editorials. Douglass consulted considerably with author Harriet Beecher Stowe after she wrote *Uncle Tom's Cabin*, the most widely read antebellum novel about the evils of slavery. Exploring his own creative writing ability, Doulass's novella, *The Heroic Slave*, was published in an 1852 book produced as a fundraising collection by the Rochester Ladies Anti-Slavery Society. At age thirty-seven, in 1855, he penned a second autobiography, *My Bondage and My Freedom*, in which he expanded his narrative of enslavement but also offered details of his career as a reformer. Providing a more nuanced overview of his life experiences, he intended the book as a work of literature and not the antislavery propaganda of his *Narrative*. The book also spoke to Douglass's independence since his break with Garrison, and to his prominent recognition by whites and blacks. In contrast to the testimony offered by Garrison and Wendell Phillips authenticating his 1845 *Narrative*, this second volume was prefaced by James McCune Smith. Praising Douglass's intellectual strength, McCune Smith's endorsement compared the book to a number of black autobiographies published in the antebellum era. Selling five thousand copies in its first two days of publication, by 1856 and 1857 second and third editions were required to keep up with demand.[18]

The appearance of *My Bondage and My Freedom* caught the attention of readers in the U.S. and abroad. Among the admirers was Ottilie Assing, a German-Jewish journalist, who came to Rochester after reading the volume, ostensibly to interview Douglass for a German magazine. Assing arrived just a few months after the departure of Julia Griffiths, and Douglass was immediately intrigued with the young German woman. Theirs was another controversial relationship across color lines that called his marital fidelity once again into question. Like Griffiths before her, Assing spent time in Douglass's home, splitting her residence between Rochester and Hoboken, New Jersey where she boarded with another German-Jewish immigrant, Clara B. Marks.[19] She translated *My Bondage and My Freedom* into her native language, arranging for the 1860 publication of a German edition. Surviving correspondence, at least Assing's letters to Douglass, indicates that theirs was an intimate relationship and possibly sexual. Their complicated connection lasted for the next twenty-six years, but Douglass's public stature and position as a black leader made it impossible for him to divorce or be openly known to be involved in an extra-marital affair.

Anna Douglass's reaction to the appearance of another white woman in her household is difficult to discern because she left no written record, but references to her occasionally appeared in Assing's correspondence with friends and relatives, suggesting theirs was a tense relationship. Perhaps out of guilt at appropriating her husband's attention, Assing often referred to Anna as "the wife" or an "old woman" who was from "the uneducated and ignorant classes."[20] It is impossible to know for certain, but Anna likely felt she had little choice but to acquiesce in her husband's infidelities. Known to be illiterate and without trade or independent means, but also holding on to the respected position as the famous Douglass's wife, it may simply have been easier to declare a truce and to treat this white woman with the same polite coolness with which she had tolerated Julia Griffiths. Whatever her true feelings, Anna made no open public objection to Assing's presence, and although Douglass and Assing often appeared in public together, their relationship was not subject to the same public criticism that his appearances with Griffiths had drawn. Rosetta Douglass also developed a special relationship with Assing, perhaps seeing the independent and career-minded woman as a role model. In correspondence with her father Rosetta often asked about Assing, and when at home in Rochester the two spent time discussing literature and contemporary affairs, subjects Anna likely had little time to pursue amidst her heavy domestic responsibilities.

As sectional tensions heated up, the Douglass household sheltered more fugitives on their way to Canada. Although Douglass served as the main conduit for these houseguests, it was Anna who provided hospitality in the form of meals, laundry, and housekeeping. Rosetta later recalled, "perhaps no other home received under its roof a more varied class of people than did our home." Among them, her mother welcomed them all from the "highest dignitaries to the lowliest person, bond or free, white or black," and Anna was "equally gracious to all." Douglass found so many fugitives seeking his assistance that he appealed to the British reform community, including Julia Griffiths, who helped raise funds to support his efforts.[21] While his wife ran their ever-changing household, Douglass increasingly turned his attention to his editorial duties and to the evolving world of abolition and politics.

Douglass's thoughts on the role of political action in bringing an end to slavery continued to develop as he absorbed and explored the political developments of the 1850s. Initially greatly influenced by Gerrit Smith's Liberty Party, Douglass came to embrace a more practical and hopeful brand of political abolition than his mentor. Awakened to the need for new tactics with the passage of the Fugitive Slave Act, Douglass and other reformers were galvanized into action by two other events in the decade. The Kansas–Nebraska Act in 1854 repealed that part of the Missouri Compromise which banned slavery in what would become the states of Kansas, Nebraska, the Dakotas, Montana, and parts of Wyoming and Colorado. Instead of an absolute ban on slavery in these territories, known as the Kansas and Nebraska Territories, Congress allowed the settlers to decide the issue of slavery in the region on their own, through "popular sovereignty." This led to a rush of settlers from the North and the South into Kansas, as people from both sections tried to influence the ultimate vote on allowing slavery there. The rapid immigration of proslavery and antislavery settlers to push their position on the territory resulted in a near-civil war, dubbed "bleeding Kansas." The conflict caused the final collapse of the Whig Party, and helped spur the creation of the northern-based Republican Party, as pro- and antislavery politicians realigned themselves over the Kansas controversy.

Loudly denouncing the Kansas–Nebraska Act in his editorials, Douglass at first urged a plan to boost the free settlers in Kansas. He called for a thousand free black families to join the rush to make Kansas a free state, arguing that Illinois senator Stephen A. Douglas, author of the bill, "has given his plan for getting slavery into Kansas; and we see not why Frederick Douglass should not submit his plan for keeping slavery out of Kansas."[22] He soon backed away from this impractical plan. As historian David Blight has noted, Douglass temporarily seemed to forget that one of the main thrusts of the Free Soil Party and ideology attracted northern support because it advocated free white labor and opposed the extension of slavery mainly to protect the developing West from attracting black settlement. The involvement of important political abolitionists in the party may have contributed to his wavering on the issue. The practical nature of the free-soil impulse would be carried over into the emerging Republican

Party and Douglass's denunciation of the Kansas bill led him into implied support of the new party. [23] His newspaper continued to publicly support Gerrit Smith's brand of pure antislavery politics, as outlined by the flailing Liberty Party, through announcements and articles, but Douglass was growing more flexible, or perhaps practical, than Smith. Still not settled on the issue, however, in June 1855 he stood with Smith and friends James McCune Smith and John Brown at the Syracuse convention that formed the successor to the Liberty Party. The new Radical Abolition Party upheld the liberty principle that the Constitution provided a means for the federal government to abolish all slavery, but went farther to endorse the use of violence to end slavery and oppression. [24]

As tensions escalated between pro- and antislavery forces in Kansas, Douglass and his friends found violence surrounding them. Reports of murder, rapes, and property attacks in Kansas were widespread by early 1856. Gerrit Smith sent $1,600 to help transport men, and provide arms and ammunition. John Brown sent five of his sons to help the free settlers, eventually joining them himself. In the nation's capital, insanity seemed to reign whenever Kansas was mentioned. Outrage over the Kansas situation prompted Massachusetts senator Charles Sumner to give a scathing congressional address attacking the "Crimes against Kansas." Incensed at Sumner's portrayal of Senator Andrew Butler, South Carolina congressman Preston Brooks savagely beat Sumner with a cane on the floor of the Senate chamber. In May, following the burning of the free-state stronghold at Lawrence, Kansas, Brown led a band of men in a middle-of-the-night attack on a proslavery settlement, using broadswords to kill five proslavery men. The so-called Pottawatomie Massacre marked Brown as both a murderer and as a champion of the extreme wing of the abolition movement. The violence awakened the consciousness of numerous eastern abolitionists but did not offend their nonresistant sensibilities. Times had certainly changed, as had thoughts on using violence to combat the slave system. Douglass defended Brown's action as he editorialized, "He is charged with murder! What could be more absurd? If he has sinned in anything, it is in that he spared lives of murderers, when he had power to take vengeance upon them." [25]

As these events roiled across the nation, Douglass found his newspaper struggling. By the time Kansas was exploding in the West, northern political support was dividing along pro- and antislavery lines. With the collapse of the Whigs, many former members of that party joined with antiextension Democrats and Free Soilers to form the Republican Party. Compared with Gerrit Smith and other radical political abolitionists, the Republicans were only nominally antislavery, adopting the free-soil idea of nonextension as its strongest stance against slavery. Gerrit Smith and his followers clung to their pure abolitionist principles in the Radical Abolition Party, but formed a very small minority voice. Although publicly Douglass supported Smith's ideology, he did so at the risk of losing subscribers to *Frederick Douglass' Paper*, and in 1856 was considering more practical matters. Following the departure of Julia Griffiths as financial manager, Douglass's paper, and his family, became almost completely reliant on Smith's philanthropy. In 1855 Smith's party had chosen another paper, the *Radical Abolitionist*, edited by William Goodell, as its official organ. Douglass complained that his weekly suffered and was as much as $1,500 in debt because it was no longer affiliated with a base of support. "My paper is not Republican—and therefore Republicans look coldly on it. It is not Garrisonian and therefore Garrisonians hate and spare no pains to destroy it. Meanwhile the colored people do very little to support."[26] It is unclear if Smith helped make up the shortfall, but shortly thereafter Douglass endorsed Republican presidential nominee John C. Frémont, although he still expressed hesitancy about supporting the new party altogether.[27]

The 1857 Supreme Court decision in the case of *Dred Scott v. Sandford* was the second influential event of the 1850s to rouse Douglass into rethinking his chosen path as an activist. Filed on behalf of an enslaved African American man who claimed freedom after he and his wife were brought into free Minnesota territory by their master, the case reached the nation's highest court. In denying their petition, the Supreme Court, then dominated by proslavery justices, stirred up a nation already reeling from sectional tensions. Declaring that African Americans, even those in the free northern states, could never be U.S. citizens, and that Congress could not ban slavery in western territories, the decision galvanized many into opposing the domination of proslavery politicians, and greatly helped spur support for the Republican Party. Addressing the annual meeting of the American Anti-Slavery Society, Douglass expressed both outrage and hope in the wake of the Supreme Court decision. He told the audience that in the wake of "this judicial incarnation of wolfishness" his "hopes were never brighter than now," that the nation would be awakened to the wrongness of the decision and the trampling of basic human rights as guaranteed in the Declaration of Independence and the Constitution.[28] His belief that outraged Americans would denounce the ruling was tempered by a warning that failure to do so might lead to more violence. "Goaded by cruelty, stung by a burning sense of wrong, in an awful moment of depression and desperation, the bondman and bondwoman at the south may rush to one wild and deadly struggle for freedom. Already slaveholders go to bed with bowie knives, and apprehend death at their dinners. Those who enslave, rob, and torment their cooks, may well expect to find death in their dinner-pots."[29] Clearly, his was no longer the nonresistant position still held by many of the Garrisonians in his audience that May.

Douglass was never as stalwartly nonresistant as his Garrisonian friends had been, so his shift toward accepting that violence might be needed to overthrow slavery should not be surprising. Even in slavery, Douglass had lashed out when necessary. He celebrated his fight with slave breaker Edward Covey as a major turning point in his life, repeating and enhancing the encounter in his autobiographies. When he and his abolitionist colleagues had come under physical attack in Pendleton, Indiana during the Hundred Conventions tour, Douglass suffered a severe beating after he raised a piece of lumber and wielded it as a club in defense of his friends. He watched his fellow abolitionists grow more daring and militant in the rescue of fugitive slaves after passage of the Fugitive Slave Act. He also spent considerable time with John Brown, often discussing and debating ways to end slavery. On more than one occasion, Douglass sponsored meetings in Rochester aimed at raising funds for Brown's free Kansas plan. In January and February 1858, two years following the dramatic events at Pottawatomie Creek, Brown spent three weeks in Douglass's Rochester home. After learning the details of Pottawatomie firsthand, Douglass was not shocked or critical of his friend, and later recalled that Brown "showed boundless courage but [also] eminent military skill." Describing Brown's influence in his last autobiography, Douglass recalled that his own "utterances became more and more tinged by the color of [Brown's] strong impressions."[30]

It is clear that Douglass was familiar with the details of Brown's plan to incite a slave insurrection in Virginia in the fall of 1859, and that Gerrit Smith was among the "secret six" who financed the affair. From their earliest meetings in the 1840s, Brown had spoken openly to Douglass about his plan to plant small bands of armed men in strategic places from which they might draw slaves off from Virginia farms and plantations into the Allegheny Mountains. Even at their first meetings, Douglass pointed out the impracticality of the plan to his new friend, arguing that the slaveholders would "employ bloodhounds to hunt you out of the mountains."[31] When Brown called on him to come to Chambersburg, Pennsylvania in August 1859, Douglass met him at a nearby stone quarry. Brown and many of the twenty-one men who would join in his plan spent much of the summer at a nearby Maryland farm making preparations for October action.

Revealing a daring plan to raid the federal arsenal at Harpers Ferry, Virginia in preparation for a slave uprising that would be the beginning of the end for slavery, Brown tried to convince Douglass to join him. If necessary, he told Douglass, he could take townspeople hostage to effect his escape. Douglass opposed it, not because it was a violent plan, but because it was an attack on the federal government and because he had no chance of success.

Douglass told Brown he was going into a "perfect steel trap."[32] Douglass felt that the raid contradicted what Brown had planned for more than ten years and he was astonished at Brown's assertion that he was willing to take innocent residents hostage. Seeing the obvious failure that was to result, Douglass tried for two days but was unable to convince Brown of the futility of his plan. He recalled that their differences came down to Brown's desire for bold action to "instantly rouse the country" and Douglass's support for Brown's original plan for "gradually and unaccountably drawing off the slaves to the mountains." On their final meeting, Douglass recalled Brown said, "come with me, Douglass; I will defend you with my life. I want you for a special purpose. When I strike, the bees will begin to swarm, and I shall want you to help hive them."[33] Douglass left Chambersburg without convincing his friend to abandon his foolhardy plan. He left behind his traveling companion, Shields Green, a fugitive slave who had been living in Rochester. One of five African American participants in the October 16 raid, Green was arrested and later hanged for his participation.

Douglass was lecturing in Philadelphia when word reached him that Brown's raid had failed and his old friend was arrested and charged with treason. Both Douglass and Gerrit Smith were implicated in the raid's planning through letters found in Brown's possession. As Brown's known associate, Douglass's arrest was only averted by sympathetic telegraph operator John W. Hurn, who managed to delay his arrest warrant long enough for him to flee back to Rochester. Within days, he crossed into Canada on much the same route as fugitive slaves. He penned a letter to the Rochester *Democrat* denying that he had ever planned to take part in the raid, noting "I have always been more distinguished for running than fighting, and, tried by the Harpers-Ferry-insurrection test, I am most miserably deficient in courage."[34] On November 12 he boarded a ship for Great Britain, a trip he claimed he had intended to make, and watched from afar as events unfolded in the U.S. Although he remained at home, Smith was so frantic that he was hospitalized for several months in the New York State Lunatic Asylum.[35]

From his vantage point abroad, Douglass witnessed the U.S. become further polarized over the issue of slavery and the violence of Harpers Ferry. David Blight has shown that, following Brown's execution on December 2, 1859, Douglass found an "effective weapon in Brown's martyrdom." The fear the specter of a slave rebellion incited in slaveholders proved a useful tool which he later exploited on the lecture circuit.[36] In the South Brown was denounced as a crazed and dangerous man, but in the North even mainstream newspapers came to admire his commitment to ending slavery. In the immediate wake of Brown's execution, however, Douglass carefully and prudently avoided any clashes with law enforcement.

Despite the hasty trip to Canada, and then on to Britain, his European trip had in fact been planned for late fall and Douglass enjoyed a reunion with many reformers whom he met during his first trip to Great Britain. Sharing the lecture platform with a number of British friends, Douglass first stayed in the home of his friend Julia Griffiths, who had married Methodist minister Henry O. Crofts earlier that year, and then traveled throughout England and Scotland. Addressing sympathetic crowds wherever he went, Douglass denied claims that John Brown was insane and began celebrating him as a martyr. Although still liable to arrest for complicity, he continued to publicly deny that he had encouraged the insurrection.[37] The trip put the necessary distance between Douglass and the events at Harpers Ferry, but was cut short when he learned that his youngest daughter Annie had died on March 13, a few days before her eleventh birthday. Unwilling to leave Anna alone with her grief and the children, he started for home.[38]

Returning to Rochester and his family's tragedy, Douglass remained out of the public spotlight until it became clear that the Congressional investigation into John Brown's raid would not target him. Upon his homecoming he also found a nation spiraling toward crisis and eventual war. He turned his attention to his editing, emphasizing a new publication called *Douglass' Monthly*, which was initially begun as a supplement to his weekly in January 1859, but soon became his only organ. With the Harpers Ferry events still at the forefront of debate, the political parties prepared for the upcoming 1860 presidential election. Douglass remained unsure about the Republican Party and questioned the commitment of its candidate, Abraham Lincoln, to the abolition of slavery. He was pleased to see the Democratic Party splintering into northern and southern factions, not over slavery per se, but over the issue of a federal slave code for the territories. Nevertheless, Douglass did not count the Republicans' support of antiextension as sufficient to win his unqualified support. Penning an open letter to his British friends, which he published in *Douglass' Monthly*, he advised them of his lukewarm endorsement. "The Republican party is only negatively anti-slavery. It is opposed to the *political power* of slavery, rather than to slavery itself, and would arrest the spread of the slave system, humble the slavepower, and defeat all plans for giving slavery any further guarantees of permanence."[39] In his opinion, the Republican Party merely opened the door to the possibility of abolition. Nevertheless, in the same issue of his journal, Douglass endorsed Lincoln's candidacy: "While we should be glad to co-operate with a party fully committed to the doctrine of 'All rights, to all men,' in the absence of all hope of rearing up the standard of such a party for the coming campaign, we can but desire the success of the Republican candidates."[40]

Wavering support for Lincoln was on Douglass's mind when he attended the Radical Abolitionist Party's nominating convention in August. He endorsed Gerrit Smith's nomination for president and was even chosen as an elector for his ticket, but he and Smith both privately believed Lincoln would carry the election.[41] Spending little time campaigning for either candidate, Douglass's energy was instead more focused toward removing the punitive $250 property qualification placed on black voters by the state of New York. Campaigning through his newspaper and on the stump, he was sorely disappointed at the failure of the equal suffrage measure placed before New York voters in November. He complained that its failure in the wake of Republican triumph was "inconsistent with every profession and principle of the triumphant party, and must surprise the enemies of equal rights as much as it certainly disappoints the expectations of colored citizens."[42]

He was halfheartedly optimistic about the prospects of Lincoln's presidency and took pains to report in his monthly that southerners were taking too much offense at the prospect of a president who upheld the legality of slavery and merely opposed its further extension. As South Carolina and other southern states moved toward secession, Douglass found their actions overly dramatic and utterly unnecessary. He argued that Lincoln's administration would be "attacked more bitterly for their pro-slavery truckling, than for doing any anti-slavery work. [Lincoln] and his party will become the best protectors of slavery where it now is."[43] Losing much hope that change would actually result from a Republican presidency, Douglass began to look outside the U.S., considering colonization for the first time. He had always dismissed black emigration to Africa or the Caribbean, arguing that, as American citizens, African Americans were determined to fight for full civil and political rights. Despite his bitter disagreement with his former newspaper partner Martin R. Delany and others in the past, the black republic of Haiti began to look more inviting, and Douglass planned a three-month exploratory trip for the spring of 1861. His trip to Haiti was postponed indefinitely as the election winter turned to spring and war erupted. Douglass put aside his Haitian plans and was cautiously hopeful that he could throw his support behind Lincoln's war plan, seeing in civil war the best opportunity to finally abolish slavery.

CHAPTER 7

DISUNION REALIZED

THE NATION'S BEST HOPE TO END SLAVERY

The firing on Fort Sumter on April 12, 1861 momentarily elated Douglass and left him hopeful that President Abraham Lincoln's response to hostilities would lead quickly to both an end to war and to the abolition of slavery. Finding little inspiring in the weeks following Lincoln's inauguration, Douglass had criticized the new president for his quiet and disguised entry into the nation's capital, comparing his journey to that of a fugitive slave on the Underground Railroad. He found Lincoln's conciliatory inaugural address to be "a double-tongued document, capable of two constructions, [that] conceals rather than declares a definite policy."[1] Indeed, Lincoln's early days in Washington seemed only to cap a decade of disappointment for immediate abolitionists. As he watched southern states leave the Union, Douglass made his own plans to make an extended visit to Haiti. Echoing the arguments of procolonizationists against whom he had argued for more than two decades, Douglass declared that the "margin of life and liberty is becoming more narrow every year. There are many instances where the black man's places are taken by the white man, but few where, in the free States, the places of the white man are taken by the man of sable hue." When news of Fort Sumter's fall reached Rochester, Douglass cancelled his trip and watched with anticipation, believing: "When the Northern people have been made to experience a little more of the savage barbarism of slavery, they may be willing to make war upon it, and in that case we stand ready to lend a hand in any way we can be of service."[2]

The outbreak of war galvanized some opponents of slavery and left others holding their breath, waiting to see what would materialize. Radical abolitionist William Lloyd Garrison abandoned his earlier attacks on the Union and cautiously expressed a new flag-waving brand of patriotism. Garrisonians found themselves caught between hope for an abolition war and their commitment to nonresistance.[3] Wendell Phillips, who had preached his doctrine of disunion even through the secession winter, quickly came to support the Union war effort. In a speech at Boston's Music Hall on April 21 he condemned the South's actions, proclaiming that "[we] welcome the tread of Massachusetts men marshaled for war." Although he and other Garrisonians had long supported the right of secession, taking as their motto, "no union with slaveholders," Phillips now declared the South's secession illegal and saw the war as a just battle to end slavery. Others, including Douglass, were more reticent. He welcomed the outbreak of hostilities, but feared that northerners would support a compromise that would reunite the nation but leave slavery intact.[4] Early in the war, Lincoln's actions clearly demonstrated he was not willing to consider abolishing slavery. While the president issued a call for volunteer troops and built up his war machine, he also adopted a conciliatory tone that urged the seceding states to return to the Union with their slaves protected. Determined to preserve the Union, and with concern to keep the border South loyal, Lincoln proceeded more carefully than abolitionists wanted.

Spending the first months of the war agitating and pushing his anti-slavery message before countless northern crowds, Douglass urged his fellow Americans to see the importance of slavery in the current conflict. In early summer, just before the first Battle of Bull Run, he addressed a crowd in Rochester, declaring the war to be "the American Apocalypse." Speaking to the role of northerners in driving the war agenda he hammered home his belief that "slavery is at the bottom of all mischief amongst us, and will be until we shall put an end to it."[5] While his words seemed to fall on deaf ears among policy makers in the nation's capital, he was encouraged by the actions of General John C. Frémont in Missouri. The former western explorer known as "The Pathfinder" had been the first Republican nominee for president in 1856 and Lincoln's choice to lead the Union's Department of the West. Aiming to bring unruly guerrilla fighting to an end, on August 30 Frémont imposed martial law in Missouri and declared that those in rebellion forfeited all property, including their slaves, whom he subsequently declared free. Douglass celebrated Frémont's order, finding it much more to his liking than the Confiscation Act passed by Congress on August 6. For while the Confiscation Act declared enslaved men and women used by the Confederate Army to be forfeit as contraband of war, the bill fell short of granting them freedom. Frémont's more radical proclamation declared the Missouri slaves seized to be "not only confiscated property, but *liberated men*."[6] Keeping with his moderate position and determination to keep the border states, including Missouri, committed to the Union, President Lincoln rescinded the order, at first demanding that Frémont make his policy conform to the Congressional Confiscation Act, then removing him from his post when he refused to do so.

In Frémont, Douglass saw the very spirit he was agitating for in the first year of the war: a northerner who hated slavery *and slaveholders*. Frémont aimed to press precisely the type of war that Douglass and other abolitionists believed just and necessary. In General Henry W. Halleck, Frémont's replacement in the West, Douglass saw the abolition position lose ground. Halleck issued General Order No. 3, which refused fugitive slaves protection behind his lines despite the Confiscation Act's directive. Although Halleck's order died in Congressional debate, Douglass despaired of the Union commanders and soldiers who "made themselves more active in kicking colored men out of their camps than in shooting rebels."[7] Despite his disappointment, Douglass continued to agitate against slavery and in favor of a more active role for African Americans in the war effort.

As 1861 came to a close, Douglass reflected on the first months of the war. In January 1862 he delivered a scathing criticism of the government's lack of sensibility in failing to make abolition a war aim. Addressing a black self-improvement society in Philadelphia with a speech entitled "Fighting the Rebels with One Hand," he argued that African Americans were necessary to a full and effective war strategy. He complained that the federal government aimed to preserve slavery in the South. Although General Benjamin Butler had declared that slaves aiding the Confederacy were contraband of war and able to seek safety behind Union lines, they were not directly freed. The Confiscation Act of 1861 was similarly demeaning because it labeled men and women contraband, a term Douglass believed applied "better to a pistol, than to a person." His plan to subdue the Confederate army required the full acceptance of black participation in the Union army: "We are striking the guilty rebels with our soft, white hand, when we should be striking with the iron hand of the black man, which we keep chained behind us."[8]

In the second year of the war, Douglass threw the full force of his energy into agitation, through multiple editorials in each issue of *Douglass' Monthly*, speeches, letters, and private conversations. His assessment of the Union Army's dismal performance eased a bit with General Ulysses Grant's successful capture of Fort Henry on the Tennessee River and Fort Donelson on the Cumberland River in early February 1862, and Grant's demand for "unconditional surrender" by the Confederates. Nevertheless, Douglass continued to condemn northern politicians and public sentiment as too lenient on the rebels. In March, he editorialized, "the North has been angry with the South only as a child is angry with a pet, and that anger soon passes away when the pet has been well kicked. We are now ready to make up and hug the darling slaveholders with a fondness as ardent as ever." To Douglass's mind it was clear that the Confederate forces were making full use of the labor of enslaved southerners and that the North should go even farther to make the ultimate policy one that would both free the slave and arm them once emancipated. Following the Union victory at the Battle of Antietam in September, 1862 he would learn that Lincoln was indeed beginning to see just such a necessity.[9]

The Emancipation Proclamation was the game-changing event that allowed Douglass and other abolitionists to push beyond agitation and into action. Although it applied only to enslaved men and women in areas of the Confederacy then under rebellion, for abolitionists it spelled the end to slavery and made the Civil War an abolition war at last. Following Lincoln's proclamation that slaves in areas under rebellion would be free on January 1, 1863, Douglass rejoiced: "We shout for joy that we live to record this righteous decree." Although he had been a frequent critic of Lincoln's inaction on the question of slavery and the role of blacks in the war effort, Douglass had no concern that the president would reverse his position on emancipation. "Abraham Lincoln may be slow, Abraham Lincoln may desire peace even at the price of leaving our terrible national sore untouched to fester on for generations, but Abraham Lincoln is not the man to reconsider, retract and contradict word and purposes solemnly proclaimed over his official signature." Instead of deliberate inaction, Douglass now saw in Lincoln's slow movement on the slavery question assurance that the president had carefully considered his options and chosen the right path. Besides, he told *Douglass' Monthly* readers, events greater than Lincoln had already "wrung this proclamation from him" and would carry emancipation forward. He charged fellow abolitionists to get to work ensuring that northern sentiment favored the implementation of the policy. Douglass sprang to action: "We are ready for this service or any other, in this, we trust, the last struggle with the monster slavery."[10] Over the next year *his* efforts would focus on the recruitment and service of African American troops in the Union Army.

Even before the preliminary Emancipation Proclamation was issued in September, the Second Confiscation Act and the Militia Act, both passed in July 1862, paved the way for African American military participation. The Second Confiscation Act freed those slaves captured at war and the Militia Act empowered the army to put African Americans to work at menial labor or "any military or naval service for which they may be found competent."[11] Under the supervision of General Benjamin F. Butler, who commanded military occupation activities in and around New Orleans, in the late summer regiments of black troops were mustered into service in Louisiana, with units soon following in South Carolina and Kansas. As many as four thousand African American troops had been raised in southern localities by the issuance of the final Emancipation Proclamation on January 1, 1863. At that point Douglass's urgent desires became reality, as the recruitment of black troops became a major thrust across the northern states. Massachusetts Governor John A. Andrew was the first to authorize a northern regiment, the 54th Massachusetts, and Douglass proudly recruited northern men for its service.

Headed by white company officers and commanded by Colonel Robert Gould Shaw, the 54th Massachusetts recruited black men from beyond the commonwealth's borders, as Massachusetts had fewer than two thousand African American men of military age in 1863. Douglass recruited in upstate New York, and fellow abolitionists Henry Highland Garnet, John Mercer Langston, and Martin R. Delany sought to fill the volunteer ranks among the citizens of New York City, Ohio, and Chicago. Blacks across the northeast were so eager to join in the fight that ranks were quickly filled in the 54th and a second black unit, the 55th, Massachusetts. Among the early volunteers were two of Douglass's sons, Charles and Lewis. Lewis, the eldest, became the regiment's first sergeant major, while his younger brother served as a private. Mustering first at Boston and then in more permanent barracks at Readville, on May 18 Governor Andrew himself came to present the unit with their regimental colors. Among the celebrants were William Lloyd Garrison and Wendell Phillips, fully shed of their pacifism, and a throng of the city's black residents. On May 28, the men of the 54th Massachusetts arrived in Boston in preparation for transport to South Carolina. There they marched to the statehouse where Governor Andrew accompanied their procession across Boston Common. Douglass was reportedly so proud of his sons' service that when the regiment sailed from Boston harbor, he rented a boat to wave the men off from the bay, although Charles had fallen ill and was not among those departing.[12]

The spring's recruiting efforts left Douglass tired but pleased that he had made a significant contribution. At the age of forty-five, he knew that his talent as an orator and agitator was better suited for a non-military role in the conflict, and he never seriously considered enlisting in the Union army. When his old friend George Luther Stearns called him back into the recruiting field, Douglass prepared to go to Philadelphia. A Massachusetts philanthropist and abolitionist who was among the "secret six" funding John Brown's Harpers Ferry raid, Stearns was the lead recruiter for the 54th and 55th Massachusetts regiments. His success in enlisting black troops in the commonwealth earned Stearns a federal major's commission at the recommendation of Secretary of War Edwin M. Stanton. Douglass felt duty-bound to continue his recruiting efforts, writing to Gerrit Smith, "The work is not to my taste—and I had enough of it while recruiting for Massachusetts: Nevertheless as this is not a time to be governed by one's taste—I shall probably go soon into the work again."[13] Understanding that his influence could be of assistance in filling out the ranks of black regiments, he rejoined Stearns's efforts.

While recruiting in Philadelphia in mid-July, Douglass learned of the violent antidraft riots that erupted in New York City and other parts of the North. As the war moved into its third year, dwindling volunteer recruitments prompted Congress to enact a conscription law declaring all men between twenty and thirty-five as well as unmarried men ages thirty-five to forty-five liable for military service. All were to be subjected to a lottery, but those who could pay $300 for a substitute were exempt. African Americans, who were still not considered full citizens of the U.S., were also excluded from the draft. The conscription lottery served to exacerbate tensions between African Americans and working-class white men, especially in northern cities where competition for limited jobs and economic opportunities had raged even before the onset of the Civil War. Combined with anger and fear emanating from the potential effects of the Emancipation Proclamation which made ending slavery a goal of the Union war effort, blacks found themselves targeted by frustrated workers and immigrants in northern cities.

Dismayed by violent attacks, and the lynching of eleven men during the riots in New York City in particular, Douglass's elation about emancipation and an expanding role for African Americans in the war effort quickly began to wane.[14] The possibility of personal loss also struck home when he received a letter from Lewis describing the engagement of the 54th Massachusetts at Fort Wagner in South Carolina. Volunteering for a recklessly dangerous attack on the fort across an open beach, the black regiment suffered 281 casualties, including their commander Colonel Robert Gould Shaw, who was mortally wounded. Lewis's description made his father's blood run cold: "I had my sword sheath blown away while on the parapet of the Fort. The grape and canister, shell and minnies swept us down like chaff, still our men went on and on, and if we had been properly supported we would have held the Fort, but the white troops could not be made to come up."[15] The 54th had been sent into great peril and likely suffered extreme casualties partly because the inept leaders failed to send the support of their white fellow soldiers. In the month following the debacle, Douglass published Lewis's letter and several others upholding the bravery of Colonel Shaw in his monthly, but his heart was heavy.[16] Coupled with the realization that participation in the Union army did little to dispel racial inequality, and the antiblack violence of the draft riots, the report of events in South Carolina served to push Douglass into a state of despair. He lost faith with Lincoln's slow steps forward on abolishing slavery and issues of racial justice.

All of Douglass's agitation for a larger role for blacks in the war effort left him bitter and frustrated at the reality of mistreatment and unequal policies emanating from the War Department, and seemingly from President Lincoln. African American soldiers were given inferior assignments, and were ineligible for commissioned officer posts. Set to manual labor in miserable and hot conditions across the South or sent into dangerous situations such as at Fort Wagner, African American soldiers clearly did not have equal standing with whites. When the Confederate Congress responded to the Union enlistment of black troops with a proclamation in May 1863 that any captured African Americans would be liable to death or sale into slavery, the president offered no assurances that they would be protected from such a fate. Instead, in June, the War Department formalized an unequal pay policy by which white privates were paid thirteen dollars per month while black privates were allowed ten dollars, from which another three dollars was deducted for clothing and equipment. Denied the ability to advance, African American sergeants, including Lewis Douglass, soon learned that white privates earned more each month. Originally enthusiastic recruiters, Douglass and other African Americans soon found it difficult to encourage men to commit to such a situation. Enlistment began to concentrate in the border states and deep South, where even impoverished blacks began to protest loudly against the policy. The War Department's policy thwarted Douglass's double battle against slavery and racism, as David Blight has noted, and strained his ability to promise black recruits that freedom and equality would be possible at war's end.[17] With potential new recruits in the northeast drying up, on August 1, Douglass wrote to Stearns declining further recruiting responsibilities. "I owe it to my long abused people, and especially those of them already in the army to expose their wrongs and plead their case. When I plead for recruits, I want to do it with all my heart, without qualification. I cannot do that now," he told Stearns.[18]

As Douglass penned these words to his old friend, he was unaware that Lincoln had acted in the wake of the debacle at Fort Wagner, after which a number of captured black enlisted men were forced into slavery. In his monthly newspaper he lashed out at Lincoln's seeming failure to insist that black prisoners be exchanged and his failure to retaliate for the atrocities black soldiers had faced at Charleston. He demanded justice: "For every black prisoner slain in cold blood, Mr. Jefferson Davis should be made to understand that one rebel officer shall suffer death, and for every colored soldier sold into slavery, a rebel shall be held as a hostage.

For our Government to do less than this, is to deserve the indignation and the execration of mankind."[19] Although not exactly the eye-for-an-eye retribution Douglass sought, the president did issue a retaliatory order on July 30, demanding that one Confederate soldier be put to hard labor for each Union soldier remanded to slavery.[20] Douglass still published his critical letter to Stearns in his monthly, but he followed it with a disclaimer noting that protections were being offered to black soldiers. He believed it to be a small concession that black troops had purchased "dearly," noting "it really seems that nothing of justice, liberty or humanity can come to us except through tears and blood."[21] He determined to agitate more fiercely for black soldiers and to do so he needed to communicate directly with the one man who had the ability to level the playing field. At the urging of Stearns, Douglass traveled to Washington to plead the case for black troops and their grievances directly to President Lincoln.

Douglass traveled to the nation's capital for the first time bearing a written endorsement from Stearns indicating his visit was officially connected to his recruiting duties. On August 10, Kansas senator Samuel C. Pomeroy helped him gain access to Secretary of War Edwin Stanton and then Lincoln. Meeting first with the businesslike Stanton, Douglass spent thirty minutes pressing the case for the equality of black troops. He argued that the War Department should make no distinction between white and black troops in all matters—pay, rations, equipment, and opportunities for officer commissions. Somewhat to his surprise, Douglass learned that Stanton already supported equal treatment, and that he had sent such a bill to Congress, but it failed to pass. Somewhat mollified by Stanton's receptiveness, and certainly influenced by his surroundings, Douglass reversed his position on recruiting. Stanton offered him an officer's commission and Douglass agreed to travel to Vicksburg, Mississippi to assist General Lorenzo Thomas in organizing black regiments in the Mississippi Valley.[22]

From Stanton's office in the War Department, Douglass and Pomeroy traveled next to the White House, where a nervous but determined Douglass waited for his first meeting with Lincoln. Buoyed by his reception at the War Department, and already making mental plans for his recruiting trip south, Douglass joined a substantial group of men lining the stairway, all waiting in hopes of a few minutes of the president's time. Expecting a lengthy wait, he was surprised when he was summoned to enter soon after his arrival, prompting someone in the crowd to mutter, "I knew they would let the nigger through."[23] He was led into an upstairs room where Lincoln preferred to work instead of his formal office. After a moment's hesitation, Douglass relaxed in the president's presence, recalling later "I was never more quickly or more completely put at ease in the presence of a great man. ... I at once felt myself in the presence of an honest man."[24] The president was resting on a sofa reading, with his work papers scattered all around him. Upon seeing his visitor, Lincoln rose and came forward to shake Douglass's hand, calling him "Mr. Douglass," indicating that he had read about him, and that his secretary of state William H. Seward had "told me all about you."[25]

Douglass began by thanking the president for signing the order extending protection to black troops, but before he could launch into his list of grievances and suggested remedies, Lincoln began a lengthy vindication of his policies on slavery and the use of African American troops. The president was certainly aware that through his editorials and speeches Douglass himself had frequently charged the president with hesitation on both emancipation and black military participation. He did not deny his slowness to act, but told Douglass, "No man can say that—once having taken the position [to support emancipation and black troops] I have contradicted it or retreated from it."[26] Indeed, before losing hope in the face of the draft riots, unequal pay policy, and atrocities aimed at black troops, Douglass himself had upheld Lincoln's methodical approach. Meeting the president and being greeted with respect restored his faith in the nation's leader. Douglass repeated his concerns about equal pay and protection for black troops as well as his belief that black soldiers performing "great and uncommon service on the battlefield" should "be rewarded by distinction and promotion" using the same criteria by which white soldiers were judged. The president assured him that he would take the matters under serious consideration, but did not offer any promise save that he would "sign any commission to colored soldiers whom his Secretary of War should commend to him."[27] Despite receiving no guarantees, Douglass came away convinced that Lincoln would stand firm on his antislavery policies and the meeting did much to assure him that the "Country would survive both Slavery and the War."[28] He returned home to Rochester to prepare for his recruiting mission, waiting and watching for the commission Stanton had promised.

Douglass was energized by his meetings with Lincoln and Stanton. In his third autobiography, he recalled that he left Washington with the "full belief that the true course to the black man's freedom and citizenship was over the battlefield, and that my business was to get every black man I could into the Union armies."[29] His mission was to join chief recruiter General Lorenzo Thomas and use his influence to encourage southern blacks, most of whom had recently been freed by the army and the Emancipation Proclamation, to enlist in newly forming regiments of the U.S. Colored Troops. In doing so, he would be joining his son Frederick Jr., who had been recruiting in the Mississippi Valley for several months. Serious about this new commitment, Douglass ceased publication of *Douglass' Monthly*, giving up the editor's pen for the first time in almost sixteen years. In the coming weeks, he received orders to report to General Thomas at Vicksburg, Mississippi with his travel paid by the government, but no official officer's commission. Instead of a military commission he received a document proclaiming Douglass to be a "loyal free man," who should be treated with respect and allowed to travel "unmolested." Issued by John Palmer Usher, secretary of the interior, and signed by Lincoln and others, the endorsement was little more than an elaborate set of papers such as those required of free African Americans across the southern states to prove their status as free men.[30] He wrote immediately to Stanton to inquire about his commission, but Assistant Adjutant General C.W. Foster informed him that he was to continue to be paid by General Stearns, and as to his official duties, Douglass was told, "it is expected that you go to aid General Thomas in any way that your influence with the colored race can be made available to advance" the recruiting effort.[31] No commission would be forthcoming, and Douglass decided not to undertake the trip without it.

There is no clear explanation for Douglass's refusal to travel to the South without a commission. Historians have speculated that his wounded pride, or perhaps his sense of practicality, prevented his acceptance of the offered terms.[32] Certainly, he relished the belief that he would be the first African American granted an advanced officer's commission in the U.S. Army. Accepting such a post would also have quelled critics who complained that he should take a more active role in the conflict. Douglass's Washington visit followed close on the heels of a letter appearing in the *Anglo African* charging him with remaining in the safety of the North instead of enlisting in the army.[33] Yet, as Douglass had admitted to Gerrit Smith, recruiting was not a job he took delight in, but something he had felt obligated to undertake. Traveling the familiar northern cities for Stearns was agreeable, but heading to the war-torn South was another matter. He was a reformer, an editor, and an orator, but not a military man. For years Douglass had publicly condemned white southerners for their refusal to see the evils of slavery and he was much hated across the region. It is not inconceivable to think that his prominence as an abolitionist would have made him the target of white violence. Without epaulets on his shoulders, Douglass would be just another black man in a slaveholding region, albeit one with a written endorsement from the president of the U.S. Although he chose to remain in the North, the meeting with Lincoln and Stanton formed a major marker in Douglass's life. The boy who began life in a Maryland slave cabin strode into the White House at the age of forty-six to advise the president of the United States. In the end, however, he determined that he could better serve the cause through familiar channels, turning once again to agitation for the end of slavery and for the uplift of his race.

Closing his newspaper office in anticipation of an officer's commission served to cement Douglass's new life direction. For the first time since 1847 he held no editorial pen, and was without the meager salary his newspaper had provided for himself and his family. Subscription income was small, but Douglass's publications had served to keep him in contact with his friends in the British reform community, who funneled money for the support of his weeklies and for *Douglass' Monthly*. Douglass tipped his hat to their support by regularly writing editorials aimed at keeping his British friends informed about events in U.S. abolition circles, politics, and the Civil War. Chief among his British allies was his old friend Julia Griffiths Crofts, who lived in Leeds, England. After acting as his business manager in Rochester from 1849 to 1855, she remained his closest friend and advisor, even following her return to England and subsequent marriage.[34] Indeed, it is likely that Crofts influenced Douglass's decision not to take the recruiting post without a commission. Once *Douglass' Monthly* ceased publication, his British friends lamented the loss of that regular channel of communication with Douglass. Receiving a letter from him written in mid-November, Crofts wrote back immediately that "never was a long looked for letter more welcome to anxious friends." Apparently speaking for a number of Douglass's British friends, she expressed relief that he had abandoned plans to go south and urged him to write frequently, for the discontinuance of his paper meant a shortage of news about his life and activities.[35]

For the remainder of 1863 and into the winter of 1864 Douglass concentrated on agitating, once again taking to the lecture circuit to call for an abolition war, and now for an abolition peace. He began to look beyond the war toward a Reconstruction that would include full equality for his race. His speeches called for an all-out attack and conquest of the South and full emancipation throughout the region. This message was hammered home again and again in a speech titled "The Mission of the War," which he delivered on numerous occasions in Rochester, Philadelphia, Boston, and other cities across the North. Its most famous delivery was on January 13, 1864 at the request of the Woman's Loyal League, which was actively working in favor of a constitutional amendment banning slavery. Given at New York's Cooper Institute before a large crowd, the speech outlined four main principles all loyal Americans needed to embrace. First, he told his audience they were compelled to recognize that the war "shall be, and of right ought to be, an Abolition war." By the same token no peace but an "Abolition peace" could be considered a satisfactory outcome. This meant that the nation must recognize the contributions of African Americans to the war and to society as a whole, and extend to blacks full rights and opportunities. Finally, he demanded that such full equality would only be achieved when the nation invested "the black man everywhere with the right to vote and to be voted for, and remove all discriminations against his rights on account of this color, whether as a citizen or as a soldier."[36]

As 1864 wore on and the prospects for an end to the war grew dimmer, with repeated military blunders and extended campaigns, Douglass's support for the president began to wane again. He watched and listened carefully to the words and actions of the Republican Party, and grew skeptical of Lincoln and his ability to wage an abolition war or to effect any type of peace. Resolution to the equal pay controversy extended well into the summer's election season and the Republicans made no move to extend suffrage to blacks in the areas of the border South under Union control. In May Douglass was among a group of abolitionists and Radical Republicans calling for a convention to meet at Cleveland to choose an alternative presidential ticket headed by John C. Frémont and John Cochrane, for president and vice president respectively. In a letter appearing in the *New York Times*, Douglass explained that if the proposed alternative convention supported black equality and suffrage rights, "I cheerfully give my name as one of the signers of the call."[37] The convention managed to attract around four hundred disaffected Republicans, but Douglass was not among their number. Although he was enamored of Frémont's role on behalf of African Americans, particularly with his emancipation policy early in the war, in the end Douglass's practicality once again prevented him from fully committing to an unlikely candidacy in such a troubling time.

Although he could not yet bring himself to openly commit to an alternative candidate, Douglass continued to be angered and disappointed with Lincoln's actions. In midsummer he was hopeful that an abolition peace was foreshadowed in the Reconstruction plan of abolitionist-minded Senator Benjamin Wade of Ohio and Maryland Congressman Henry Winter Davis. Passing both houses of Congress on July 2, 1864, the Wade–Davis Bill would have imposed a firm Republican hand on the South, requiring among other things that residents in states seeking readmission to the Union take an iron-clad loyalty oath. Preferring his own more generous and lenient Reconstruction plan, Lincoln exercised a pocket veto, allowing the bill to expire without acting on it.

The president faced growing criticism on other fronts as well, when the nation learned of an attempt by *New York Tribune* editor Horace Greeley to negotiate a peaceful end to the war with agents supposedly representing the Confederate government. Spurred on by the growing influence of the antiwar Democrats, known as Copperheads, Lincoln wrote the editor agreeing to meet with any southern representatives bearing a written peace proposition penned by Confederate President Jefferson Davis, provided that it supported restoring the Union and ending slavery. As it turned out, Greeley's southern contacts were independent agitators who had no connection to the Confederate government. In the end, Lincoln's embarrassment over the fiasco was second to the criticism the president endured because of the contents of his letter to Greeley, which appeared in print for all to read. In making the "abandonment of slavery" a condition for peace, Lincoln drew the ire of Democrats and moderate Republicans. But for Douglass, Lincoln's language sounded close to his own desire for an abolition war. When the anguished president called on Douglass to meet with him in Washington, he put aside his criticism and rushed to help.[38]

When Douglass arrived at the White House on August 19 for his second meeting with Lincoln, he found the president downtrodden and looking older than he had at their first encounter just a year before. In the wake of recent criticism and with the November election looming large before him, Lincoln sought Douglass's advice on how to satisfy his critics and the nation on the issue of emancipation. He also asked for the abolitionist's help on a plan to hasten the demise of slavery and any support slave labor brought to the Confederacy. At the same time, he was drafting a letter, he told Douglass, conceding his willingness to accept a peace without the abolition of slavery if Congress and the people so wanted. Alarmed that all he had fought so earnestly for was about to crumble before him, Douglass urged Lincoln to destroy the letter and to continue to push for an end to slavery.

It is not likely that Douglass exerted much influence on the president and the second subject of their meeting suggests that Lincoln was not really considering conceding to his opponents. Douglass later recalled that Lincoln expressed concern that the number of slaves moving across Union lines to freedom was smaller than expected. Word of the Emancipation Proclamation was not spreading fast enough to affect the Confederate war effort. The president proposed a plan reminiscent of John Brown's early scheme to draw slaves out of the South and into the Appalachian mountains, although this time with the full sanction of the U.S. government. Lincoln asked Douglass to devise an arrangement by which slaves would be made acquainted with the possibility of freedom and a way "for bringing them into our lines."[39] Taking this request with utmost seriousness, Douglass left the meeting already planning to engage important African American leaders in crafting the plan. Ten days after their meeting, he outlined his ideas in a letter to Lincoln. He advised the president to appoint a general agent who would in turn deploy as many as two dozen men to go south among the slaves and move as many as possible behind Union lines. Possibly recalling his own recent disappointment with the War Department, he recommended that the general agent be granted a "kind of roving commission within our lines, so that he may have a more direct and effective oversight of the whole work."[40] Douglass did not ask that he be appointed to the post, and the entire plan proved unnecessary when a tide of Union victories by the fall of 1864 brought freedom to an increasing number of slaves as they came behind U.S. Army lines.

Douglass came away from these interactions with the president convinced that Lincoln opposed slavery on moral grounds and that his issuance of the Emancipation Proclamation was more than an expedient war measure. Lincoln's respect for Douglass as an individual was also evident. Shortly after their second meeting, the president invited Douglass to take tea with him at the Soldier's Home in Washington, where Lincoln often went to relax and think. Although a previous speaking engagement kept Douglass from accepting the invitation, he was flattered.[41] Once the Democrats nominated peace advocate and former general George McClellan as their presidential candidate, Douglass became a strong supporter of Lincoln's reelection, although he did not campaign publicly. He confided in his friend Theodore Tilton, "I am not doing much in this Presidential canvass for the reason that Republican committees do not wish to expose themselves to the charge of being the 'N—r' party."[42] Despite treating blacks as "deformed children," the Republicans and Lincoln's candidacy offered the only possible hope for advocates of freedom, Douglass told William Lloyd Garrison. He urged all to work for the "utter defeat and political annihilation" of McClellan.[43] In late September, Frémont withdrew from the race, providing an even clearer reason for Republicans to stand behind the president. Douglass celebrated Lincoln's reelection, which served to silence the Copperhead movement and foreshadowed the death of the Confederacy.[44]

The last months of the war found Douglass assuming his old role as a black leader and orator. Following the election he embarked on a speaking tour that brought him to his home state of Maryland for the first time since escaping slavery twenty-six years before. He was drawn to speak before large Baltimore crowds in celebration of the state's new constitution, which had recently abolished slavery. Among the six lectures Douglass delivered in Baltimore, he gave one on November 17 at the Bethel AME Church. He entered the church of his youth for the first time as a free man and in the company of his sister Eliza Bailey Mitchell, whom he had not seen for more than thirty years. The war brought Douglass the freedom to travel to the South, but it was a bittersweet homecoming. Although he was warmly welcomed by the black community, his planned reunion with his former mistress, Sophia Auld, who had kindly taught Douglass to read as a boy, was aborted when her son Benjamin refused to allow the meeting. Douglass returned to Rochester without the closure that encounter might have brought him.[45]

The winding down of the war brought a reunion of the Douglass family, near and far. Through his father's influence, Charles, who had been ill and unable to fight for much of his army service, had been transferred to the 5th Massachusetts Cavalry in March 1864. While his unit was stationed in Maryland, Charles managed to visit his Bailey relatives on the Eastern Shore, the first of Douglass's children to connect with their southern family members. Although promoted to sergeant, Charles continued to suffer from a respiratory ailment, perhaps asthma. In August, following their second White House meeting, Douglass asked Lincoln to intercede so that his son could be discharged. The president complied, and Charles Douglass was mustered out of service on September 15. Frederick Jr. had completed his recruiting in the South without major incident and returned to the North where he remained until he and his older brother Lewis embarked on a short-lived business venture in Denver. Rosetta, who had married Nathan Sprague on Christmas Eve in 1863, gave birth to Douglass's first granddaughter, Annie, in late 1864. Last to arrive home was Lewis Douglass, who remained a part of the 54th Massachusetts until mid-1865. When his regiment was stationed briefly at Royal Oak in Talbot County, Maryland, in early June, Lewis walked to St. Michaels for his own reunion with the Bailey clan. There they celebrated the freedom from slavery extended to them all.[46]

The winter and spring of 1865 marked another important milestone in Douglass's life and in the life of the nation. On February 1, about a month before Lincoln's second inauguration, the House of Representatives joined the Senate in passing the Thirteenth Amendment, which, when ratified later in the year, banned slavery everywhere in the United States. Douglass rejoiced that the long-fought battle for the abolition of slavery was won, although he had no illusions that an abolition peace would result in immediate equality for members of his race. In the coming months and years he would work tirelessly to achieve those goals, but as the long war moved toward a close he celebrated the dawn of a post-slavery America. He traveled to Washington to attend the second inauguration of Lincoln with a lively step and a light heart. On March 4 he joined the swelling crowd outside the Capitol to hear his president call for the reunion of the nation, "with malice toward none, with charity for all," in a rousing inaugural address Douglass later remembered as "more like a sermon than like a state paper."[47]

At a reception later that day Douglass had his final personal encounter with Lincoln, the details of which are recorded only in Douglass's third autobiography, written more than fifteen years later. No African American had ever attended the inaugural day festivities at the White House, but Douglass believed that the spirit of freedom embodied in the recent passage of the Thirteenth Amendment would extend to his presence at the executive mansion. Accompanied by Louise Dorsey, the wife of prominent African American Philadelphia caterer Thomas Dorsey, Douglass tried to enter the reception, but was denied. He recalled that two large policemen took him "rudely by the arm" and informed him that their instructions were to admit no black persons. Refusing to believe that any "such order could have emanated from President Lincoln," Douglass would not leave until he saw the president. He called out to a passing acquaintance to please be so "kind as to say to Mr. Lincoln that Frederick Douglass is detained by officers at the door." In Douglass's memory he was soon admitted to the East Room where he was greeted by the president's welcome: "Here comes my friend Douglass."[48] The president asked Douglass's opinion of his oration, and spoke with him for a few minutes. Douglass returned to Rochester honored and hopeful for the future struggle.

He was at home in Rochester six weeks later when he learned that crazed southern sympathizer John Wilkes Booth had shot the president while he attended a play at Ford's Theater in Washington. He died in the early morning hours of April 15. Lincoln's assassination shocked the nation and hit Douglass especially hard. He had harbored much hope that the president's second term would put the nation on the path toward a color-blind future. Mayor Daniel David Tompkins Moore called upon Douglass to offer up an impromptu eulogy to a crowd gathered late that afternoon at the Rochester City Hall. Although he had not anticipated being called upon to speak, Douglass remarked eloquently on his friend, telling the crowd that the "blood of our beloved martyred President will be the salvation of our country." Yet he was already looking forward, warning, "let us not be in too much haste in the work of restoration." To do justice to Lincoln's legacy and his memory meant doing justice to black Americans. The right way to remember the slain leader was to "know no man hereafter in all these States by his complexion, but know him by his loyalty, and wherever there is a patriot in the North or South, white or black, helping in a good cause, hail him as a citizen, a kinsman, a clansman, a brother beloved!"[49] With this expression, Douglass entered into the postwar world and began the struggle he hoped would finally bring his nation and his race together.

CHAPTER 8

TOWARD A NEW NATIONAL ERA

The Civil War's conclusion was bittersweet for Douglass and all who saw Lincoln's presidency as the dawn of a new era for African Americans. The president's assassination and succession of the southerner Andrew Johnson somewhat tempered the emancipation celebration secured by the passage of the Thirteenth Amendment, which became law with its final ratification by the states in December 1865. An abolition peace was won, but at the high cost of more than 620,000 American lives. The nation was entering the post-slavery era and beginning the process of Reconstruction. For Douglass, the end of the war brought a renewed sense of purpose. He rejoiced in emancipation and gloriously claimed his rightful role in bringing about slavery's demise, but he also realized that racial equality would not automatically follow on the heels of abolition. In the months following the war's end, Douglass already began to ponder a new path through the struggle that lay ahead. His belief that the fight for equality was only beginning was not shared by some of his longtime abolitionist colleagues.

In the spring of 1865 William Lloyd Garrison called for the disbanding of the American Anti-Slavery Society (AASS). During the war, any animosity remaining between Douglass and Garrison seemed to evaporate as the pair relished the imminent realization of their life's work. Tensions returned, however, once emancipation became a reality. The annual meeting of the AASS fell a mere three weeks after the president's death and there a heated debate raged when Garrison suggested that the society's work was complete and the organization no longer necessary.[1] The huge turnout at New York's Cooper Institute should have been a rousing celebration of the success of the abolition movement, but instead the meeting marked a new turning point in the reform community, separating those who intended to continue to fight for black civil rights from those who believed their goals had been achieved. Addressing the crowd, Garrison proclaimed, "My vocation, as an Abolitionist, thank God, is ended."[2] But others in the room, including Wendell Phillips, strongly disagreed. Garrison's motion to dissolve the Society failed by a vote of 118 to 48. Leadership of the group transferred to Phillips, who had long agreed with Douglass that abolition meant much more than just ending slavery. By the end of the year, though, the field of abolitionists had rapidly cleared. Garrison ceased publication of the *Liberator*, and most of his Boston circle of reformers followed him into retirement. Even Douglass's British allies, Elizabeth Pease and Richard Webb among them, considered their work complete.[3] Douglass found that he could still rely on Gerrit Smith and a few other white colleagues, but in the postwar era his circle of influence became ever more linked with leaders in the black community and with the Republican Party.

In 1865 Douglass urgently sought to cast off his role as America's most famous former slave. Once slavery was no more, he turned to a host of reforms and platforms that cemented his reputation as an African American statesman. Although he had long been the most prominent spokesman for the slave, he sought to be a leader for his race in freedom, and although he was eager for political patronage, he also needed a steady income. Turning his oratorical skill into a professional career, Douglass engaged the Redpath Lyceum Bureau of Boston to book an extensive speaking tour each winter, and was paid an average of $100 to $200 per appearance, earning a nice living. He perfected a series of lectures, some of which dealt with contemporary political issues, such as one on Santo Domingo and another reflecting on his career as an antislavery lecturer. Moving into the postwar era, he sought to shake off his standing as simply an abolitionist and former slave. Douglass was popular with African Americans, but also broadened his repertoire with orations that appealed to a range of mixed-race audiences. Some speeches demonstrated the breadth of his intellect, emulating the best speakers of his time. An oft-repeated speech was "William the Silent," which offered an historical account of a sixteenth-century Dutch revolt against Spanish control. Although it received mixed reviews, Douglass maintained it in his regular schedule because it was based on extensive historical research and he believed it would help audiences get beyond his image as a "self educated former slave."[4]

Lecturing was his vocation and paid the bills, but Douglass's postwar calling and passion lay in his push for civil and political rights. He styled himself as one of several spokesmen for African Americans. Along with George T. Downing, he headed a delegation of blacks at a February 1866 meeting with President Johnson, where they addressed concerns including black suffrage. The meeting foreshadowed the eventual fight between

Radical Republicans (and even mainstream moderate Republicans) and the president. Calling himself the "Moses" who would lead blacks from "bondage to freedom," Johnson dismissed Douglass's call for voting rights. Declaring that pushing for universal suffrage could lead to a race war, Johnson argued for the supremacy of states' rights on issues such as suffrage and claimed that it would be "tyrannical ... to attempt to force such upon them without their will." If the freed people could not find employment or a place in society, he told the delegation, they should consider emigrating elsewhere. Clearly, African Americans did not have an advocate in the racist former slaveowner who had succeeded Lincoln.[5]

By mid-1866 Douglass was an even more determined promoter of extending suffrage to African Americans. His political leanings fell strongly in the camp of the Radical Republicans, and many of his orations were before mixed audiences on behalf of black civil and political rights. He was bitterly disappointed in June when the Fourteenth Amendment draft presented to the state legislatures by the Congress failed to include a provision for black suffrage. Instead it strengthened the federal citizenship guarantee offered in the Civil Rights Act of 1866, which became law only after Congress overrode President Johnson's veto. The amendment guaranteed due process and equal protection, but Douglass and others were convinced that without suffrage rights African Americans could never gain equality with whites. For Douglass, Reconstruction was largely a political problem and including African Americans among the electorate provided a certain means of advancing the Radical agenda.

His intense advocacy for black suffrage put Douglass at odds with the women's rights activists with whom he had long shared a unified reform agenda. During the height of the abolition movement in the 1840s and 1850s many recognized a natural link between the plight of the enslaved and women. Abolitionist circles opened their organizations to middle-class women reformers, and Douglass shared meaningful friendships with a number of them including Abby Kelley Foster, Lydia Maria Child, and British friends Julia Griffiths Crofts and Anna Richardson. Although the single male speaker at the 1848 Seneca Falls Convention to support a resolution on woman suffrage, during the fight over the Reconstruction amendments, Douglass temporarily abandoned the cause of his old friends, including Susan B. Anthony and Elizabeth Cady Stanton. Believing strongly that any suffrage amendment would fail if women were included, Douglass appealed to practicality and temporarily deserted their cause. Responding to a request to speak in favor of woman suffrage in Washington from long-time abolitionist colleague Josephine S.W. Griffing, Douglass told her that, while he was quite willing to "hold up both my hands in favor of this right," he could not accept the invitation. Then occupied full time in the fight for black suffrage, he chided Griffing for siding with Anthony and Stanton on the principle that the struggle of both women and black men must necessarily be linked. Postwar violence made his cause the critical one, he argued: "While the Negro is mobbed, beaten, shot, stabbed, hanged, burnt, and is the target of all that is malignant in the North and all that is murderous in the South his claims may be preferred by me without exposing in any wise myself to the imputation of narrowness or meanness toward the cause of woman."[6] The women who had long stood beside Douglass in the struggle to end slavery were shocked and dismayed at this attitude. Segments of the reform community soon divided over the issue and it would take Douglass years to repair the damage.

Black suffrage also became a contentious issue dividing Republicans, with southern Republicans and loyalists clamoring for the black vote to enhance their numbers and prevent former Confederates from regaining control of the South, and northern racists in the party strongly opposing it. Those supporting President Johnson's lenient policies of southern restoration and states' rights held a National Union convention in August. Moderate and Radical Republicans planned their own "Southern Loyalists' Convention" the following month. Douglass's election by the citizens of Rochester as a delegate to the Radical-sponsored loyalists' convention in Philadelphia foreshadowed the beginnings of his role as a minor politico, but also demonstrates the deep-seated racism among northern white Republicans. Some white delegates warned that his presence would cause more problems and urged that he stay away. Naturally incensed, Douglass later recalled his response: "Gentlemen, with all respect, you might as well ask me to put a loaded pistol to my head and blow my brains out, as to ask me to keep out of this convention."[7] He and other black delegates were largely ignored during the official proceedings, but Douglass was invited to address a private meeting of convention delegates, and there made a strong plea for black suffrage: "I go for this right because our Government is a democratic one; because it is based upon the principle of universal suffrage; and the right cannot be denied on account of complexion."[8] As was true of his antebellum encounters with segregation on public conveyances, the racial discrimination he and other black delegates endured simply encouraged him to press the case for suffrage even more strongly, and to fight for a place for African Americans in the United States and within the Republican Party.

While Douglass's public life became more entwined with party politics, his family life grew more complex, as the war's end brought both family reunion and saw his children struggle to branch out on their own. Douglass also opened his home temporarily to his friend Ottilie Assing, the German journalist who had befriended him in the 1850s and completed a German translation of his second autobiography. Assing found herself without means when the journal for which she had long been a reporter folded. She left her boarding house in Hoboken, New Jersey, where Douglass had visited her frequently before and during the war, and traveled to Rochester. Like the presence of Julia Griffiths in the previous decade, Assing's nine-month residence complicated family life. It was with Assing and not his wife that Douglass discussed his plans for the lecture circuit, his political aspirations, and his intellectual yearnings. It is also possible that he shared her bed. Whatever the true nature of Douglass and Assing's relationship, a white woman living among the extended family was a shock and certainly intensified the tension between Anna Douglass and her husband.[9] Anna remained mute on Assing's boarding arrangement, but must have been happy to see her get on a train for New York in October 1866. Tensions over Assing's presence may also have acted as a catalyst to push at least two of their adult children to establish their own households, although none was able to stand on their own for long.

His children's continual inability to succeed in life became a deep and lasting disappointment to Douglass. Rosetta and Nathan Sprague moved with three-year-old Annie to a house in downtown Rochester, where Nathan tried and failed to operate a hack service, soon falling into conflict with the city's other carriage drivers. Charles married Mary Elizabeth Murphy, known as Libbie, in 1866, and subsequently moved to Washington, D.C., once his father secured a clerkship for him in the Freedmen's Bureau. He would remain dependent on his father's connections to gain minor federal appointments, including as a Treasury Department clerk and a later role in the U.S. consulate in Santo Domingo.

Instead of remaining in Rochester following their military service, Lewis and Frederick Jr. headed west to Denver, where both worked as clerks in the printing office of the Red, White, and Blue Mining Company. But they too benefited from their father's connections, as it was his old friend Henry O. Waggoner who taught them the typography trade. Lewis was apparently the more skilled typographer, working in Denver until 1869, when he accepted a post at the Government Printing Office in Washington. The same year he married Helen Amelia Loguen, daughter of the Syracuse AMEZ minister and abolitionist Jermain Wesley Loguen. Frederick Jr. had already returned east in 1868, working somewhat sporadically at a Washington printing office. In 1871 Frederick Jr. married Virginia Hewlett from Cambridge, Massachusetts.

By 1870, then, most of Douglass's family resided permanently in the nation's capital, and he was soon to follow. Although their children were all operating at least semi-independently, there was other family to attend to before he and Anna could contemplate relocating. Douglass had reunited with his sister Eliza in 1864, and had always known she was living on Maryland's Eastern Shore, but in February 1867 he received a communication from a man named Perry Downs, proclaiming himself to be his brother. Separated from the family more than forty years earlier, Douglass's oldest brother Perry Bailey had apparently ended up in Texas, where his wife had been sold. Douglass arrived home from a Virginia lecture tour in early July to find his brother waiting, along with his wife Maria and four children. He was elated to be reunited with Perry, but Douglass's joy was not shared by his adult children. Having been reared in northern middle-class circumstances, the Douglass children had little in common with these unknown relatives, who were only recently removed from slavery. Disappointed that their presence in Rochester would keep his father away from an event in Washington and a little concerned about the character of his newfound relatives, Charles wrote his father, "From what I have heard of their conduct, I should be afraid even to have them in the same neighborhood and more especially when you are away in the winter."[10] But Perry and his family did stay on in Rochester, and Anna was once again saddled with long-term houseguests thanks to her husband's generosity. Douglass even had a small cottage constructed on his property where the Baileys lived for the next two years. No record offers Anna's opinion of this extended family, but their presence must have added to her household responsibilities. Bailey's impoverished status certainly further taxed their already overextended resources. Finally, in 1869, the Baileys returned to Maryland's Eastern Shore, but continued to struggle financially. When Perry Bailey died in 1880, Douglass paid his funeral expenses.[11]

These family matters distracted Douglass and kept him away from the nation's capital, where he longed to be engaging in the work of Reconstruction. About the time his brother and family arrived in Rochester, Charles Douglass wrote his father with news that it was rumored that General Oliver O. Howard, head of the Freedmen's Bureau, was to be replaced with a black man. From his minor clerk's post at the agency, Charles heard a rumor that Douglass might be named to command the bureau. William Slade, steward at the White House, had already written an unofficial letter on White House stationery urging Douglass to take the post and offering to help intercede with the president, and a host of other black leaders maneuvered for Douglass's appointment. Although Slade believed he could procure the appointment, there is no evidence that President Johnson had any intention of appointing an African American, or that he was contemplating removing Howard. Through his son, Douglass also learned that John Mercer Langston, a prominent attorney and former abolitionist from Ohio, who would become Douglass's chief rival for black leadership, was actively seeking the appointment. Considering Johnson's disdain for Howard, he may have actually considered his removal, but Langston's involvement made Douglass cautious. Although he relished the thought of directing education and other opportunities for the freedpeople, he declined Slade's offer to intercede with the president on his behalf. Howard remained at the head of the Bureau, and Douglass learned a lesson in the art of political dealing. He would put his newfound skills to good use as soon as he joined his son in Washington.[12]

Yet Douglass was still dealing with family concerns and keeping up a busy lecture schedule in the early winter of 1868. He was touring Ohio and Illinois when events in Washington erupted. The Radical Republicans in Congress finally exhausted their tolerance for the intemperate Andrew Johnson's obstruction of their Reconstruction agenda. While Douglass was lecturing crowds on the importance of black suffrage and sidestepping criticism from women's rights activists who believed he had abandoned their cause, Congress moved to impeach the president. Although the prosecution failed by one vote in the Senate, the unprecedented trial bespoke of a nation still deeply divided and in tremendous turmoil over the very issues Douglass held dear. In July, the Fourteenth Amendment was formally ratified, and although progress on suffrage was slow, in the fall Douglass and other black leaders found reason to be hopeful in the presidential candidacy of Ulysses S. Grant. The famous general's run for the presidency represented a turning point in Republican politics and in the implementation of Reconstruction. Douglass campaigned on Grant's behalf and remained a stalwart supporter during his two terms in the White House. Although later disappointed that his loyalty was not rewarded with an important political appointment, Douglass was buoyed by Grant's inaugural address in which he pledged to push for ratification of the Fifteenth Amendment, which had passed the post-Johnson era Congress just days before he took office. Guaranteeing the right to vote to all men without regard to race, the amendment would achieve one of Douglass's lifelong goals.

Around the time of Grant's inauguration, Douglass was invited to edit a new African American weekly called the *New Era*, to be published in Washington. The venture was funded by a consortium of prominent blacks including J. Sella Martin and George T. Downing, who believed that African Americans needed a journal that addressed their interests. As the editor of the nation's longest-running black newspaper, Douglass was a natural choice but he initially declined because, in his opinion, the mere $5,000 the group had raised was insufficient to fund a *"first class journal."* Instead he offered the editors his advice and wisdom as an experienced journalist and took on the minor role of corresponding editor. Before long Douglass was increasingly drawn into the venture. His son Lewis became the paper's compositor, giving Douglass a stake in ensuring the weekly's success. In less than a year, his concerns about financial stability proved accurate, and the paper was on the verge of failure. Traveling to Washington, Douglass purchased the paper and soon renamed it the *New National Era*. His vision was to create an organ addressing the concerns of both blacks and whites in and around the nation's capital, but in reality the weekly attracted few white subscribers. Lasting from 1870 into 1874, the newspaper provided employment for sons Lewis and Frederick Jr., who were both floundering in their careers. It also cemented Douglass as the most recognized black spokesman in Washington. Although he turned over most of the operations to his sons, the *New National Era* gave Douglass the public voice he had lost when he discontinued his monthly publication in 1863.[13] His editorials and letters appeared in almost every issue. From the pages of the weekly Douglass urged blacks toward self-reliance, thrift, sobriety, and hard work. These qualities, he opined, would see the realization of equality and full citizenship.[14]

The editing venture also established Douglass as a man of Washington, although his family and home still remained in Rochester. Dividing his time between the lecture circuit that supported his extended family and attending to the newspaper, he still remained politically involved. David Blight has argued that, after 1870, Douglass's career underwent major changes, bolstering his unfailing adherence to the party of Lincoln. After establishing himself in Washington, he began to speak before larger black audiences than most of his earlier lecture tours allowed. Following the ratification of the Fifteenth Amendment in March 1870, Douglass attended numerous celebratory gatherings where he often shared the stage with other emerging black leaders, including John Mercer Langston and *New Era* partners J. Sella Martin and George T. Downing. This gave him an even larger presence as a race leader, but Douglass longed to be recognized as an important contributor to the Republican Party through a federal appointment.

In the first decade of Reconstruction his stalwart Republican allegiance brought him little in the way of patronage, however. Douglass must have been bitterly disappointed when in 1870 he was passed over for appointment as minister to Haiti. Although his name had been circulated for the post, this first major diplomatic appointment of an African American went to Ebenezer Bassett, a free-born northern educator who had recruited black troops along with Douglass. The following year, Grant appointed Douglass to accompany an official delegation to Santo Domingo, which the U.S. was already contemplating annexing to establish a desirable naval post in the Caribbean. Leaving in January 1871, Douglass joined the three official commissioners, including Ohio Senator Ben Wade and Cornell University President A.D. White, on a three-month tour of the island nation. The only black on the mission, and clearly the lowest-ranking member of the group, Douglass's name was not even included in the official diplomatic papers of introduction. As an assistant secretary with few official duties he found the mission disappointing. Upon his return to the U.S., he wrote to Secretary of State Hamilton Fish that he regretted "that my services in the capacity authorized by the terms of my appointment were inconsiderable and unimportant."[15] Although his traveling companions treated him with respect during the trip, he was denied service in the dining room on the return steamer, and was later excluded from Grant's White House dinner honoring the commissioners.[16]

Although disappointed in his first official government trip abroad, he did not speak out against Grant's administration. Instead, within months of the Santo Domingo trip he accepted appointment as one of three black representatives to the first District of Columbia Legislative Council, which governed the newly consolidated capital as a single political entity. Since the capital fell under federal jurisdiction, council seats were conferred by the president on the advice of the U.S. Senate. Ultimately he found the mundane work of local governance unsatisfying. Finding the "many matters of local legislation" incompatible with his frequent absences on the lecture circuit, Douglass lasted only a short time on the council. When resigning on June 21, however, he did use his influence to see his son Lewis appointed to fill his seat.[17]

Despite Grant's dismal disappointment as president and as a patron to African Americans, Douglass rarely spoke out against his party's leader. Even with the numerous scandals surrounding the White House he remained loyal to the Republicans, and in 1872 he became firmly cemented in the stalwart camp of the party. That year also proved to be a personal turning point for the Douglass family. Spending most of the spring in the nation's capital, on June 3 Douglass received the shocking news that his Rochester home had burned, but thankfully his family escaped unharmed. Rushing to catch a train northward, he arrived in the middle of the night to find that his home of more than twenty years was no longer habitable, and his family, though badly shaken, was safe in the care of his Rochester friends. Douglass's initial impulse was to believe that the blaze was the work of an arsonist, remarking that "while Rochester is the most liberal of Northern cities, it nevertheless has its full share of that Ku-Klux spirit," but no charges were ever brought.[18] Some furniture and mementos escaped harm, but many personal papers, including his personal collection of his newspapers, the *North Star, Frederick Douglass' Paper,* and *Douglass' Monthly,* were lost.

Securing temporary residence for the Douglass clan in Washington, he turned his attention to Grant's reelection bid, acting as a paid stump speaker for his 1872 campaign. The masthead of the *New National Era* announced his allegiance: "Frederick Douglass, Editor; Douglass Brothers, Publishers: For President, U.S. Grant."[19] In some respects, Douglass's faithfulness to the Republican Party and Grant marked a turning point and a separation from the reform community. When Douglass had not been invited to the president's dinner for the Santo Domingo commissioners, his old friend Gerrit Smith was more insulted than Douglass. Defending the president, Douglass told Smith he judged Grant by his opportunities, not his actions. Considering the episode just one of many countless snubs and insults endured on account of his race, Douglass proclaimed that nevertheless he was "confident of the ultimate improvement in the civilization of my countrymen."[20] For him the path toward social equality required adherence to the president despite his faults. Just as pragmatism led him to at least temporarily abandon the woman suffrage movement in favor of male suffrage under the Fifteenth Amendment, Douglass optimistically hoped for the best from Grant and the Republican Party. If that loyalty was rewarded with a political appointment, so much the better, but no offer ever came from Grant's administration.

Beneath Douglass's confidence that the Republican Party would bring racial justice and a possible political career for himself was a deep-seated fear that events in the South would worsen without the party's pressure on Reconstruction enforcement. The early 1870s saw the eruption of racial violence and the rise of the Ku Klux Klan, as white southerners pushed back against the policies of Grant. Republicans in Congress responded with a series of laws aimed at curbing the violence, but not all northerners endorsed the physical enforcement of Reconstruction. The Supreme Court ruling in the 1873 *Slaughterhouse* Cases also struck fear into the hearts of civil rights activists. In the midst of escalating southern violence, Justice Samuel F. Miller's ruling denied that the privilege and immunities clause of the Fourteenth Amendment had removed any distinction between state and national citizenship. Douglass understood the dangers implied in the ruling. If there was no federal guarantee of citizenship, southern conservatives could easily push back the meager civil rights gains of the Reconstruction Era.[21]

A fracturing within the party further exacerbated Douglass's fears, as *New York Tribune* editor Horace Greeley led a Liberal Republican movement that opposed the corruption of Grant's administration while also trying to reconcile the North and the South. The movement attracted considerable southern support and Greeley, an early founder of the Republican Party, ended up receiving the Democratic nomination for president. Douglass's stump speeches urged the nation to remain loyal to Grant, and under the circumstances he could hardly have been openly critical of the president. Although he had already relocated his family to Washington, Douglass was chosen an elector at large for New York and was given the honor of carrying the state's sealed electoral votes to the nation's capital. Grant's reelection was secured not only by the popular vote, but by the death of Greeley before the electoral votes were tallied. Douglass later recalled, perhaps somewhat disingenuously, that he had "neither received nor sought" office from Grant.[22]

Instead of a federal appointment, in 1874 Douglass became president of the Freedman's Savings and Trust Company. Chartered as a multi-state savings bank by the Congress in 1865, the Freedman's Bank, as it was known, aimed to support the development of the African American business sector following emancipation and provide a safe haven for the nickels and pennies of hardworking men and women. The elegant Pennsylvania Avenue headquarters stood diagonal to the White House, but the bank had branch offices in numerous cities, including Baltimore, Louisville, and even New York. The first officers and trustees of the bank had been reform-minded white men, but within its first years of operation leadership fell to the African American community. Unfortunately when Douglass took the president's post in March the bank was already insolvent, and it teetered toward the collapse that occurred less than four months into his tenure. Suffering from a series of bad investments, including unreliable railroad bonds and dubious loans to prominent depositors, the bank's trustees sought out Douglass not because of his financial experience, which was negligible, but because he was the most visible black leader in the nation. Although ignored by the Grant administration, Douglass's reputation among blacks as a prominent statesman was growing and he was pleased to make an effort to save the institution. On his first day as president he declared his desire to manage operations with complete honesty and to strive to keep the bank alive.[23]

Unfortunately the Freedman's Bank required more than the boost of confidence Douglass or any black leader could provide. Trustees named physician Charles B. Purvis vice president and John Mercer Langston, then head of Howard University's law school, chair of the finance committee, but neither had any experience in the day-to-day operations of a bank. Douglass seems to have spent most of his time reassuring depositors and investors of the bank's solvency, expending little effort to actually stop its failure. Although he went so far as to loan the bank $10,000 of his own money, by the time he appealed to the Senate Finance Committee for assistance it was too late. The bank closed its doors in July and Douglass's reputation was tarnished, with many in the African American community blaming him for their lost deposits and investments. Some of the criticism was well founded. He had no experience with financial matters but

Douglass could and should have sought intervention sooner. Describing the episode in his final autobiography, he noted, "it is not altogether without a feeling of humiliation that I must narrate my connection with 'The Freedman's Savings and Trust Company'."[24] Angry depositors blamed him for their lost funds and Douglass steadfastly avoided discussing the matter beyond the brief account in his 1881 narrative.

Douglass's disappointments continued later in the year when the *New National Era* folded in October 1874. The costs of production began to outweigh the meager subscription base as the weekly failed to attract the integrated and informed readership Douglass had imagined in postwar Washington. He returned to the lecture circuit in 1875, traveling across the northeast and Midwest in the winter and fall, managing to earn a nice living, but Douglass and Anna continued to live in a small rented house on A Street. Much of his energy was concentrated on his grown children, who continued to flounder personally and financially. Charles, a clerk in the Treasury Department, struggled with marital and financial problems. Rosetta's husband Nathan Sprague outspent his income, and they were forced to relocate to Washington after losing their Rochester home. There Sprague ended up employed as a stable hand at the home of Salmon P. Chase's daughter, Kate Chase Sprague.[25] Always in fragile health, Frederick Jr. remained in the nation's capital, but was also dependent on his father to help him secure employment following the newspaper's closure, working first in the federal marshal's office and later the office of the Recorder of Deeds. A bit more independent, Lewis sometimes traveled with Douglass on the lecture circuit and later worked in real estate.

Douglass was relieved to turn his attention back to the political realm as the presidential election of 1876 loomed. Remaining stalwart through a series of corruption scandals that wracked the Grant administration, by late 1876 Douglass watched in dismay as the specter of racial equality and the promise of civil rights for the freedpeople slowly slipped away. Many in the Republican Party backed away from promises to enforce the guarantees of the Fourteenth and Fifteenth Amendments, and conservatives and former Confederates began to seize control of political power in areas of the South. Some African American leaders were lured into support for the Democratic Party, but Douglass stood firm behind the party of Lincoln. Despite the growing problems, he continually argued that the Republicans offered the only real hope for African Americans. His support was not complacent: instead of deserting the party, he took pride in "waving the bloody shirt," chiding Republicans for abandoning the cause for which the nation had suffered through four years of war and all its consequences. Invited to address the party's national convention for the first time in June 1876, Douglass demanded that Republicans finish the work of

Reconstruction. "What does it all amount to, if the black man, after having been made free by the letter of your law, is unable to exercise that freedom; and after having been freed from the slaveholders' lash he is to be subject to the slaveholders' shotgun?" He urged Republicans to make good on their promises to apply the guarantees of the Constitution to all.[26]

The complicated compromise that allowed the Republicans to hold on to the presidency after 1876 spelled further doom for the enforcement of Reconstruction in the South, but ultimately gave Douglass the federal appointment he had long sought. During negotiations over disputed electoral votes, Douglass was one of many who met with Republican candidate Rutherford B. Hayes to discuss the condition of African Americans in the southern states. Of that meeting, Hayes recorded in his diary, "I talked yesterday with Fred Douglass and Mr. Poindexter, both colored, on the Southern question. I told them my views. They approved. Mr. Douglass gave me many useful hints about the whole subject."[27] On March 4, 1877, Hayes was confirmed as the next president and on March 17 Douglass was appointed federal marshal for the District of Columbia. Soon after assuming office, however, Hayes agreed to withdraw the remaining federal troops occupying the deep South and fell closer in line to the reconciliationists in the party.

In the wake of events, Douglass's appointment left him open to criticism, especially from blacks. He did meet with Hayes before the so-called "compromise of 1877" was finalized, and perhaps the southern policy outlined in that meeting differed substantially from the final form. However, to the African American community it seemed Douglass had acquiesced in the nonenforcement of Reconstruction in exchange for personal gain, or as one critic later put it, "a fat office gagged him."[28] Many African Americans believed that the appointment of Douglass and other blacks to minor federal posts was aimed at curtailing criticism of Hayes's southern policies. Despite events surrounding his appointment, Douglass continued to believe that the Republican Party was the best hope—indeed the only hope—for black equality. As he had done with Grant, Douglass worked hard to separate Hayes the president from his Reconstruction policies, but he was deeply disappointed. Finally a Washington insider, Douglass found his reputation tied to the man associated with reconciliation and reunion. As David Blight has argued, what Douglass really wanted was "racial justice, promised in law, demonstrated in practice, and preserved in memory."[29] In the end he managed to effect that separation, if only in his own memory. In addition to serving warrants and federal notices, the District of Columbia's marshal had traditionally served as a master of ceremonies for formal events at the White House, introducing diplomatic guests. Douglass was not invited to fill that role, and he did not enjoy a close relationship with the president. Nevertheless, appointment even as a minor Republican official won out over any sense of outrage, and Douglass later described Hayes as a man with a "noble and generous spirit."[30]

Demonstrating his willingness to criticize white society as well as black, soon after assuming the marshal's post Douglass delivered a speech in Baltimore that managed to draw the ire of white professionals in the capital, leading a number of Washington attorneys to initiate a petition for his removal. Later published in regional newspapers, his "Our National Capital" speech condemned prominent Washingtonians as complicit in slavery before the Civil War and as blatantly racist in 1877. The controversy drew the attention of the national press and led one of his guarantors to threaten to remove support from the $20,000 bond required to secure the marshal's position. President Hayes refused to bow to pressure to remove him, and Douglass's sureties remained, but the African American community did not rush to his defense. Only his former associate at the Freedman's Bank, Charles B. Purvis, spoke out in his favor. Douglass's failure to keep the bank afloat and his persistent support for the failing Republican agenda placed him at odds with many prominent blacks.[31] Somewhat bitter that his leadership role was called into question, he later recalled that, rather ironically, although African Americans abandoned him in the wake of the election and the Baltimore speech controversy, he continued to receive dozens of requests from blacks seeking his help to secure a position in Washington.

In 1877 Douglass also received an invitation from his old friend Charles Caldwell to return to St. Michaels, Maryland, thirty-nine years after escaping slavery. There he was scheduled to address a mixed crowd of blacks and whites. Sporting his new federal appointment, he found himself about to effect his own reconciliation when he learned that his former master, Thomas Auld, wanted to see him. Douglass met Auld, then eighty-two and bedridden, at the home of Auld's son-in-law, William H. Bruff. A flood of memories overwhelmed Douglass as he entered Auld's sick room. Before him lay the master who had "made property of my body and soul, reduced me to chattel," he recalled, yet Douglass was prepared to make amends. He noted that, since slavery had been abolished, they stood on equal ground: "He was to me no longer a slaveholder either in fact or in spirit, and I regarded him as I did myself, a victim of the circumstances of birth, education, law, and custom."[32] Douglass's return to St. Michaels was widely reported in the press, where his conciliatory behavior further raised the ire of the black community. Younger African Americans were especially angry that Douglass would acquiesce in the meeting with Auld, and further incensed by his deferential approach to the encounter. Several newspapers reported that when Auld called him Marshal Douglass, he "instantly broke up the formal nature of the meeting by saying, 'not *Marshal*, but Frederick to you as formerly'."[33] He came away from the encounter feeling a sense of closure on many events from his youth, but in the eyes of the black press his behavior was out of character for Douglass the militant opponent of slavery and black oppression. Reports that he wept with the deep emotion of the meeting served to convince some that, in conjunction with his unwavering support for Hayes, he had abandoned his life's work for racial equality in favor of personal gain and reunion.

Douglass's living arrangements, too, soon served to further worsen African Americans' perception of him. During the four years he held the marshal's post he enjoyed true financial stability for the first extended period in his life as a free man. With the assistance of Charles Purvis, he bought a house and nine acres in Uniontown (later known as Anacostia), a village just across the river from Washington. The 1850s era house the Douglasses named Cedar Hill included twenty-one rooms of living space, more than enough room to accommodate visits from their growing extended family. Douglass and Anna moved from A Street in September 1878, and soon after purchased additional acreage, giving them a veritable estate just outside the capital's borders.[34] The white house on a hill, although frame and of modest construction, marked Douglass apart from the majority of African Americans, and certainly a lifetime away from his modest beginnings in slavery. Douglass found his political home in the Republican Party, and he would spend the remainder of his life at Cedar Hill.

At age sixty in 1878, Douglass was patriarch of a large and dysfunctional family. His children continued to struggle and he constantly intervened on their behalf. Ironically, while Douglass preached a doctrine of self-reliance to black audiences across the nation, his own family remained dependent on him for their livelihood and emotional stability. He supported Rosetta and her children while Nathan Sprague traveled to Nebraska to try again to establish himself. Charles's wife Libbie died in 1879, and the family divided their children among several households, leaving Anna and Douglass with young children underfoot. Frederick Jr. and his wife welcomed two of Charles's children, but needed additional financial support from Douglass to meet household expenses. Soon thereafter, Douglass's brother Perry and his daughter came to live with them. Perhaps partly due to the stress of caring for such an extended household of children and family (Perry was quite ill), Anna Douglass's health began to fail.[35]

Douglass began the postwar era at odds with abolitionist colleagues, who believed that their work on behalf of African Americans was chiefly completed. By the end of Reconstruction he was coming to terms with his earlier reform years. When Garrison died in May, 1879, Douglass put aside differences and offered a stirring tribute to his old mentor at a Washington service honoring the great reformer. Instead of a conflict with his early abolitionist colleagues, Douglass ended the era at odds with some African American leaders who believed that he "had deserted to the old master class and that [he] was a traitor" to his race.[36] The practicality and hopeful attitude that sustained him in the face of numerous challenges in the struggle for the abolition of slavery did not transfer as well into the Reconstruction Era. Although Douglass's adherence to the Republicans allowed him to prosper through appointment as marshal and helped him gain lesser patronage for his children, he continued to struggle for recognition among his black peers and to help his children achieve the self-reliance he felt so important.

CHAPTER 9

AGING REFORMER AND STATESMAN

At the end of Reconstruction, the United States moved toward an era of reconciliation between North and South that allowed the return of white, Democratic office holders (including former Confederates) across the South. As the country hovered at the edge of the industrial era, it was easy for many to push the struggle for racial equality to the margins in favor of the emerging concerns of modernity. Douglass's old radical associates fell out of favor within the Republican Party, and many African Americans flirted with new party associations. The most radical of all Republicans were gone. Thaddeus Stevens had died in 1868. Charles Sumner, the most consistent supporter of black rights in the Senate, had died in 1874, leaving as his legacy the Civil Rights Act of 1875. It would be the last federal legislation protecting racial equality until the mid-twentieth century. Enforcement was lax, however, and the Act was a dead letter after the Supreme Court undermined its validity in the *Civil Rights Cases* in 1883.[1] In the face of such declining support for the black agenda, the Republican Party found maintaining the loyalty of African Americans essential but increasingly difficult. With his leadership stretching back to before the Civil War, Republicans looked to Douglass to use his influence to keep the black vote in line. After 1880, he continued to be a party loyalist, but many of his personal decisions and actions left Douglass at odds with his race. As the new century approached, emerging black leaders such as Booker T. Washington, W.E.B. DuBois, T. Thomas Fortune, and others seemed more in touch with the needs of African Americans born near the end of slavery or even after the Civil War. The last two decades of Douglass's life found him struggling to maintain his influence in the black community and still working to overcome his legacy as America's most famous former slave. He often disappointed blacks for being insensitive to their concerns, and whites for his "arrogant" assumptions and expectations regarding the position of African Americans as equal in U.S. society.

Douglass stumped for Republican candidate James A. Garfield across the South and Midwest in 1880 and hoped to be rewarded with a prominent post in Garfield's administration. He felt assured that at least he would hold on to his post as marshal, and was dismayed when Garfield offered the office to another supporter. Leading the procession into the capitol's rotunda at the new president's inauguration was one of the last ceremonial duties he performed as marshal. However, Garfield did not totally shut Douglass off from patronage, appointing him Recorder of Deeds for the District of Columbia, an office he held until August 1886 when he was succeeded by James G. Matthews.[2] The office was not a prestigious one, but proved more lucrative than his marshal's post as he collected a fee on land and estate transactions within the capital. Although disappointed yet again because he was not rewarded with an appointment, when Garfield was assassinated a mere six months into his presidency Douglass offered a stirring introduction to a series of eulogies honoring the fallen leader at Washington's Fifteenth Street Presbyterian Church.[3] Chester A. Arthur, Garfield's successor, owed Douglass nothing, so he was fortunate to hang on to the Recorder's office through the new president's term. Because political patronage may have motivated Garfield's killer, Arthur further committed to a reform of the nation's civil service system aimed at limiting patronage appointment in lower-level federal positions, making it even harder to gain a patronage appointment.

During this turbulent period, Douglass maintained his liaison with Ottilie Assing. As only her side of their correspondence survives, it is difficult to discern the full nature of their relationship, but it is clear that she was intimately knowledgeable about his life and career. Assing had been in Washington while Douglass was publishing the *New National Era*, and may even have lived with the family for short periods in their rented house on A Street. She left for Europe in 1876 and maintained a correspondence with Douglass during her extended travels. Assing had hoped Douglass would join her, but his appointment as marshal in 1877 made that impossible. Returning to the U.S. the following summer, she visited the Douglasses soon after they were settled at Cedar Hill. After returning to her boarding house in Hoboken, New Jersey, Assing wrote Douglass, "Whatever there may be distressing in the conditions under which we only can meet, yet your company for me has such a charm and affords me a gratification the like of which I never feel elsewhere."[4] Among those distressing conditions were Douglass's extended family, and, of course, a disapproving Anna, who appeared to barely tolerate the white woman's visits in her household.

As with Julia Griffiths in Rochester, it was with Assing and not his wife that Douglass shared the intimate details of the ambitions for his career.

A journalist and author herself, Assing began urging Douglass to pen a third autobiography, suggesting "John Brown, political and abolitionist reminiscences, intercourse with prominent men, such as Lincoln, Sumner, Grant, etc, deliverance from religious bondage and so many other interesting topics [he] might treat."[5] Despite his many responsibilities as Recorder, he began to rewrite the story of his life in early 1881, including again the narrative of his enslavement, but also a much longer treatment of his many years as a reformer and public servant. Douglass penned the entire manuscript in less than six months and the first edition of the *Life and Times of Frederick Douglass* was published by the Park Publishing Company of Hartford, Connecticut in November 1881.[6] Never as successful as his first two autobiographies, *Life and Times* nevertheless was published in numerous editions, including an 1892 version to which Douglass appended a lengthy third part updating readers on his activities in the 1880s.

A third autobiography granted Douglass a forum for responding to his critics. The Freedman's Bank failure and Douglass's continued adherence to the Republican Party left him at odds with many in the African American community. *Life and Times* reminded readers of Douglass's prominence in the antebellum and Civil War era struggles for civil and political rights. His friendship with John Brown, recruitment activities for the Union army, and meetings with Abraham Lincoln stand out in its pages. Never one to back down from his opinions, even those considered controversial, shortly before agreeing to write *Life and Times*, Douglass had further raised the ire of many blacks by publicly opposing the Exoduster Movement. The end of Reconstruction in the South left many freedpeople struggling with unfair labor practices, restrictive Black Codes, and stripped of their political rights. Many former abolitionists including William Lloyd Garrison and Wendell Phillips encouraged the migration of Lower South blacks to Kansas and other points in the Midwest. Some African American leaders, including Douglass's rival John Mercer Langston and his old friends Henry Highland Garnet and Sojourner Truth, also encouraged the exodus. Douglass's prominence as a black leader made his opposition particularly irksome to migration advocates. It also suggests that he was out of touch with the plight of many southern African Americans.[7] Their struggle to survive in the post-Reconstruction South was certainly unlike anything Douglass had experienced.

Douglass outlined his reasons for opposing the migration in a paper prepared for a meeting of the American Social Science Association, although he did not attend the meeting himself. Without fully assessing the dire economic conditions in the South, Douglass claimed that blacks needed to stay put in the South. In language and reasoning akin to his antebellum attacks on colonizationists, he appeared unable to empathize with those trapped in the share-cropping economy. Many black leaders lashed out at him, with some accusing him of doing a disservice to his race.[8] Reprinting large parts of the paper in *Life and Times*, the autobiography furnished Douglass a forum for rebuttal. Angry over the personal attack, he argued that there was "something sinister in this so-called exodus, for it transpired that some of the agents most active in promoting it had an understanding with certain railroad companies," from which they received a recruiting fee. In Douglass's mind, many of the migrants were being duped into a situation of "extremest destitution," in the West.[9] Indeed, although some African Americans were able to gain title to free land, and several black communities persisted, many found the arid weather and unfamiliar farming conditions difficult.

While maintaining a reasonable presence in the Recorder of Deeds office, Douglass took to the lecture stage again in the fall of 1881 and winter of 1882. Although he had declined an invitation to speak at their July Fourth celebration in 1867, Douglass returned to Maryland's Eastern Shore in November, delivering a speech in Easton. There he visited with the families of many he had known in his youth. Returning by boat across the Chesapeake, just as he had left as an enslaved boy many years before, this time he was welcomed in the front door of Wye House. Edward Lloyd VII, grandson of the plantation's owner in Douglass's youth, was away on business, but his son greeted him and together they toured the house and gardens. Perhaps reflecting on how far his life had departed from his youth in slavery, Douglass found his reception to be in "every way gratifying."[10]

Similarly rewarding was the following winter and early spring spent in and around Washington. Douglass appeared often before largely black audiences offering both paid and benefit lectures. He returned to Rochester in May 1882 to deliver a Decoration Day address. Known later as Memorial Day, the holiday was observed in many cities across the nation to honor and reflect on the service of those who lost their lives during the Civil War. Unbeknownst to Douglass, he would soon be making a second trip to Rochester to honor the life of his closest companion. In mid-July, his world was shaken when sixty-nine-year-old Anna Murray Douglass suffered a serious stroke. Dozens of close friends wrote inquiring after her condition as she lingered in miserable condition for three weeks. All of Douglass's children rushed to be by her side and offer care, but she died on August 4. Douglass, his daughter Rosetta, and granddaughter Annie, traveled to Rochester where she was buried.[11]

His forty-four year marriage over, Douglass returned to Cedar Hill and worked to pull his life together. Work in the Recorder's office and lecturing occupied much of his time, but all accounts suggest he was deeply depressed following Anna's death. Although theirs was a complicated relationship and she rarely shared in his public life, they had five children together and a growing number of grandchildren. Anna managed his household and kept peace among their extended kin. Shortly after her death, Douglass wrote to a friend, "the main pillar of my house has fallen."[12] Still adjusting to life as a widower, in the summer of 1883 he recuperated with old anti-slavery friends at Poland Springs in Maine.

He reemerged on the public stage as chair of a National Convention of Colored Men scheduled for September 1883 in Louisville, Kentucky. Aimed at confronting the persistent problem of racial inequality and the erosion of political and civil rights in the South, preparations for the event illustrate Douglass's conflict with emerging African American leaders. In the early 1880s he clashed with Richard T. Greener, dean of the law school at Howard University, and black historian George Washington Williams over the Exoduster Movement, once accusing Williams of lying. The plans for the upcoming convention exacerbated tensions. Originally scheduled for the nation's capital, T. Thomas Fortune, editor of the *New York Globe*, publicly accused Douglass of acquiescing to the conference's venue change to Louisville at the demand of President Arthur. Printed in the pages of Fortune's newspaper, Douglass's reply expressed outrage, but did not mention that several conservative delegates and those from the South and southwest strongly supported a venue change. A number of prominent white Republicans did fear that the black convention would in reality be an anti-Republican meeting, as some African Americans began deserting the party of Lincoln. Before departing for Louisville, Douglass outlined his expectations for the convention and chastised his critics in a lengthy interview with the *New York World*. The controversy over the venue change resulted in many important leaders boycotting the meeting, but Douglass did preside over nearly three hundred delegates at the convention.[13]

While black leaders gathered in September, the Supreme Court decided *The Civil Rights Cases* (1883) with an opinion more devastating to the nation's hopes for black equality than the internecine rivalries among African American leaders. In five cases consolidated from lower courts, the eight-to-one majority ruling announced in October 1883 effectively struck down the Civil Rights Act of 1875. The most radical of all legislation emerging from Reconstruction, it had guaranteed equal access to all in public accommodations. Although rarely fully imposed, with the Civil Rights Act on the books blacks could at least push for its enforcement. Without it, Douglass understood that the civil rights agenda was a dead letter. He and other blacks put aside their differences to mobilize against the onslaught of segregation and second-class citizenship the ruling foretold.

On October 22 he gathered at Washington's Lincoln Hall with more than two thousand outraged blacks and some whites in protest at the decision. Douglass told the stunned crowd, "We have been, as a class, grievously wounded, wounded in the house of our friends, and this wound is too deep and too painful for ordinary and measured speech."[14]

Despite his outrage, Douglass was careful to temper his response to avoid publicly criticizing members of the Supreme Court. He was, after all, a public office holder and wanted to continue as Recorder of Deeds. In 1882 he hired Helen Pitts as a clerk in the Recorder's office, and in the months following Anna's death their business association transformed into a romantic relationship. The daughter of white New York abolitionists whom Douglass had encountered in the 1840s, Pitts benefited from a middle-class upbringing. Educated at Mount Holyoke College, she worked to educate freed blacks in Virginia and later Indiana. Coming to Washington in 1880 to work as a journalist, Pitts's uncle helped her secure the clerkship in the Recorder's office two years later. On January 2, 1884 Douglass married the forty-six-year-old Helen in Washington.[15]

The union sparked almost universal controversy. Both Douglass's and Pitts's families opposed the union, and Helen's father, once Douglass's abolitionist colleague, refused to give his blessing. Douglass's children were appalled that their father had married someone so soon after their mother's passing, and that Helen was a white woman only added insult to injury. Reaction outside family circles was even more venomous. Their union was attacked in both the white and black press. Douglass was outraged and lashed out at the detractors who "would have had no objection to my marrying a person much darker in complexion than myself, but to marry one much lighter, and of the complexion of my father rather than that of my mother, was, in the popular eye, a shocking offense."[16] Regardless of the tensions their marriage caused, Helen and Douglass were well matched and enjoyed a happy life together. Unlike his first wife who kept to the domestic sphere and rarely appeared in public with her husband, Helen and Douglass traveled extensively and often entertained guests at Cedar Hill.[17]

Among those shocked by Douglass's marriage was his longtime friend Ottilie Assing. Traveling in Italy when word of Anna's death reached her, she did not immediately return to the U.S., but instead traveled back to her native Germany and then to France. If Douglass once intended to pursue a romantic relationship with her after his wife's death, that no longer seemed to be the case. Although their letters from this period do not survive, apparently Douglass did not invite her to come to his side, nor did he travel to Europe. Scant evidence remains to puzzle out the true nature of their relationship, but it is clear from Assing's letters that their friendship, spanning more than twenty-five years, was a close one before Douglass met Helen Pitts. Yet, since Douglass did not even make his family and friends in Washington aware of his impending nuptials, it is unlikely that he wrote to Assing of his intent to marry Helen. According to her biographer, devastated by news of Douglass's marriage to a woman more than twenty years her junior, Assing withdrew from normal work patterns and social interactions. Soon after she learned she was suffering from incurable breast cancer and wrote to Douglass of her ailment. On August 21, 1884 she walked into a Paris public park and committed suicide by swallowing potassium cyanide, her body lying in the morgue for two weeks before being identified. Although many of Assing's friends speculated that Douglass's recent marriage pushed her to the edge, he chose only to reflect on his own loss at her passing. He wrote to a friend, "you will easily believe that this is a distressing stroke for me—for I ever held her as one of my most precious friends. I never had one more sincere." Much to the chagrin of her relatives, Assing left her meager estate to Douglass.[18]

If his marriage to Helen alienated his family and Assing, anger over the public attacks on his union helped mend fences with some old friends in the women's rights movement. During the struggle to ratify the Fifteenth Amendment in 1870, Douglass curtailed his longtime activism on behalf of equality for women. Claiming that the amendment would be doomed if women were attached to the black suffrage amendment, he drew the ire of Susan B. Anthony, Elizabeth Cady Stanton, and others. In the wake of the personal attacks on his interracial marriage, however, Stanton wrote expressing support. Douglass responded with gratitude, telling her "you have made both Mrs. Douglass and myself very glad and happy by your letter." Douglass's letter saw him particularly pleased that Helen could complete the addressing and mailing of his reply while he rushed off to a convention in Chicago. He told Stanton, "how good it is to have a wife who can read and write, and who can as Margaret Fuller says cover one in all his range."[19] In coming years Douglass returned to a full support of woman suffrage, often delivering public lectures before women's groups, and in this cause he received the full support of his wife.

Following their wedding, Douglass and Helen remained in Washington except for a brief trip to visit Helen's family in upstate New York. Duties in the Recorder's office postponed an extended honeymoon trip until 1886 when Douglass was released from his position. In 1884 Democrat Grover Cleveland broke the nearly twenty-five-year hold Republicans had enjoyed with his narrow defeat of James G. Blaine. Although he held onto his post for more than a year into Cleveland's presidency, Douglass's replacement was inevitable. Although the Recorder of Deeds was a local, not federal, position, the District of Columbia fell under the president's jurisdiction and all city officials served at the executive's pleasure. On August 10, 1886, Douglass settled accounts with the newly appointed James G. Matthews, a graduate of Albany Law School, and the following month he and Helen embarked on a lengthy tour of Europe and North Africa.[20]

Pre-war travel had taken Douglass to Ireland and Great Britain, but he was eager to explore Europe and other regions of the world. In Ireland and England he introduced Helen to a few surviving friends from his abolitionist travels in the 1840s and 1850s, and delivered several lectures. With both recording their experiences in travel journals, the couple moved from London to Paris in late October, then spent the winter exploring France and Italy. Deciding to extend their trip, in mid-February they boarded the steamer *Ormuz* for Egypt, and onboard ship Douglass celebrated turning sixty-nine, although he did not know the exact date of his actual birth and believed he was seventy. Reflecting on how far his life had departed from his meager beginnings, "I could but congratulate myself, that born as I was a slave marked for life under the lash," but was now "free and previleged to see these distant lands so full of historical interest."[21] Fascinated with Egypt, Douglass wrote most extensively of his time there, later recounting climbing the great pyramid even at his advanced age, although he remembered having "two Arabs before me pulling, and two at my back pushing."[22]

Douglass and Helen passed through Greece in March on their return to Italy. Arriving in Florence, they visited the grave of Unitarian minister and abolitionist Theodore Parker, who had died there during a visit to Elizabeth Barrett Browning and her husband in 1860. Douglass reflected on the "brave stand" Parker took as one of the major supporters of John Brown's raid on Harpers Ferry.[23] After extensive touring in Italy and Paris, they returned to London, where Helen received word that her mother had fallen gravely ill in New York and she departed for home alone, as he was still unwelcome in her family circle. Douglass finished the final few lectures scheduled in Britain and rejoined Helen at Cedar Hill in August 1887, her mother having recovered fully from her ailment.[24]

After more than a year abroad, it took Douglass little time to adjust to his familiar surroundings. Less than two weeks after returning from Europe, he took to the lecture stage, addressing a large crowd at the Unitarian Church in Nantucket, Massachusetts, the very city where he had given his first public address more than forty-five years earlier. In September the Washington African American community welcomed him home with a more formal reception at the Metropolitan AME Church and in December he gave a two-part recounting of his trip abroad.[25] Returning to the circuit more or less as a profession, he spoke before crowds in and around Washington throughout the fall and winter months. On February 12 he addressed the Republican National League on the seventy-ninth anniversary of Lincoln's birth, then in March headed south to address crowds in South Carolina and Georgia.[26]

As the national election approached in 1888, Douglass devoted his time to ousting Democratic president Grover Cleveland. His first choice for the Republican nomination, John Sherman of Ohio, seemed the most likely to support the enfranchisement of southern blacks, and he spoke out in favor of his nomination at the national convention in Chicago. Although not an official delegate, when invited to briefly address the convention, Douglass urged his party to come to the aid of southern blacks facing violence and intimidation at the voting box. "Be not deterred from duty by the cry of 'bloody shirt,'" he shouted, "Let that shirt be waved so long as blood shall be found upon it."[27] His use of the Reconstruction Era rhetoric of the Radical Republicans expressed his frustration at the party's continuing retreat from postwar promises, but it made the crowd uncomfortable. The late nineteenth-century evolution of the modern pro-business Republican Party was well underway and his remarks drew criticism from within the party and the national press.[28]

When the convention nominated Indiana's Benjamin Harrison over Sherman, Douglass accepted his party's choice and took to the stump in his favor. Although over seventy, he campaigned tirelessly across the Midwest, addressing crowds in Indiana, Michigan, and even as far west as Kansas. Many African Americans and Douglass's former abolitionist colleagues had deserted the Republicans by 1888, with many supporting the Democratic incumbent, Cleveland. However, Douglass stood solidly behind the party, even as it abandoned its commitment to its Civil War era principles. With the main issues of the campaign the desirability of a protective tariff and fear of free trade, racial equality and black civil rights were off the table. Dismayed at the departure of so many colleagues, Douglass's persistent loyalty again left him open to the criticism that he clung to the party for his own benefit, or perhaps that he was out of step with the modernizing world. One New England newspaper called him out: "Mr. Frederick Douglass cannot understand why the representatives of all the great anti-slavery families of Massachusetts are in favor of the Democratic ticket in this election. But the answer is very easy. They are working for present reforms, not past ones."[29] Although his commitment to civil rights can hardly be called into question, his long-held hope of an important official appointment lingered and was finally realized. He applied twice for reappointment as Recorder of Deeds, and also asked for a diplomatic appointment in Cairo, Egypt. Instead, in 1889 Harrison appointed Douglass as minister resident and consul general to the republic of Haiti.

Beginning with the Grant administration, the (ambassadorial) ministries of the largely black republics of Haiti and Liberia were held by African

Americans. Republicans appointed Ebenezer Basset and then John Mercer Langston to the Haitian post, and even Democrat Grover Cleveland continued the tradition by appointing John E.W. Thompson. Douglass had been waiting in the wings, so to speak, for his turn at a diplomatic post, and Harrison made him wait a little longer, finally offering the ministry in June. Although he hoped for a more prominent station, he accepted at once, and along with Helen made preparations for their departure. However, political unrest in Haiti delayed their travel until the fall.

The conflicts and controversies of recent years followed Douglass to Haiti. He was delighted that he, a runaway slave from Maryland, was to serve as his nation's minister to the republic created in 1804 by Toussaint L'Overture's revolution to overthrow bondage and French domination. It was the reward due him for his longtime Republican loyalty, but it came at an inopportune time. Even before his arrival in the capital of Port-au-Prince, a second Haitian revolution left the island nation struggling as rival military leaders fought for control. Events surrounding the revolution and its aftermath figured prominently in the news and when word of Douglass's appointment became public, his recent actions and personal choices clouded public response. Those members of the black press supporting Douglass argued that the appointment was beneath a man of his stature and standing. Critics in the black press argued that a younger man should hold the post, suggesting that Douglass's ideas were old and no longer relevant. A number of his friends advised Douglass to refuse the appointment for health reasons, but to no avail. He was, after all, seventy-one, and the tropical climate of the Caribbean would expose him to harsh conditions that could take a toll on his health. Mainstream newspapers, including the *New York Times*, argued that at such a crucial moment in international relations the Haitian people preferred to deal with a white man.[30]

In reality it was more likely that the mainstream press and a number of prominent Republicans preferred that a white man hold the post, for 1889 was a crucial moment in U.S.–Haitian relations. Poised to enlarge naval capacity in the wake of an expanding global imperial thrust, even before Harrison's election, the U.S. had its eye on a Caribbean coaling or refueling station for the nation's naval fleet. Haiti's Môle St. Nicolas, a lengthy and elevated limestone peninsula with a spacious deep harbor, appeared to fit the bill. An independent republic for almost all of the nineteenth century, in the late 1880s Haiti became a pawn in the rush of Europeans and Americans for control of the region. Douglass assumed his ministry in the midst of international controversy, arriving just at the revolution's conclusion, only later learning of his government's role in its inducement. When the Haitian dictator fell in 1888, two military generals fought over presidential succession and each sought foreign aid. England and France came to the aid of François Légitime, but U.S. businesses with interests in Haiti and many in Harrison's administration funneled aid to the rival Florvil Hyppolite.[31]

Delaying until fighting ceased, Douglass and Helen sailed for Port-au-Prince in October, arriving just as the U.S.-favored Hyppolite was elected president. After clearing up some confusion over his appointment documentation, Douglass began to learn the delicate nature of his role. He supported America's expansionist agenda in the Caribbean to a degree, but enjoyed a respect for the Haitian people and their cherished independence, which they had enjoyed since the overthrow of French colonial rule and enslavement in 1804. As a part of Grant's 1871 Caribbean delegation, Douglass had supported the proposed annexation of Santo Domingo. His official dispatches from Haiti and during his ministry also indicated that he believed that increased trade with the U.S. would be of benefit to the Haitian people and the nearby Dominican Republic, but he was an inexperienced diplomat. Before long it became apparent that the American business interests and naval officers with whom he had to work did not appreciate his measured method of dealing with the Haitians. He soon faced criticism from the mainstream white press for siding with the black Haitians against the needs of the U.S. government. Unable to satisfy any segment of the American populace, when he tried to chart a balanced path that would satisfy expansionists and be fair to Haiti, he came under attack in the black press for exploiting the black republic for his support of U.S. intervention.[32]

Convincing the Haitian government to lease the Môle to the U.S. was a priority. Another considerable part of Douglass's ministry involved complex negotiation of an exclusive shipping contract for the Clyde Steamship Line, which had also provided Hyppolite considerable support in his struggle against Légitime. Assuming Hyppolite's government would eagerly allow the Môle lease, the U.S. sent Rear Admiral Bancroft Gherardi to help with negotiations and to survey the area for the best location of a naval base. However, when Gherardi anchored his flagship in the deep water harbor off the peninsula and his men began exploring the Môle, some Haitians took alarm and feared that the U.S. had designs on annexing the entire country.

The racism that Douglass fought all his life was also obvious in the majority American view of the Haitian people, and of him as minister. Bigotry was especially blatant in the press supportive of an expansionist agenda, including the influential *New York Times*. Disdain for black Haitians and Douglass as an African American complicated his ministry. In the late nineteenth-century era of advancing imperialism worldwide, when Africa, Asia, and other parts of the world were being claimed and divided among expanding European empires, Haitian fears of a U.S. threat to their independence were not unreasonable. The American press did little to allay Haitian concerns. An article in the hawkish *New York Times* appeared around the time of Douglass's arrival proclaiming that Haiti needed "an infusion of white blood" and that "white capital and white energy" would soon flow there.[33] A wave of nationalistic opposition within Haiti put Hyppolite's presidency in jeopardy and although Douglass continued to receive cordial treatment, Admiral Gherardi's actions were viewed with suspicion and even disdain. In the shaky year and a half that followed, Douglass became increasingly embroiled in complex international negotiations well beyond his depth of experience. With no formal diplomatic training, he was out of his element and was often blamed for the actions of others and for events beyond his control.

The tense winter of 1890 saw Gherardi aim to mend fences with Haitian officials, but at the same time he moved a naval squadron into the Môle's harbor. The admiral's show of strength exacerbated tensions, but it was Douglass who came under regular attack in the press for the strain between U.S. and Haitian officials. Although Hyppolite's government seemed to stabilize as spring approached, the chances for the Môle lease faded. The Clyde concession was finalized, but at a less than generous figure. The fiasco required a scapegoat, and Douglass fit the bill. The *New York Times* worried that an African American minister could never negotiate in America's favor because of his natural sympathies with the black republic, a claim that Douglass repeatedly denied. Helping to stir tension between Douglass and Gherardi, the *Times* also reported that Secretary of State James G. Blaine "has finally come to the conclusion that as long as the United States is represented in Hayti by a colored man he must leave the question as to whether our Government shall have a coaling station in Hayti to Admiral Gherardi."[34]

In the spring, with little movement on the lease, however, Gherardi and his fleet departed for home. Still hoping to secure a deal, Secretary of State Blaine intervened along with William Clyde, and in June 1890 proposed a revised concession contract for Clyde, but also included a ninety-nine year lease of the Môle St. Nicholas. Proposing that American warships have exclusive use of the harbor for the duration, it also guaranteed Haiti U.S. military protection. To the minister and many Haitians, the proposal sounded like an imperialistic takeover. Douglass disapproved of the terms, not because he felt a special fellowship with the black Haitians, but because he simply believed the terms unfair. He refused to press the issue in the Haitian legislature, and was again publicly attacked for his actions as U.S. minister. This time the black leader T. Thomas Fortune, editor of the *New York Age*, accused Douglass of damaging his reputation as a black leader by engaging in interventionist politics. Pressing Blaine's agenda, Fortune warned, was tantamount to acting "with the guns of three wartubs leveled at the head of Hyppolite."[35] When the legislature adjourned without acting on the proposal, Douglass was blamed for failing to press the issue with Hyppolite.

Douglass returned to Washington for a planned two-month respite in the summer of 1890, and unbeknownst to him the State Department continued to approach Hyppolite's government in his absence. When his scheduled return was delayed, speculation raged that he would be removed from his post and that Harrison planned to replace him with a white man or even former minister Ebenezer Bassett. Although, that was not the case and Douglass returned to Port-au-Prince in late December with verbal instructions from Blaine to press the Môle lease issue, in reality the authority for the negotiations bypassed the minister. He continued to meet with Anténon Firmin, the Haitian foreign minister, and to report to Blaine, but soon became aware that during his absence others, including an agent of the Clyde shipping line, had known more about happenings than did he. Returning with his flagship *Philadelphia*, Gherardi had also usurped his role as chief diplomatic officer. The Secretary designated the admiral a special commissioner in charge of the Môle negotiations, and he presented orders that Douglass was to assist him as necessary.[36]

Naturally angry and affronted, Douglass's first inclination was to resign the ministry, and according to one report he penned a letter of resignation to Blaine, but did not mail it.[37] Instead, Douglass arranged and attended several meetings between Gherardi and Firmin, but in February negotiations halted when the Haitian minister abruptly demanded to see Gherardi's official authorization to speak on behalf of the U.S. president. With talks stalled until Gherardi's papers arrived, rumors that the U.S. planned to seize the Môle by force began to circulate around the island. Fears escalated when four American warships arrived on April 18. Douglass could do little to reassure the Haitian minister that the U.S. had no such plan because he was not in control of events and had little influence with Gherardi or the State Department. It is not surprising that, once the admiral's delayed documentation finally arrived in mid-April 1891, the Haitian government refused to grant a lease of the Môle. Douglass's brief telegram to Secretary Blaine said simply, "Hayti has declined lease of Môle."[38]

The issue now a dead letter, it was Douglass's ministry that again shouldered the blame, with press attacks coming even before the deal fell through. Especially cruel, the *Times* assailed both his race and his advanced age: "Mr. Douglass is seventy-four years of age. He is a sentimentalist and is carried away by the ideal of a free and enlightened republic of his own race. He does not see, and his color prevents him from detecting, the barbarism that is rampant about him, and from acknowledging, what is patent to the world, what a travesty upon democracy is the so-called Republic of Haiti."[39] Angry and frustrated, Douglass requested a two-month leave of absence from his post, claiming a need to escape the tropical climate in the heat of summer, and then resigned his post on July 30. Secretary Blaine acknowledged his ministry's end on August 11, 1891.

Eager to tell his side of the story and clear his name, once at home Douglass gave a series of newspaper interviews and published a lengthy essay in the *North American Review*. His justifications reveal a remnant of his old hopeful nature that made him appear naive in the late-nineteenth-century climate of declining race relations in the U.S. "I believed that duty called me to Hayti," he told one reporter, "I hoped that I would be able to serve the United States by securing the concession of Mole St. Nicholas and at the same time I hoped to so improve the opportunity which residence in Hayti gave as to make it patent to all the civilized nations of the world that my people are as other peoples—amenable to improvement and endowed with all desirable qualities."[40] His optimism for the economic uplift of the Haitians and his own nation's willingness to see their inherent worth was misplaced in the 1890s' climate of worsening race relations that saw Jim Crow segregation laws enacted across the South. The *Times* headline announcing Douglass's initial arrival in the Caribbean nation—"The Only Hope for Hayti: White Men Must Develop the Country"—should have foretold the impenetrable barrier descending between whites and blacks in America. Douglass's interviews and essays were careful to honestly present the role of Gherardi and the State Department, and he presented his role without anger or attacks. As he had with his accounts of his life in slavery, Douglass let events speak for themselves, trusting readers to see the truth.[41]

Free from diplomatic service, at seventy-three, Douglass began to think about his legacy and to reflect on his role in history. Deeply hurt and concerned that events in Haiti might cause permanent damage to his reputation and his place in history, he decided to update his third autobiography. Adding a third part comprised of a hastily compiled thirteen chapters, he contracted with DeWolfe, Fiske and Company of Boston to publish the new edition in 1892. In it he commented on some of the most momentous events of his life which had occurred since the initial publication of *Life and Times* in 1881. He responded to critics of his Republican loyalty, offered his opinion of Presidents Garfield, Cleveland, and Harrison, detailed his actions as Recorder of Deeds, and bemoaned the demise of the Civil Rights Act of 1875. The volume also offered the most detailed account of his Haitian ministry. At more than 750 pages, the self-indulgent and weighty volume did not sell well and received very little critical attention. By mid-1893, some newspapers were advertising it for sale at the discounted rate of $2.50.[42]

The summer of 1892 also turned out to be a sad time for Douglass and his family. Always the most physically and emotionally fragile among his children, his son Frederick Jr. struggled in adulthood to find an independent path, but perhaps found it impossible to emerge from the shadow of his famous father. Always reliant on his father for career guidance, he became even more fragile following his wife's death in 1890 during an influenza epidemic. He died at his home in Washington on July 26.

Shaking off family tragedy, Douglass found a final platform for clearing his name and reputation when the Haitian government invited him to serve as its commissioner to the World's Columbian Exposition (World's Fair) held in Chicago in 1893. A clear sign that the Haitians held him in high regard, Douglass accepted the post and cherished it as one of the highest honors of his life.[43] The event celebrated the four-hundredth anniversary of Christopher Columbus's arrival in the New World. Honoring his landing on the island now occupied by Haiti and the Dominican Republic, Douglass believed the fair would pay particular tribute to black people of the Caribbean and the U.S. He was sadly disappointed. Instead of repairing his name, critics viewed President Hyppolite's appointment of Douglass as evidence that he had worked against U.S. interest during his ministry. He was also distressed at the lack of African American participation in the World's Fair. No exhibit featured African American life, and the entire fair counted not one black face among its employees or guards.

Although the fair was designed to exhibit human progress, in its exclusion of black Americans it simply pointed to the fading hope for racial equality as the new century approached. Even while the fair was still underway, Douglass sponsored the writing of a pamphlet titled *The Reason Why the Colored American Is Not in the World's Columbian Exposition*. Penned by well-known anti-lynching crusader and journalist, Ida B. Wells, Douglass expressed his dismay in the pamphlet's introduction: "We would like ... to tell our visitors that the moral progress of the American people has kept even pace with their enterprise and their material civilization ... that two hundred and sixty years of progress and enlightenment have banished barbarism and race hate from the United States ... that no man on account of his color, race or condition, is deprived of life, liberty or property without due process of law; that mobs are not allowed to supercede courts of law or usurp the place of government; that here Negroes are not tortured, shot, hanged or burned to death, merely on suspicion of crime and without ever seeing a judge, a jury or advocate; that the American

Government is in reality a Government of the people, by the people and for the people, and for all the people."[44] But unfortunately that was not the case in 1893.

Despite his advanced age, Douglass maintained an active lecture schedule, speaking before more than two dozen audiences in 1893 and nearly as many in 1894. While still attending to his duties at the World's Fair he penned "The Lessons of the Hour," one of his most important and powerful speeches. He delivered it several times in the Midwest in 1893 and eventually before a large audience gathered at Washington's Metropolitan AME Church on January 9, 1894.[45] Reflecting on what many were calling the "Negro problem," the oration and subsequent pamphlet expressed his dismay at the erosion of hard-won rights for his race, but contained strains of his ever-hopeful nature. Beginning with the Supreme Court's decision to strike down the 1875 Civil Rights Act, a nadir of race relations reversed the gains that Douglass and others had worked their entire lives to achieve. Waves of disfranchisement, advancing Jim Crow laws, and the horrors of lynching were the new reality. Still mustering some hope, however, Douglass appealed to his faith in the Declaration of Independence's ability to overcome the ills of the era and looked forward to the "advent of a nation, based upon human brotherhood and the self-evident truths of liberty and equality."[46]

Douglass would leave the work of rebuilding a civil rights foundation to a new generation of black leaders. On February 20, 1895, seventy-seven-year-old Douglass left his Anacostia home to attend a meeting of the National Council of Women. Escorted into the hall by his old friend, Susan B. Anthony and Anna Shaw, he made a few remarks to those gathered, then afterward remained to chat with several of the delegates. Returning home for an early evening meal with Helen, the two prepared to depart for a meeting at the nearby Hillsdale African Church, where Douglass was to lecture. While awaiting the arrival of their carriage, Douglass collapsed and died of an apparent heart attack.[47]

Shocked and dismayed at his sudden passing, family, close friends, and the public marked his death with the respect due a great reformer and statesman. Telegrams from around the nation and abroad reached Cedar Hill in packets. His body lay on display at the Metropolitan AME Church, and a stream of important individuals viewed his open casket. Among those paying respects were the entire faculty of Howard University, Supreme Court Justice John Marshall Harlan, and senators John Sherman and George Hoar. African American schools in Washington were closed so that hundreds of students could file past. Within days Helen and Douglass's remaining children Rosetta, Lewis, and Charles accompanied his body to Rochester. There he was laid to rest in Mount Hope Cemetery near his first wife Anna and their daughter Annie. Setting aside earlier criticism, the *New York Times* offered its kindest words at his passing: "He was of inestimable service to the members of his own race, and rendered distinguished service to his country from time to time in various important offices that he held under the Government. Mr. Douglass, perhaps more than any other man of his race, was instrumental in advancing the work of banishing the color line."[48] Across the nation, thousands mourned the loss of a great American reformer and statesman.

Douglass's death left a void in race leadership that was not fully filled in the coming half century. Emerging leaders, including Booker T. Washington and W.E.B. DuBois, never approached his reputation as the singular voice for African Americans. Although their works influenced generations to come, neither enjoyed the recognition Douglass claimed. For more than fifty years he was the most widely recognized black face in America, and that legacy extended far beyond his death. Early in his career, his fiery rhetoric demanded that the nation break the bonds of slavery. Douglass risked personal and material security to aid his fellow men and women to escape slavery as he had, never wavering in his demand for immediate and complete abolition. For most, realizing self-emancipation was a momentous achievement, but for Douglass it was a new beginning.

Although his work as an abolitionist was important, Douglass became much more than an advocate for the slave. He championed universal reform, speaking out on behalf of women's rights, temperance, and the rights of labor. In doing so, he became a vocal critic of American society, but also one of its strongest defenders. In demanding equal rights for African Americans and others, he embraced the Declaration of Independence, the U.S. Constitution, and the American political system. Once slavery was abolished, Douglass embarked on a new campaign for his race and for all those denied full participation in U.S. society. Arguing that America was his country, he determined to work within the existing system to gain citizenship and voting rights for blacks, and for women. His cause was truly an agenda of universal reform.[49] Because of his broad range of concerns, Douglass's influence extends far beyond the black community. His ability to embrace and articulate the natural rights liberalism of the American Revolution and the nation's founding documents makes him not just a black leader of the nineteenth century, but a leading American voice in modern times. As scholar Peter C. Myers has noted, Douglass's vision of justice was deeply rooted in American principles. His ability to argue for and affirm those principles made him an "invincible adversary of black alienation, an exemplar and apostle of peculiarly American and African American forms of hopefulness."[50] For these reasons he will continue to stand as an iconic American reformer and statesman.

Documents

DOUGLASS FIGHTS WITH COVEY

When, after spending several years with Hugh Auld's family in Baltimore, Douglass returned to rural slavery on Maryland's Eastern Shore he was angry and defiant. An argument between the Auld brothers had led Thomas to remove the fifteen-year-old slave from his brother's care. Douglass knew nothing of farming or rural life and did not adapt well to the change. In order to break his strong will, his master Thomas Auld leased him to work on the farm of Edward Covey, a small farmer with a reputation as a slave breaker. Covey's ability to bring slaves into line allowed him the privilege of leasing labor at a considerable discount. Slave leasing was common, especially in the Upper South states, where tobacco cultivation had shifted to less labor-intensive food crops. It helped cement support for slave ownership among the middling white community, allowing those who could not afford the full purchase price to benefit from slave labor on a temporary basis. Leases were generally an annual contract beginning in January. At Covey's farm, Douglass was introduced to the harsh realities of farm labor and field work, and in an effort to break his spirit, he experienced regular beatings from the slave breaker's lash. In the following famous scene from his first autobiography, Douglass recounts his resistance to Covey's lash. He later often recounted his fight with Covey, marking it as a major turning point in his life. Douglass's chronology is confused in his *Narrative*—his year with Covey actually began on January 1, 1834.

I had left Master Thomas's house, and went to live with Mr. Covey, on the 1st of January, 1833. I was now, for the first time in my life, a field hand. In my new employment, I found myself even more awkward than a country boy appeared to be in a large city. … I lived with Mr. Covey one year. During the first six months, of that year, scarce a week passed without his whipping me. …

I have already intimated that my condition was much worse, during the first six months of my stay at Mr. Covey's, than in the last six. The circumstances leading to the change in Mr. Covey's course toward me form an epoch in my humble history. You have seen how a man was made a slave; you shall see how a slave was made a man. On one of the hottest days of the month of August, 1833, Bill Smith, William Hughes, a slave named Eli, and myself, were engaged in fanning wheat. Hughes was clearing the fanned wheat from before the fan. Eli was turning, Smith was feeding, and I was carrying wheat to the fan. The work was simple, requiring strength rather than intellect; yet, to one entirely unused to such work, it came very hard. About three o'clock of that day, I broke down; my strength failed me; I was seized with a violent aching of the head, attended with extreme dizziness; I trembled in every limb.

Mr. Covey was at the house, about one hundred yards from the treading-yard where we were fanning. On hearing the fan stop, he left immediately, and came to the spot where we were. He hastily inquired what the matter was. Bill answered that I was sick, and there was no one to bring wheat to the fan. I had by this time crawled away under the side of the post and rail-fence by which the yard was enclosed, hoping to find relief by getting out of the sun. He then asked where I was. He was told by one of the hands. He came to the spot, and, after looking at me awhile, asked me what was the matter. I told him as well as I could, for I scarce had strength to speak. He then gave me a savage kick in the side, and told me to get up. I tried to do so, but fell back in the attempt. He gave me another kick, and again told me to rise. I again tried, and succeeded in gaining my feet; but, stooping to get the tub with which I was feeding the fan, I again staggered and fell. While down in this situation, Mr. Covey took up the hickory slat with which Hughes had been striking off the half-bushel measure, and with it gave me a heavy blow upon the head, making a large wound, and the blood ran freely; and with this again told me to get up. I made no effort to comply, having now made up my mind to let him do his worst. In a short time after receiving this blow, my head grew better. Mr. Covey had now left me to my fate. At this moment I resolved, for the first time, to go to my master, enter a complaint, and ask his protection. In order to do this, I must that afternoon walk seven miles; and this, under the circumstances, was truly a severe undertaking … .

[Master Thomas] asked me what I wanted. I told him, to let me get a new home; that as sure as I lived with Mr. Covey again, I should live with but to die with him; that Covey would surely kill me; he was in a fair way for it. Master Thomas ridiculed the idea that there was any danger of Mr. Covey's killing me, and said that he knew Mr. Covey; that he was a good man, and that he could not think of taking me from him; that, should he do so, he would lose the whole year's wages; that I belonged to Mr. Covey for one year, and that I must go back to him, come what might; and that I must not trouble him with any more stories, or that he would himself GET HOLD OF ME. ...

I fell in with Sandy Jenkins, a slave with whom I was somewhat acquainted. Sandy had a free wife who lived about four miles from Mr. Covey's; and it being Saturday, he was on his way to see her. I told him my circumstances, and he very kindly invited me to go home with him. I went home with him, and talked this whole matter over, and got his advice as to what course it was best for me to pursue. I found Sandy an old adviser. He told me, with great solemnity, I must go back to Covey; but that before I went, I must go with him into another part of the woods, where there was a certain ROOT, which, if I would take some of it with me, carrying it ALWAYS ON MY RIGHT SIDE, would render it impossible for Mr. Covey, or any other white man, to whip me. He said he had carried it for years; and since he had done so, he had never received a blow, and never expected to while he carried it. I at first rejected the idea, that the simple carry-ing of a root in my pocket would have any such effect as he had said, and was not disposed to take it; but Sandy impressed the necessity with much earnestness, telling me it could do no harm, if it did no good. To please him, I at length took the root, and, according to his direction, carried it upon my right side. This was Sunday morning. I immediately started for home; and upon entering the yard gate, out came Mr. Covey on his way to meeting. He spoke to me very kindly, bade me drive the pigs from a lot near by, and passed on towards the church. Now, this singular conduct of Mr. Covey really made me begin to think that there was something in the ROOT which Sandy had given me; and had it been on any other day than Sunday, I could have attributed the conduct to no other cause than the influence of that root; and as it was, I was half inclined to think the ROOT to be something more than I at first had taken it to be. All went well till Monday morning. On this morning, the virtue of the ROOT was fully tested. Long before daylight, I was called to go and rub, curry, and feed, the horses. I obeyed, and was glad to obey. But whilst thus engaged, whilst in the act of throwing down some blades from the loft, Mr. Covey entered the stable with a long rope; and just as I was half out of the loft, he caught hold of my legs, and was about tying me. As soon as I found what he was up to, I gave a sudden spring, and as I did so, he holding to my legs, I was brought sprawling on the stable floor. Mr. Covey seemed now to think he had me, and could do what he pleased; but at this moment—from whence came the spirit I don't know—I resolved to fight; and, suiting my action to the resolution, I seized Covey hard by the throat; and as I did so, I rose. He held on to me, and I to him. My resistance was so entirely unexpected that Covey seemed taken all aback. He trembled like a leaf. This gave me assurance, and I held him uneasy, causing the blood to run where I touched him with the ends of my fingers. Mr. Covey soon called out to Hughes for help. Hughes came, and, while Covey held me, attempted to tie my right hand. While he was in the act of doing so, I watched my chance, and gave him a heavy kick close under the ribs. This kick fairly sickened Hughes, so that he left me in the hands of Mr. Covey. This kick had the effect of not only weakening Hughes, but Covey also. When he saw Hughes bending over with pain, his courage quailed. He asked me if I meant to persist in my resistance. I told him I did, come what might; that he had used me like a brute for six months, and that I was determined to be used so no longer. With that, he strove to drag me to a stick that was lying just out of the stable door. He meant to knock me down. But just as he was leaning over to get the stick, I seized him with both hands by his collar, and brought him by a sudden snatch to the ground. By this time, Bill came. Covey called upon him for assistance. Bill wanted to know what he could do. Covey said, "Take hold of him, take hold of him!" Bill said his master hired him out to work, and not to help to whip me; so he left Covey and myself to fight our own battle out. We were at it for nearly two hours. Covey at length let me go, puffing and blowing at a great rate, saying that if I had not resisted, he would not have whipped me half so much. The truth was, that he had not whipped me at all. I considered him as getting entirely the worst end of the bargain; for he had drawn no blood from me, but I had from him. The whole six months afterwards, that I spent with Mr. Covey, he never laid the weight of his finger upon me in anger. He would occasionally say, he didn't want to get hold of me again. "No," thought I, "you need not; for you will come off worse than you did before."

This battle with Mr. Covey was the turning point in my career as a slave. It rekindled the few expiring embers of freedom, and revived within me a sense of my own manhood.

SOURCE

Frederick Douglass, *Narrative of the Life of Frederick Douglass, An American Slave Written by Himself* (Boston: The Anti-slavery Office, 1845), ch. 10, 62–75. Electronic Text Center, University of Virginia, http://etext.virginia.edu/etcbin/toccer-new2?id=DouNarr.sgm&images=images/modeng&data=/texts/english/modeng/parsed&tag=public&part=11&division=div1 (accessed February 10, 2012).

INTRODUCTION TO THE ABOLITIONISTS

Escaping slavery in September 1838, Douglass soon settled in the shipbuilding town of New Bedford, Massachusetts. A haven for fugitive slaves, the town was also home to many abolitionists who believed slavery was morally wrong. Douglass attended his first antislavery meetings there, and became associated with a number of local activists. He subscribed to William Lloyd Garrison's weekly antislavery newspaper, the *Liberator*, and from it learned of the larger world of reform. Abolitionists used a series of tactics to persuade others about the evils of slavery, including petitions, pamphlets, but especially antislavery lectures and conventions. At these gatherings, white and black abolitionists spoke out against slavery, and on occasion former slaves gave firsthand accounts of the horrors of bondage. In 1841 Douglass was invited to speak at an antislavery convention held in nearby Nantucket. A very nervous Douglass gave an account of his life in slavery, captivating the crowd with his honesty and natural charisma. At the end of the night he was offered a three-month contract as a field lecturer for the Massachusetts Anti-Slavery Society. At the end of his temporary contract, Douglass was hired as a permanent field agent, and before long was one of the most well-known abolitionists in the North.

In the summer of 1841, a grand anti-slavery convention was held in Nantucket, under the auspices of Mr. Garrison and his friends. Until now, I had taken no holiday since my escape from slavery. Having worked very hard that spring and summer, in Richmond's brass foundery—sometimes working all night as well as all day—and needing a day or two of rest, I attended this convention, never supposing that I should take part in the proceedings. Indeed, I was not aware that any one connected with the convention even so much as knew my name. I was, however, quite mistaken. Mr. William C. Coffin, a prominent abolitionist in those days of trial, had heard me speaking to my colored friends, in the little school house on Second street, New Bedford, where we worshiped. He sought me out in the crowd, and invited me to say a few words to the convention. Thus sought out, and thus invited, I was induced to speak out the feelings inspired by the occasion, and the fresh recollection of the scenes through which I had passed as a slave. My speech on this occasion is about the only one I ever made, of which I do not remember a single connected sentence. It was with the utmost difficulty that I could stand erect, or that I could command and articulate two words without hesitation and stammering. I trembled in every limb. I am not sure that my embarrassment was not the most effective part of my speech, if speech it could be called. At any rate, this is about the only part of my performance that I now distinctly remember. But excited and convulsed as I was, the audience, though remarkably quiet before, became as much excited as myself. Mr. Garrison followed me, taking me as his text; and now, whether I had made an eloquent speech in behalf of freedom or not, his was one never to be forgotten by those who heard it. Those who had heard Mr. Garrison oftenest, and had known him longest, were astonished. It was an effort of unequaled power, sweeping down, like a very tornado, every opposing barrier, whether of sentiment or opinion. For a moment, he possessed that almost fabulous inspiration, often referred to but seldom attained, in which a public meeting is transformed, as it were, into a single individuality—the orator wielding a thousand heads and hearts at once, and by the simple majesty of his all controlling thought, converting his hearers into the express image of his own soul. That night there were at least one thousand Garrisonians in Nantucket! At the close of this great meeting, I was duly waited on by Mr. John A. Collins—then the general agent of the Massachusetts anti-slavery society—and urgently solicited by him to become an agent of that society, and to publicly advocate its anti-slavery principles. I was reluctant to take the proffered position. I had not been quite three years from slavery—was honestly distrustful of my ability—wished to be excused; publicity exposed me to discovery and arrest by my master; and other objections came up, but Mr. Collins was not to be put off, and I finally consented to go out for three months, for I supposed that I should have got to the end of my story and my usefulness, in that length of time.

Here opened upon me a new life a life for which I had had no preparation. I was a "graduate from the peculiar institution," Mr. Collins used to say, when introducing me, "*with my diploma written on my back!*" The three years of my freedom had been spent in the hard school of adversity.

My hands had been furnished by nature with something like a solid leather coating, and I had bravely marked out for myself a life of rough labor, suited to the hardness of my hands, as a means of supporting myself and rearing my children.

Now what shall I say of this fourteen years' experience as a public advocate of the cause of my enslaved brothers and sisters? The time is but as a speck, yet large enough to justify a pause for retrospection—and a pause it must only be.

Young, ardent, and hopeful, I entered upon this new life in the full gush of unsuspecting enthusiasm. The cause was good; the men engaged in it were good; the means to attain its triumph, good; Heaven's blessing must attend all, and freedom must soon be given to the pining millions under a ruthless bondage. My whole heart went with the holy cause, and my most fervent prayer to the Almighty Disposer of the hearts of men, were continually offered for its early triumph. "Who or what," thought I, "can withstand a cause so good, so holy, so indescribably glorious. The God of Israel is with us. The might of the Eternal is on our side. Now let but the truth be spoken, and a nation will start forth at the sound!" In this enthusiastic spirit, I dropped into the ranks of freedom's friends, and went forth to the battle. For a time I was made to forget that my skin was dark and my hair crisped. For a time I regretted that I could not have shared the hardships and dangers endured by the earlier workers for the slave's release. I soon, however, found that my enthusiasm had been extravagant; that hardships and dangers were not yet passed; and that the life now before me, had shadows as well as sunbeams.

Among the first duties assigned me, on entering the ranks, was to travel, in company with Mr. George Foster, to secure subscribers to the *Anti-slavery Standard* and the *Liberator*. With him I traveled and lectured through the eastern counties of Massachusetts. Much interest was awakened—large meetings assembled. Many came, no doubt, from curiosity to hear what a Negro could say in his own cause. I was generally introduced as a *"chattel"*—a *"thing"*—a piece of southern *"property"*—the chairman assuring the audience that *it* could speak. Fugitive slaves, at that time, were not so plentiful as now; and as a fugitive slave lecturer, I had the advantage of being a *"brand new fact"*—the first one out. Up to that time, a colored man was deemed a fool who confessed himself a runaway slave, not only because of the danger to which he exposed himself of being retaken, but because it was a confession of a very *low* origin! Some of my colored friends in New Bedford thought very badly of my wisdom for thus exposing and degrading myself. The only precaution I took, at the beginning, to prevent Master Thomas from knowing where I was, and what I was about, was the withholding my former name, my master's name, and the name of the state and county from which I came. During the first three or four months, my speeches were almost exclusively made up of narrations of my own personal experience as a slave. "Let us have the facts," said the people. So also said Friend George Foster, who always wished to pin me down to my simple narrative. "Give us the facts," said Collins, "we will take care of the philosophy." Just here arose some embarrassment. It was impossible for me to repeat the same old story month after month, and to keep up my interest in it. It was new to the people, it is true, but it was an old story to me; and to go through with it night after night, was a task altogether too mechanical for my nature. "Tell your story, Frederick," would whisper my then revered friend, William Lloyd Garrison, as I stepped upon the platform. I could not always obey, for I was now reading and thinking. New views of the subject were presented to my mind. It did not entirely satisfy me to *narrate* wrongs; I felt like *denouncing* them. I could not always curb my moral indignation for the perpetrators of slaveholding villainy, long enough for a circumstantial statement of the facts which I felt almost everybody must know. Besides, I was growing, and needed room. "People won't believe you ever was a slave, Frederick, if you keep on this way," said Friend Foster. "Be yourself," said Collins, "and tell your story." It was said to me, "Better have a *little* of the plantation manner of speech than not; 'tis not best that you seem too learned." These excellent friends were actuated by the best of motives, and were not altogether wrong in their advice; and still I must speak just the word that seemed to *me* the word to be spoken *by* me.

At last the apprehended trouble came. People doubted if I had ever been a slave. They said I did not talk like a slave, look like a slave, nor act like a slave, and that they believed I had never been south of Mason and Dixon's line. "He don't tell us where he came from—what his master's name was—how he got away—nor the story of his experience. Besides, he is educated, and is, in this, a contradiction of all the facts we have concerning the ignorance of the slaves." Thus, I was in a pretty fair way to be denounced as an impostor. The committee of the Massachusetts anti-slavery society knew all the facts in my case, and agreed with me in the prudence of keeping them private. They, therefore, never doubted my being a genuine fugitive; but going down the aisles of the churches in which I spoke, and hearing the free spoken Yankees saying, repeatedly, *"He's never been a slave, I'll warrant ye,"* I resolved to dispel all doubt, at no distant day, by such a revelation of facts as could not be made by any other than a genuine fugitive.

In a little less than four years, therefore, after becoming a public lecturer, I was induced to write out the leading facts connected with my experience in slavery, giving names of persons, places, and dates—thus putting it in the power of any who doubted, to ascertain the truth or falsehood of my story of being a fugitive slave. This statement soon became known in Maryland, and I had reason to believe that an effort would be made to recapture me.

It is not probable that any open attempt to secure me as a slave could have succeeded, further than the obtainment, by my master, of the money value of my bones and sinews. Fortunately for me, in the four years of my labors in the abolition cause, I had gained many friends, who would have suffered themselves to be taxed to almost any extent to save me from slavery. It was felt that I had committed the double offense of running away, and exposing the secrets and crimes of slavery and slaveholders. There was a double motive for seeking my reenslavement—avarice and vengeance; and while, as I have said, there was little probability of successful recapture, if attempted openly, I was constantly in danger of being spirited away, at a moment when my friends could render me no assistance. In traveling about from place to place—often alone—I was much exposed to this sort of attack. Any one cherishing the design to betray me, could easily do so, by simply tracing my whereabouts through the anti-slavery journals, for my meetings and movements were promptly made known in advance. My true friends, Mr. Garrison and Mr. Phillips, had no faith in the power of Massachusetts to protect me in my right to liberty. Public sentiment and the law, in their opinion, would hand me over to the tormentors. Mr. Phillips, especially, considered me in danger, and said, when I showed him the manuscript of my story, if in my place, he would throw it into the fire. Thus, the reader will observe, the settling of one difficulty only opened the way for another; and that though I had reached a free state, and had attained position for public usefulness, I was still tormented with the liability of losing my liberty. How this liability was dispelled, will be related, with other incidents, in the next chapter.

Source

Frederick Douglass, *My Bondage and My Freedom* (New York: Miller, Orton & Mulligan, 1855), ch. 2, 358–364. Electronic Text Center, University of Virginia, http://etext.virginia.edu/toc/modeng/public/DouMybo.html (accessed February 10, 2012).

FREDERICK DOUGLASS TO HENRY CLAY

This letter to Kentucky Senator Henry Clay appeared in the first issue of Frederick Douglass's newspaper, the *North Star*. In 1847 the nation was in the midst of the Mexican War (1846–1848) and preparing to annex a considerable amount of territory, including California and what became the southwest states of Arizona, New Mexico, and Nevada. A major point of debate was whether slavery should be extended into this new territory. Henry Clay was the Whig Party's presidential candidate in 1844, and hoping to gain his party's nomination again in 1848, he delivered a speech in Lexington, Kentucky in which he critiqued the Democrats' motivations behind the war effort. Although he owned slaves, Clay's speech declared slavery to be an evil, but argued that emancipation would lead to chaos in the social system and would result in the "extinction or expulsion" of blacks from the United States. Douglass takes Clay to task for his speech, especially arguing that free African Americans had a rightful place in American society.

LETTER TO HENRY CLAY.

SIR—I have just received and read your Speech, delivered at the Mass Meeting in Lexington, Kentucky, 13th November 1847, and after a careful and candid perusal of it, I am impressed with the desire to say a few words to you on one or two subjects which form a considerable part of that speech: You will, I am sure, pardon the liberty I take in thus publicly addressing you, when you are acquainted with the fact, that I am one of those "UNFORTUNATE VICTIMS" whose case you seem to commiserate, and have experienced the cruel wrongs of Slavery in my own person.

It is with no ill will, or bitterness of spirit that I address you. My position under this government, even in the State of N.Y., is that of a disfranchised man. I can have, therefore, no political ends to serve, nor party antipathy to gratify. My "intents" are not wicked but truly charitable. I approach you simply in the character of one of the unhappy millions enduring the evils of Slavery, in this otherwise highly favored and glorious land.

In the extraordinary speech before me, after dwelling at length upon the evils, disgrace, and dangers of the present unjust, mean, and iniquitous war waged by the United States upon Mexico, you disavow for yourself and the meeting, "in the most positive manner," any wish to acquire any foreign territory whatever for the purpose of introducing slavery into it. As one of the oppressed, I give you the full expression of sincere gratitude for this declaration, and the pledge which it implies, and earnestly hope that you may be able to keep your vow unsullied by compromises, (which, pardon me,) have too often marred and defaced the beauty and consistency of your humane declarations and pledges on former occasions. It is not, however, any part of my present intention to reproach you invidiously or severely for the past. Unfortunately for the race, you do not stand alone in respect to deviations from a strict line of rectitude. Poor, erring and depraved humanity, has surrounded you with a throng of guilty associates, it would not, therefore, be magnanimous in me to reproach you for the past, above all others.

Forgetting the things that are behind, I simply propose to speak to you of what you are at this time—of the errors and evils of your present, as I think, wicked position, and to point out to you the path of repentance, which if pursued, must lead you to the possession of peace and happiness, and make you a blessing to your country and the world.

In the speech under consideration, you say, "My opinions on the subject of slavery are well known; they have the merit, if it be one, of consistency, uniformity and long duration."

The first sentence is probably true. Your opinions on slavery may be well known, but that they have the merit of consistency or of uniformity, I cannot so readily admit. If the speech before me be a fair declaration of your present opinions, I think I can convince you that even this speech abounds with inconsistencies such as materially to affect the consolation you seem to draw from this source. Indeed if you are uniform at all, you are only so in your inconsistencies.

You confess that "Slavery is a great evil, and a wrong to its victims, and you would rejoice if not a single slave breathed the air within the limits of our country."

These are noble sentiments, and would seem to flow from a heart over-borne with a sense of the flagrant injustice and enormous cruelty of slavery, and of one earnestly and anxiously longing for a remedy. Standing alone, it would seem that the author had long been in search of some means to redress the wrongs of the "unfortunate victims" of whom he speaks—that his righteous soul was deeply grieved, every hour, on account of the foul blot inflicted by this course on his country's character.

But what are the facts? You are yourself a Slaveholder at this moment, and your words on this point had scarcely reached the outer circle of the vast multitude by which you were surrounded, before you poured forth one of the most helpless, illogical, and cowardly apologies for this same wrong, and "great evil" which I ever remember to have read. Is this consistency, and uniformity? if so, the oppressed may well pray the Most High that you may be soon delivered from it.

Speaking of "the unfortunate victims" of this "great evil," and "wrong," you hold this most singular and cowardly excuse for perpetuating the wrongs of my "unfortunate" race.

"But here they are to be dealt with as well as we can, with a due consideration of all circumstances affecting the security and happiness of both races."

What do you mean by the security, safety and happiness of both races? do you mean that the happiness of the slave is augmented by his being a slave, and if so, why call him an "unfortunate victim." Can it be that this is mere cant, by which to seduce the North into your support, on the ground of your sympathy for the slave. I cannot believe you capable of such infatuation. I do not wish to believe that you are capable of either the low cunning, or the vanity which your language on this subject would seem to imply, but will set it down to an uncontrollable conviction of the innate wickedness of slavery, which forces itself out, and defies even your vast powers of concealment.

But further, you assert,

"Every State has the supreme, uncontrolled and exclusive power to decide for itself whether slavery shall cease or continue within its limits without any exterior intervention from any quarter."

Here I understand you to assert the most profligate and infernal doctrine, that any State in this union has a right to plunder, scourge and enslave any part of the human family within its borders, just so long as it deems it for its interest so to do, and that no one or body of persons beyond the limits of said state has a right to interfere by word or deed against it. Is it possible that you hold this monstrous and blood-chilling doctrine? If so, what confidence can any enlightened lover of liberty place in your pretended opposition to Slavery. I know your answer to all this, but it only plunges you into lower depths of infamy than the horrible doctrines avowed above. You go on to say:

"In States where the Slaves outnumber the whites, as is the case in several (which I believe are only two out of fifteen) the blacks could not be emancipated without becoming the governing power in these states."

This miserable bug-bear is quite a confession of the mental and physical equality of the races. You pretend that you are a Republican. You loudly boast of your Democratic principles: why then do you object to the application of your principles in this case. Is the democratic principle good in one case, and bad in another? Would it be worse for a black majority to govern a white minority than it now is for the latter to govern the former? But you conjure up an array of frightful objections in answer to this.

"Collisions and conflicts between the two races would be inevitable, and after shocking scenes of rapine and carnage, the extinction or expulsion of the blacks would certainly take place."

How do you know that any such results would be inevitable? Where, on the page of history, do you find anything to warrant even such a conjecture? You will probably point me to the Revolution in St. Domingo, the old and thread-bare falsehood under which democratic tyrants have sought a refuge for the last forty years. But the facts in that direction are all against you. It has been clearly proven that that revolution was not the result of emancipation, but of a cruel attempt to re-enslave an already emancipated people. I am not aware that you have a single fact to support your truly terrible assertion, while on the other hand I have many all going to show what is equally taught by the voice of reason and of God, "THAT IT IS ALWAYS SAFE TO DO RIGHT." The promise of God is, "that thy light shall break forth as the morning, and thy health shall spring forth speedily, and thy righteousness shall go before thee, the glory of the Lord shall be thy reward: then shalt thou call and the Lord shall answer; thou shalt cry and he will say, Here I am."

The history of the world is in conformity with the words of inspired wisdom. Look, for instance, at the history of Emancipation in the British West Indies. There the blacks were and still are, an overwhelming majority. Have there been any "shocking scenes of rapine and carnage, extinction or expulsion." You know there have not. Why then do you make use of this unfounded and irrational conjecture to frighten your fellow-countrymen from the righteous performance of a simple act of justice to millions now groaning in almost hopeless bondage.

I now give your argument in support of the morality of your position.

"It may be argued that, in admitting the injustice of slavery, I admit the necessity of an instantaneous reparation of that injustice. Unfortunately, however, it is not always safe, practicable or possible in the great movements of States or public affairs of nations, to remedy or repair the infliction of previous injustice. In the inception of it, we may oppose and denounce it by our most strenuous exertions, but, after its consummation, there is often no other alternative left us but to deplore its perpetration, and to acquiesce as the only alternative, in its existence, as a less evil than the frightful consequences which might ensue from the vain endeavor to repair it. Slavery is one of these unfortunate instances."

The cases which you put in support of the foregoing propositions, are only wanting in one thing, and that is analogy. The plundering of the Indians of their territory, is a crime to which no honest man can look with any degree of satisfaction. It was a wrong to the Indians then living, and how muchsoever we might seek to repair that wrong, the victims are far beyond any benefit of it; but with reference to the slave, the wrong to be repaired is a present one, the slave holder is the every day robber of the slave, of his birthright to liberty, property, and the pursuit of happiness—his right to be free is unquestionable—the wrong to enslave him is self evident—the duty to emancipate him is imperative. Are you aware to what your argument on this point leads? do you not plainly see that the greatest crimes that ever cursed our common earth, may take shelter under your reasoning, and may claim perpetuity on the ground of their antiquity?

Sir, I must pass over your allusions to that almost defunct and infernal scheme which you term "unmixed benevolence" for expelling not the slave but the free colored people from these United States, as well as your charge against the Abolitionists.

"It is a philanthropic and consoling reflection that the moral and physical condition of the African in the United States in a state of slavery is far better than it would have been had their ancestors not been brought from their native land."

I can scarce repress the flame of rising indignation, as I read this cold blooded and cruel sentence; there is so much of Satan dressed in the livery of Heaven, as well as taking consolation from crime, that I scarcely know how to reply to it. Let me ask you what has been the cause of the present unsettled condition of Africa? Why has she not reached forth her hand unto God? Why have not her fields been made Missionary grounds, as well as the Feejee Islands? Because of this very desolating traffic from which you seem to draw consolation. For three hundred years Christian nations, among whom we are foremost, have looked to Africa only as a place for the gratification of their lust and love of power, and every means have been adopted to stay the onward march of civilization in that unhappy land.

Your declaration on this point, places your consolation with that of the wolf in devouring the lamb. You next perpetrate what I conceive to be the most revolting blasphemy. You say:

"And if it should be the decree of the Great Ruler of the Universe, that their descendants shall be made instruments in his hands in the establishment of civilization and the Christian religion throughout Africa —our regrets on account of the original wrong will be greatly mitigated."

Here, Sir, you would charge home upon God the responsibility of your own crimes, and would seek a solace from the pangs of a guilty conscience by sacriligiously assuming that in robbing Africa of her children, you acted in obedience to the great purposes, and were but fulfilling the decrees of the Most High God; but as if fearing that this refuge of lies might fail, you strive to shuffle off the responsibility of this "great evil" on Great Britain. May I not ask if you were fulfilling the great purposes of God in the share you took in this traffic, and can draw consolation from that alleged fact, is it honest to make England a sinner above yourselves, and deny her all the mitigating circumstances which you apply to yourselves?

You say that "Great Britain inflicted the evil upon you." If this be true, it is equally true that she inflicted the same evil upon herself; but she has had the justice and the magnanimity to repent and bring forth fruits meet for repentance. You copied her bad example, why not avail yourself of her good one also?

Now, Sir, I have done with your Speech, though much more might be said upon it. I have a few words to say to you personally.

I wish to remind you that you are not only in the "autumn," but in the very WINTER of life: Seventy-one years have passed over your stately brow. You must soon leave this world, and appear before God, to render up an account of your stewardship. For fifty years of your life you have been a slaveholder. You have robbed the laborer who has reaped down your fields, of his rightful reward. You are at this moment the robber of nearly fifty human beings, of their liberty, compelling them to live in ignorance. Let me ask if you think that God will hold you guiltless in the great day of account, if you die with the blood of these fifty slaves clinging to your garments. I know that you have made a profession of religion, and have been baptized, and am aware that you are in good and regular standing in the church, but I have the authority of God for saying that you will stand rejected at his bar, unless you "put away the evil of your doings from before his eyes—cease to do evil, and learn to do well—seek judgment, relieve the oppressed—and plead for the widow." You must "break every yoke, and let the oppressed go free," or take your place in the ranks of "EVIL DOERS," and expect to "reap the reward of corruption."

At this late day in your life, I think it would be unkind for me to charge you with any ambitious desires to become the President of the United States. I may be mistaken in this, but is seems that you cannot indulge either the wish or expectation. Bear with me, then, while, I give you a few words of further counsel, as a private individual, and excuse the plainness of one who has FELT the wrongs of Slavery, and fathomed the depths of its iniquity.

Emancipate your own slaves. Leave them not to be held or sold by others. Leave them free as the Father of his country left his, and let your name go down to posterity, as his came down to us, a slaveholder, to be sure, but a repentant one. Make the noble resolve, that so far as you are personally concerned, "AMERICA SHALL BE FREE."

In asking you to do this, I ask nothing which in any degree conflicts with your argument against general emancipation. The dangers which you conjecture of the latter cannot be apprehended of the former. Your own slaves are too few in number to make them formidable or dangerous. In this matter you are without excuse. I leave you to your conscience, and your God,

And subscribe myself,

Faithfully, yours,

FREDERICK DOUGLASS.

Source

"Letter to Henry Clay," *North Star*, December 3, 1847.

LETTER TO MY OLD MASTER

On the tenth anniversary of his escape from slavery, Frederick Douglass penned this open letter to his former master, Thomas Auld, and subsequently published it in his weekly newspaper. In 1848, Auld still lived in St. Michaels, Maryland, where he operated a general store and owned property. Public letters were a common form of discourse in the nineteenth century. Addressed to an individual, they were often meant for a wider audience. Although most such letters were addressed "to the editor" of a journal, at times they were directed at an individual. This letter allows Douglass to critique the slave system, and his former master in particular, but also contrasts his life in freedom with his experience in slavery. Meant for both the abolitionist-minded readers of the *North Star* as well as Auld, the letter stands as another form of antislavery propaganda, offering a personalized attack on slaveholders.

———————

To My Old Master.

THOMAS AULD—SIR:—The long and intimate, though by no means friendly, relation which unhappily subsisted between you and myself, leads me to hope that you will easily account for the great liberty which I now take in addressing you in this open and public manner. The same fact may possibly remove any disagreeable surprise which you may experience on again finding your name coupled with mine, in any other way than in an advertisement, accurately describing my person, and offering a large sum for my arrest. In thus dragging you again before the public, I am aware that I shall subject myself to no inconsiderable amount of censure. I shall probably be charged with an unwarrantable if not a wanton and reckless disregard of the rights and proprieties of private life. There are those North as well as South, who entertain a much higher respect for rights which are merely conventional, than they do for rights which are personal and essential. Not a few there are in our country who, while they have no scruples against robbing the laborer of the hard-earned results of his patient industry, will be shocked by the extremely indelicate manner of bringing your name before the public. Believing this to be the case, and wishing to meet every reasonable or plausible objection to my conduct, I will frankly state the ground upon which I justify myself in this instance, as well as on former occasions when I have thought proper to mention your name in public. All will agree that a man guilty of theft, robbery or murder, has forfeited the right to concealment and private life; that the community have a right to subject such persons to the most complete exposure. However much they may desire retirement, and aim to conceal themselves and their movements from the popular gaze, the public have a right to ferret them out, and bring their conduct before the proper tribunals of the country for investigation. Sir, you will undoubtedly make the proper application of these generally-admitted principles, and will easily see the light in which you are regarded by me. I will not, therefore, manifest ill-temper, by calling you hard names. I know you to be a man of some intelligence, and can readily determine the precise estimate which I entertain of your character. I may therefore indulge in language which may seem to others indirect and ambiguous, and yet be quite well understood by yourself.

I have selected this day on which to address you, because it is the anniversary of my emancipation; and knowing of no better way, I am led to this as the best mode of celebrating that truly important event. Just ten years ago this beautiful September morning, yon bright sun beheld me a slave—a poor degraded chattel—trembling at the sound of your voice, lamenting that I was a man, and wishing myself a brute. The hopes which I had treasured up for weeks of a safe and successful escape from your grasp, were powerfully confronted at this last hour by dark clouds of doubt and fear, making my person shake and my bosom to heave with the heavy contest between hope and fear. I have no words to describe to you the deep agony of soul which I experienced on that never-to-be-forgotten morning—(for I left by daylight.)—I was taking a leap in the dark. The probabilities, so far as I could by reason determine them, were stoutly against the undertaking. The preliminaries and precautions I had adopted previously, all worked badly. I was like one going to war without weapons—ten chances of defeat to one of victory. One in whom I had confided, and one who had promised me assistance, appalled by fear at the trial-hour, deserted me, thus leaving the responsibility of success or failure solely with myself. You, sir, can never know my feelings. As I look back to them, I can scarcely realize that

I have passed through a scene so trying. Trying however as they were, and gloomy as was the prospect, thanks be to the Most High, who is ever the God of the oppressed, at the moment which was to determine my whole earthly career, His grace was sufficient, my mind was made up. I embraced the golden opportunity, took the morning tide at the flood; and a free man, young, active, and strong, is the result.

I have often thought I should like to explain to you the grounds upon which I have justified myself in running away from you. I am almost ashamed to do so now, for by this time you may have discovered them yourself. I will, however, glance at them. When yet but a child about six years old, I imbibed the determination to run away. The very first mental effort that I now remember on my part, was an attempt to solve the mystery, Why am I a slave? and with this question my youthful mind was troubled for many days, pressing upon me more heavily at times than others. When I saw the slave-driver whip a slave-woman, cut the blood out of her neck, and heard her piteous cries, I went away into the corner of the fence, wept and pondered over this mystery. I had, through some medium, I know not what, got some idea of God, the Creator of all mankind, the black and the white, and that he had made the blacks to serve the whites as slaves. How he could do this and be good, I could not tell. I was not satisfied with this theory, which made God responsible for slavery, for it pained me greatly, and I have wept over it long and often. At one time, your first wife, Mrs. Lucretia, heard me singing and saw me shedding tears, and asked of me the matter, but I was afraid to tell her. I was puzzled with this question, till one night, while sitting in the kitchen, I heard some of the old slaves talking of their parents having been stolen from Africa by white men, and were sold here as slaves. The whole mystery was solved at once. Very soon after this, my aunt Jinny and uncle Noah ran away, and the great noise made about it by your father-in-law, made me for the first time acquainted with the fact, that there were free States as well as slave States. From that time, I resolved that I would some day run away. The morality of the act, I dispose of as follows: I am myself; you are yourself; we are two distinct person[s], equal persons. What you are I am. You are a man, and so am I.—God created both, and made us separate beings. I am not by nature bound to you, or you to me. Nature does not make your existence depend upon me, or mine to depend upon yours. I cannot walk upon your legs, or you upon mine. I cannot breathe for you, or you for me; I must breathe for myself, and you for yourself. We are distinct persons, and are each equally provided with faculties necessary to our individual existence. In leaving you, I took nothing but what belonged to me, and in no way lessened your means of obtaining an honest living. Your faculties remained yours, and mine became useful to their rightful owner. I therefore see no wrong in any part of the transaction. It is true, I went off secretly, but that was more your fault than mine. Had I let you into the secret, you would have defeated the enterprise entirely; but for this, I should have been really glad to have made you acquainted with my intention to leave.

You may perhaps want to know how I like my present condition. I am free to say, I greatly prefer it to that which I occupied in Maryland. I am, however, by no means prejudiced against that State as such. Its geography, climate, fertility and products, are such as to make it a very desirable abode for any man; and but for the existence of slavery there, it is not impossible that I might again take up my abode in that State. It is not that I love Maryland less, but freedom more. You will be surprised to learn that people at the North labor under the strange delusion that if the slaves were emancipated at the South, they would all flock to the North. So far from this being the case, in that event, you would see many old and familiar faces back again at the South. The fact is, there are few here who would not return to the South in the event of emancipation. We want to live in the land of our birth, and to lay our bones by the side of our fathers'; and nothing short of an intense love of personal freedom keeps us from the South. For the sake of this, most of us would live on a crust of bread and a cup of cold water.

Since I left you, I have had a rich experience. I have occupied stations which I never dreamed of when a slave. Three out of the ten years since I left you, I spent as a common laborer on the wharves of New Bedford, Massachusetts. It was there I earned my first free dollar. It was mine. I could spend it as I pleased. I could buy hams or herring with it, without asking any odds of anybody. That was a precious dollar to me. You remember when I used to make seven or eight, and even nine dollars a week in Baltimore, you would take every cent of it from me every Saturday night, saying that I belonged to you, and my earnings also. I never liked this conduct on your part—to say the best, I thought it a little mean. I would not have served you so. But let that pass. I was a little awkward about counting money in New England fashion when I first landed in New Bedford. I like to have betrayed myself several times. I caught myself saying phip, for fourpence; and one time a man actually charged me with being a runaway, whereupon I was silly enough to become one by running away from him, for I was greatly afraid he might adopt measures to get me again into slavery, a condition I then dreaded more than death.

I soon, however, learned to count money, as well as to make it, and got on swimmingly. I married soon after leaving you: in fact, I was engaged to be married before I left you; and instead of finding my companion a burden, she was truly a helpmeet. She went to live at service, and I to work on the wharf, and though we toiled hard the first winter, we never lived more happily. After remaining in New Bedford for three years, I met with Wm. Lloyd

Garrison, a person of whom you have possibly heard, as he is pretty generally known among slaveholders. He put it into my head that I might make
myself serviceable to the cause of the slave by devoting a portion of my time
to telling my own sorrows, and those of other slaves which had come under
my observation. This was the commencement of a higher state of existence
than any to which I had ever aspired. I was thrown into society the most
pure, enlightened and benevolent that the country affords. Among these, I
have never forgotten you, but have invariably made you the topic of conversation—thus giving you all the notoriety I could do. I need not tell you that
the opinion formed of you in these circles, is far from being favorable. They
have little respect for your honesty, and less for your religion.

But I was going on to relate to you something of my interesting experience. I had not long enjoyed the excellent society to which I have referred,
before the light of its excellence exerted a beneficial influence on my mind
and heart. Much of my early dislike of white persons was removed, and
their manners, habits and customs, so entirely unlike what I had been used
to in the kitchen-quarters on the plantations of the South, fairly charmed
me, and gave me a strong disrelish for the coarse and degrading customs
of my former condition. I therefore made an effort so to improve my mind
and deportment, as to be somewhat fitted to the station to which I seemed
almost Providentially called. The transition from degradation to respect-
ability was indeed great, and to get from one to the other without carrying
some marks of one's former condition, is truly a difficult matter.—I would
not have you think that I am now entirely clear of all plantation peculiarities, but my friends here, while they entertain the strongest dislike to them,
regard me with that charity to which my past life somewhat entitles me,
so that my condition in this respect is exceedingly pleasant. So far as my
domestic affairs are concerned, I can boast of as comfortable a dwelling
as your own. I have an industrious and neat companion, and four dear
children—the oldest a girl of nine years, and three fine boys, the oldest
eight, the next six, and the youngest four years old. The three oldest are
now going regularly to school—two can read and write, and the other can
spell with tolerable correctness words of two syllables. Dear fellows! they
are all in comfortable beds, and are sound asleep, perfectly secure under
my own roof. There are no slaveholders here to rend my heart by snatching
them from my arms, or blast a proud mother's dearest hopes by tearing
them from her bosom. These dear children are ours—not to work up into
rice, sugar and tobacco, but to watch over, regard, and protect, and to rear
them up in the nurture and admonition of the gospel—to train them up in
the paths of wisdom and virtue, and, as far as we can, to make them useful
to the world and to themselves. Oh! sir, a slaveholder never appears to me
so completely an agent of hell, as when I think of and look upon my dear

children. It is then that my feelings rise above my control. I meant to have said more with respect to my own prosperity and happiness, but thoughts and feelings which this recital has quickened, unfits me to proceed further in that direction. The grim horrors of slavery rise in all their ghastly terror before me, the wails of millions pierce my heart, and chill my blood. I remember the chain, the gag, the bloody whip, the deathlike gloom overshadowing the broken spirit of the fettered bondman, the appalling liability of his being torn away from wife and children and sold like a beast in the market. Say not that this is a picture of fancy. You well know that I wear stripes on my back inflicted by your direction; and that you, while we were brothers in the same church, caused this right hand, with which I am now penning this letter, to be closely tied to my left, and my person dragged at the pistol's mouth, fifteen miles, from the Bay side to Easton, to be sold like a beast in the market, for the alleged crime of intending to escape from your possession. All this and more you remember, and know to be perfectly true, not only of yourself, but of nearly all the slaveholders around you.

At this moment, you are probably the guilty holder of at least three of my own dear sisters, and my only brother in bondage. These you regard as your property. They are recorded on your ledger, or perhaps have been sold to human flesh mongers, with a view to filling your own ever-hungry purse. Sir, I desire to know how and where these dear sisters are. Have you sold them? or are they still in our possession? What has become of them? are they living or dead? And my dear old grandmother, whom you turned out like an old horse, to die in the woods—is she still alive? Write and let me know all about them. If my grandmother be still alive, she is of no service to you, for by this time she must be nearly eighty years old—too old to be cared for by one to whom she has ceased to be of service, send her to me at Rochester, or bring her to Philadelphia, and it shall be the crowning happiness of my life to take care of her in her old age. Oh! she was to me a mother, and a father, so far as hard toil for my comfort could make her such. Send me my grandmother! that I may watch over and take care of her in her old age. And my sisters, let me know all about them. I would write to them, and learn all I want to know of them without disturbing you in any way, but that, through your unrighteous conduct, they have been entirely deprived of the power to read and write. You have kept them in utter ignorance, and have therefore robbed them of the sweet enjoyments of writing or receiving letters from absent friends and relatives. Your wickedness and cruelty committed in this respect on your own fellow-creatures, are greater than all the stripes you have laid upon my back, or theirs. It is an outrage upon the soul—a war upon the immortal spirit, and one for which you must give account at the bar of our common Father and Creator.

The responsibility which you have assumed in this regard is truly awful—and how you could stagger under it these many years is marvellous. Your mind must have become darkened, your heart hardened, your conscience seared and petrified, or you would have long since thrown off the accursed load and sought relief at the hands of a sin forgiving God. How, let me ask, would you look upon me, were I some dark night in company with a band of hardened villains, to enter the precincts of your own elegant dwelling and seize the person of your own lovely daughter Amanda, and carry her off from your family, friends and all the loved ones of her youth—make her my slave—compel her to work, and I take her wages—place her name on my ledger as property—disregard her personal rights—fetter the powers of her immortal soul by denying her the right and privilege of learning to read and write—feed her coarsely—clothe her scantily, and whip her on the naked back occasionally; more and still more horrible, leave her unprotected—a degraded victim to the brutal lust of fiendish overseers who would pollute, blight, and blast her fair soul—rob her of all dignity—destroy her virtue, and annihilate all in her person the graces that adorn the character of virtuous womanhood? I ask how would you regard me, if such were my conduct? Oh! the vocabulary of the damned would not afford a word sufficiently infernal, to express your idea of my God-provoking wickedness. Yet sir, your treatment of my beloved sisters is in all essential points, precisely like the case I have now supposed. Damning as would be such a deed on my part, it would be no more so than that which you have committed against me and my sisters.

I will now bring this letter to a close, you shall hear from me again unless you let me hear from you. I intend to make use of you as a weapon with which to assail the system of slavery—as a means of concentrating public attention on the system, and deepening their horror of trafficking in the souls and bodies of men. I shall make use of you as a means of exposing the character of the American church and clergy—and as a means of bringing this guilty nation with yourself to repentence. In doing this I entertain no malice towards you personally. There is no roof under which you would be more safe than mine, and there is nothing in my house which you might need for your comfort, which I would not readily grant. Indeed, I should esteem it a privilege, to set you an example as to how mankind ought to treat each other.

I am your fellow man but not your slave, FREDERICK DOUGLASS.

P.S.—I send a copy of the paper containing this letter, to save postage.—F.D.

Source

"To My Old Master," *North Star*, September 8, 1848.

What to the Slave is Your Fourth of July?

Douglass delivered his most famous oration on July 5, 1852 at Corinthian Hall in Rochester, New York. Invited by the Rochester Ladies Anti-Slavery Society to deliver the annual Independence Day oration, he declined and instead spoke the following day. Nineteenth-century American communities celebrated the Fourth of July with a ceremonial reading of the Declaration of Independence, which was generally followed by an oration or speech dedicated to the celebration of independence, the American Revolution, and glorifying the nation's Founding Fathers. Believing that African Americans, especially those millions enslaved in the South, did not share in the revolutionary heritage, Douglass's speech offered a masterfully crafted critique of the holiday and of the nation's complicity in maintaining slavery. Within weeks the speech was published in pamphlet form and read widely across the North. It stands today as an articulate expression of what it meant to be excluded from the republican experiment that resulted in the creation of the United States of America.

Mr. President, Friends and Fellow-Citizens:

He who could address this audience without a quailing sensation, has stronger nerves than I have. The task before me is one which requires much previous thought and study for its proper performance. I know that apologies of this sort are generally considered flat and unmeaning. I trust, however, that mine will not be so considered. Should I seem at ease, my appearance would much misrepresent me. The little experience I have had in addressing public meetings, in country school-houses, avails me nothing on the present occasion.

The papers and placards say, that I am to deliver a 4th July oration. This, certainly, sounds large, and out of the common way, for me. It is true that I have often had the privilege to speak in this beautiful Hall, and to address many who now honor me with their presence. But neither their familiar faces, nor the perfect gage I think I have of Corinthian Hall, seems to free me from embarrassment.

The fact is, ladies and gentlemen, the distance between this platform and the slave plantation, from which I escaped, is considerable—and the difficulties to be overcome in getting from the latter to the former, are by no means slight. That I am here to-day, is, to me, a matter of astonishment as well as of gratitude. You will not, therefore, be surprised, if I evince no elaborate preparation, nor grace my speech with a high sounding exordium. With little experience and with less learning[,] I have been able to throw my thoughts hastily and imperfectly together; and trusting to your patient and generous indulgence, I will proceed to lay them before you.

This, for the purpose of this celebration, is the 4th of July. It is the birth-day of your National Independence, and of your political freedom. This, to you, is what the Passover was to the emancipated people of God. It carries your minds back to the day, and to the act of your great deliverance; and to the signs, and to the wonders, associated with that act; and that day. This celebration also marks the beginning of another year of your national life; and reminds you that the Republic of America is now 76 years old.

I am glad, fellow-citizens, that your nation is so young. Seventy-six years, though a good old age for a man, is but a mere speck in the life of a nation. Three score years and ten is the allotted time for individual men; but nations number their years by thousands. According to this, you are, even now, only in the beginning of your national career, still lingering in the period of childhood. I say, I am glad this is so. There is hope in the thought, and hope [is] much needed, under the dark clouds which lower about us. The eye of the reformer is met with angry flashes, portending disastrous times; but his heart may well beat lighter at the thought that America is young, and that she is still in the impressible stage of her existence. May he not hope that high lessons of wisdom, of justice and of truth, may yet give direction to her destiny[?] Were the nation older, the patriot's heart might be sadder, and the reformer's brow heavier.

Fellow-citizens, I shall not presume to dwell at length on the associations that cluster about this day. The simple story of it is, that, 76 years ago, the people of this country were British subjects. The style and title of your "sovereign people" (in which you now glory) was not then born. You were under the British Crown. Your fathers esteemed the English Government as the home government; and England as the fatherland. This home government, you know, although a considerable distance from home did, in the exercise of its parental prerogatives, impose upon its colonial children, such restrainings, burdens and limitations, as, in its mature judgment, it deemed wise, right and proper.

But, your fathers, who had not adopted the fashionable ideas of this day, of the infallibility of government, presumed to differ from the home government in respect to the wisdom and the justice of some of those burdens and restraints. They went so far in their excitement as to pronounce the measures of government unjust, unreasonable, and oppressive, and altogether such as ought not to be quietly submitted to. I scarcely need say, fellow-citizens, that my opinion of those measures fully accords with that of your fathers. Such a declaration of agreement on my part, would not be worth much to anybody. It would, certainly, prove nothing, as to what part I might have taken in the great controversy of 1776. To say *now* that America was right, and England wrong, is exceedingly easy. Everybody can say it; the dastard, not less than the noble brave, can flippantly discant on the tyranny of England towards the American Colonies. It is fashionable to do so; but there was a time when, to pronounce against England, and in favor of the cause of the colonies, tried men's souls. They who did so were accounted in their day, plotters of mischief, agitators and rebels, dangerous men. To side with the right, against the wrong, with the weak against the strong, and with the oppressed against the oppressor! *here* lies the merit, and the one which, of all others, seems unfashionable in our day. But, to proceed.

Feeling themselves harshly and unjustly treated, by the home government, your fathers, like men of honesty, and men of spirit, earnestly sought redress. They petitioned and remonstrated, they did so in a decorous, respectful, and loyal manner.—Their conduct was wholly unexceptionable. This did not answer the purpose. They saw themselves treated with sovereign indifference, coldness and scorn. Yet they persevered. They were not the men to look back.

On the 2d of July, 1776, the old Continental Congress, to the dismay of the lovers of ease and the worshippers of property, clothed that dreadful idea with all the authority of national sanction. They did so in the form of a resolution; and as we seldom hit upon resolutions, drawn up in our day, whose transparency is at all equal to this, it may refresh your minds and help my story if I read it.

Resolved, That these united colonies *are,* and of right, ought to be free and independent States; that they are absolved from all allegiance to the British Crown; and that all political connection between them and the State of Great Britain *is,* and ought to be, dissolved.

Citizens, your fathers made good that resolution. They succeeded; and to-day you reap the fruits of their success. The freedom gained is yours; and you, therefore, may properly celebrate this anniversary. The 4th of July is the first great fact in your nation's history—the very ring-bolt in the chain of your yet undeveloped destiny.

Pride and patriotism, not less than gratitude, prompt you to celebrate and to hold it in perpetual remembrance. I have said that the Declaration of Independence is the RING-BOLT to the chain of your nation's destiny; so, indeed, I regard it. The principles contained in that instrument are saving principles. Stand by those principles, be true to them on all occasions, and in all places.

From the round top of your ship of state, dark clouds may be seen. Heavy billows, like mountains in the distance, disclose to the leeward huge forms of flinty rocks! That bolt drawn, that chain broken, and all is lost. *Cling to this day—cling to it,* and to its principles, with the grasp of a storm-tossed mariner to a spar at midnight.

I am not wanting in respect for the fathers of this republic. The signers of the Declaration of Independence were brave men. They were great men too—great enough to give fame to a great age. It does not often happen to a nation to raise at one time such a number of truly great men. The point from which I am compelled to view them is not, certainly, the most favorable; and yet I can not contemplate their great deeds with less than admiration. They were statesmen, patriots and heroes and for the good they did, and the principles they contended for, I will unite to honor their memory.

They loved their country better than their own private interests; and, though this is not the highest form of human excellence, all will concede that it is a rare virtue, and that when it is exhibited it ought to command respect. He who will, intelligently, lay down his life for his country, is a man whom it is not in human nature to despise. Your fathers staked their lives, their fortunes, and their sacred honor, on the cause of their country.

They were peace men; but they preferred revolution to peaceful submission to bondage. They were quiet men; but they did not shrink from agitating against oppression.—They showed forbearance; but that they knew its limits. They believed in order; but not in the order of tyranny. With them, nothing was "*settled*" that was not right.—With them, justice, liberty and humanity were "*final;*" not slavery and oppression.—You may well cherish the memory of such men. They were great in their day and generation. Their solid manhood stands out the more as we contrast it with these degenerate times.

How circumspect, exact and proportionate were all their movements! How unlike the politicians of an hour! Their statesmanship looked beyond the passing moment, and stretched away in strength into the distant future. They seized upon eternal principles, and set a glorious example in their defence. Mark them!

Fully appreciating the hardships to be encountered, firmly believing in the right of their cause, honorably inviting the scrutiny of an on-looking world, reverently appealing to heaven to attest their sincerity, soundly comprehending the solemn responsibility they were about to assume, wisely measuring the terrible odds against them, your fathers, the fathers of this republic, did, most deliberately, under the inspiration of a glorious patriotism, and with a sublime faith in the great principles of justice and freedom, lay deep, the corner-stone of the national superstructure, which has risen and still rises in grandeur around you.

Of this fundamental work, this day is the anniversary. Our eyes are met with demonstrations of joyous enthusiasm. Banners and pennants wave exultingly on the breeze. The din of business, too, is hushed. Even mammon seems to have quitted his grasp on this day. The ear-piercing fife and the stering drum unite their accents with the ascending peal of a thousand church bells.—Prayers are made, hymns are sung, sermons are preached in honor of this day; while the quick martial tramp of a great and multitudinous nation, echoed back by all the hills, valleys and mountains of a vast continent, bespeak the occasion one of thrilling and universal interest—a nation's jubilee.

Friends and citizens, I need not enter further into the causes which led to this anniversary. Many of you understand them better than I do. You could instruct me in regard to them. That is a branch of knowledge in which you feel, perhaps, a much deeper interest than your speaker. I leave, therefore, the great deeds of your fathers to other gentlemen whose claim to have been regularly descended will be less likely to be disputed than mine!

THE PRESENT.

My business, if I have any here to-day, is with the present. The accepted time with God and his cause is the ever-living now. But pardon me, allow me to ask, why am I called upon to speak here to-day? What have I, or those I represent, to do with your national independence? Are the great principles of political freedom and of natural justice, imbodied in that Declaration of Independence, extended to us? and am I, therefore, called upon to bring our humble offering to the national altar, and to confess the benefits and express devout gratitude for the blessing resulting from your independence to us?

I am not included in the pale of this glorious anniversary! Your high independence only reveals the immeasurable distance between us. The blessings in which you, this day, rejoice, are not enjoyed in common. The rich inheritance of justice, liberty, prosperity and independence, bequeathed by your fathers, is shared by you, not by me. The sunlight that brought life and healing to you, has brought stripes and death to me. This Fourth [of] July is *yours,* not *mine. You* may rejoice, *I* must mourn. To drag a man in fetters into the grand illuminated temple of liberty, and call upon him to join you in joyous anthems, were inhuman mockery and sacrilegious irony. Do you mean, citizens, to mock me by asking me to speak today? If so, there is a parallel to your conduct. You are copying the example of a nation whose crimes, towering up to heaven, were thrown down by the breath of the Almighty, burying that nation in irrecoverable ruin!

Above your national, tumultuous joy, I hear the mournful wail of millions! whose chains heavy and grievous yesterday, are, to-day rendered more intolerable by the jubila shouts that reach them. If I do forget, if I do not faithfully remember those bleeding children of sorrow this day, "may my right hand forget her cunning, and may my tongue cleave to the roof of my mouth!" To forget them, to pass lightly over their wrongs, and to chime in with the popular theme, would be treason most scandalous and shocking, and would make me a reproach before God and the world. My subject, then, fellow citizens, is AMERICAN SLAVERY. I shall see, this day, and its popular characteristics, from the slave's point of view. Standing, there, identified with the American bondman, making his wrongs mine, I do not hesitate to declare, with all my soul that the character and conduct of this nation never looked blacker to me than on this 4th of July!—Whether we turn to the declarations of the past, or to the professions of the present, the conduct of the nation seems equally hideous and revolting. America is false to the past, false to the present, and solemnly binds herself to be false to the future. Standing with God and the crushed and bleeding slaves on this occasion, I will, in the name of humanity which is outraged, in the name of liberty which is fettered, in the name of the constitution and the bible, which are disregarded and trampled upon, dare to call in question and to denounce, with all the emphasis I can commend, everything that serves to perpetuate slavery—the great sin, and shame of America! "I will not equivocate; I will not excuse;" I will use the severest language I can command; and yet not one word shall escape me that any man, whose judgment is not blinded by prejudice, or who is not at heart a slaveholder, shall not confess to be right and just.

But I fancy I hear some one of my audience say, it is just in this circumstance that you and your brother abolitionists fail to make a favorable impression on the public mind. Would you argue more, and denounce less, would you persuade more, and rebuke less, your cause would be much more likely to succeed. But, I answer, where all is plain there is nothing to be argued. What point in the anti-slavery creed would you have me argue? On what branch of the subject do the people of this country need light? Must I undertake to prove that the slave is a man? That point is conceded already. Nobody doubts it. The slaveholders themselves acknowledge it in the enactment of laws for the government. They acknowledge it when they punish disobedience on the part of the slave. There are seventy-two crimes in the State of Virginia, which, if committed by a black man, (no matter how ignorant he be,) subject him to the punishment of death; while only two of the same crimes will subject a white man to the like punishment. What is this but the acknowledgement that the slave is a moral, intellectual and responsible being. The manhood of the slave is conceded.

Would you have me argue, that man is entitled to liberty? that he is the rightful owner of his own body? You have already declared it. Must I argue the wrongfulness of slavery? Is that a question for Republicans? Is it to be settled by the ruler of logic and argumentation, as a matter beset with great difficulty, involving a doubtful application of the principle of justice, hard to be understood? How should I look to-day, in the presence of Americans, dividing, and subdividing a discourse, to show that men have a natural right to freedom? speaking of it relatively, and positively, negatively, and affirmatively. To do so, would be to make myself ridiculous, and to offer an insult to your understanding. There is not a man beneath the canopy of heaven, that does not know that slavery is wrong *for him.*

What, am I to argue that it is wrong to make men brutes, to rob them of their liberty, to work them without wages, to keep them ignorant of their relations to their fellow men, to beat them with sticks, to flay their flesh with the lash, to load their limbs with irons, to hunt them with dogs, to sell them at auction, to sunder their families, to knock out their teeth, to burn their flesh, to starve them into obedience and submission to their masters? Must I argue that a system thus marked with blood, and stained with pollution, is *wrong?* No! I will not.—I have better employment for my time and strength, than such arguments would imply.

What, then, remains to be argued? Is it that slavery is not divine; that God did not establish it; that our doctors of divinity are mistaken? There is blasphemy in the thought. That which is inhuman, cannot be divine! *Who* can reason on such a proposition? They that can, may; I cannot. The time for such argument is past.

What, to the American slave, is your 4th of July? I answer; a day that reveals to him, more than all other days in the year, the gross injustice and cruelty to which he is the constant victim. To him, your celebration is a sham; your boasted liberty, an unholy lisence; your national greatness, swelling vanity; your sounds of rejoicing are empty and heartless; your denunciations of tyrants, brass-fronted impudence; your shouts of liberty and equality, hollow mockery: your prayers and hymns, your sermons and thanksgivings, with all your religious parade, and solemnity, are, to him, [mere] bombast, fraud, deception, impiety, and hypocrisy—a thin veil to cover up crimes which would disgrace a nation of savages. There is not a nation of savages. There is not a nation on the earth guilty of practices, more shocking and bloody, than are the people of these United States, at this very hour.

Go where you may, search where you will, roam through all the monarchies and despotisms of the old world, travel through South America, search out every abuse, and when you have found the last, lay your facts by the side of the every day practices of this nation, and you will say with me, that for revolting barbarity and shameless hypocrisy, America reigns without a rival.

Take the American slave-trade, which we are told by the papers, is especially prosperous just now. Mr. Benton tells us that the price of men was never higher than now. This trade is one of the peculiarities of American institutions. It is carried on in all the large towns and cities in one half of this confederacy; and millions are pocketed every year, by dealers in this horrid traffic. In several states, this trade is a chief source of wealth. It is called (in contradistinction to the foreign slave-trade) *"the internal slave trade."* It is, probably, called so, too, in order to divert from it the horror with which the foreign slave-trade is contemplated.

Behold the practical operation of this internal slave-trade, the American slave-trade, sustained by American politics and American religion. Here you will see men and women reared like swine for the market. You know what is a swine-drover. I will show you a man-drover. They inhabit all our Southern States. They perambulate the country, and crowd the highways of the nation, with droves of human stock. You will see one of these human flesh jobbers, armed with pistol, whip and bowie-knife, driving a company of a hundred men, women, and children, from the Potomac to the slave-market, at New Orleans. These wretched people are to be sold singly, or in lots, to suit purchaser. They are food for the cotton-field, and the deadly sugar-mill. Mark the sad procession, as it moves wearily along, and the inhuman wretch who drives them. Hear his savage yells, and his blood-chilling oaths, as he hurries his affrighted captives! There, see the old man, with locks thinned and gray. Cast one glance, if you please, upon that young mother, whose shoulders are bare to the scorching sun, her briny tears falling on the brow of the babe in her arms. See, too, that girl of thirteen, weeping, *yes!* weeping, as she thinks of the mother from whom she has been torn! Tell me WHERE, under the sun, you can witness a spectacle more fiendish and shocking. Yet this is but a glance at the American slave-trade, as it exists, at this moment, in the ruling part of the United States.

I was born amid such sights and scenes.—To me, the American slave-trade is a terrible reality.

Fellow-citizens, this murderous traffic is, to-day, in active operation in this boasted republic. In the solitude of my spirit, I see clouds of dust raised on the highways of the South; I see the bleeding footsteps; I hear the doleful wail of fettered humanity, on the way to the slave-markets, where they are to be sold like *horses, sheep*, and *swine*, knocked off to the highest bidder. There I see the tenderest ties ruthlessly broken, to gratify the lust, caprice and rapacity of the buyers and sellers of men. My soul sickens at the sight. But a still more inhuman, disgraceful, and scandalous state of things remains to be presented.

By an act of the American Congress, not yet two years old, slavery has been nationalized in its most horrible and revolting form. By that act, Mason and Dixon's line has been obliterated; New York has become as Virginia; and the power to hold, hunt, and sell men, women and children, as slaves, remains no longer a mere state institution, but is now an institution of this whole United States.—The power is co-extensive with the star-spangled banner, and American Christianity.—Where these go, may also go the merciless slave-hunter. Where these are, man is not sacred. By that most foul and fiendish of all human decrees, the liberty and person of every man are put in peril. Your broad republican domain is hunting ground for *men*. *Not* for thieves and robbers, enemies of society, but for men guilty of no crime. Your law-makers have commanded all good citizens to engage in this hellish sport. Your President, your Secretary of State, your *lords*, *nobles*, and ecclesiastics, enforce it as a duty you owe to your free and glorious country, and to your God, that you do this accursed thing. Not fewer than forty Americans, have, within the past two years, been hunted down, and, without a moment's warning, hurried away in chain[s], and consigned to slavery and excruciating torture.—Some of these have had wives and children, dependent on them for bread; but of this, no account was made. The right of the hunter to his prey stands superior to the right of marriage, and to *all* rights in this republic, the rights of God included. For black men, there are neither law, justice, humanity, nor religion, in this land. The Fugitive Slave *Law* makes MERCY TO THEM, A CRIME; and bribes the judge who tries them. An American JUDGE GETS TEN DOLLARS FOR EVERY VICTIM HE CONSIGNS to slavery, and five, when he fails to do so. The oath of any two villains is sufficient, under this hell-black enactment, to send the most pious and exemplary black man into the remorseless jaws of slavery! His own testimony is nothing. He can bring no witnesses for himself. The minister of American justice is bound, by the law, to hear but *one* side; and *that* side, is the side of the oppressor. Let this damning fact be perpetually told. Let it be thundered around the world, that, in tyrant-killing, king-hating, people-loving, democratic, Christian America, the seats of justice are filled with judges, who hold their offices under an open and palpable *bribe*, and are bound, in deciding in the case of a man's liberty, *to hear only his accusers!*

At the very moment that they are thanking God for the enjoyment of civil and religious liberty, and for the right to worship God according to the dictates of their own consciences, they are utterly silent in respect to a law which robs religion of its chief significance, and makes it utterly worthless to a world lying in wickedness. The fact that the church of our country, (with fractional exceptions,) does not esteem "the Fugitive Slave Law" as a declaration of war against religious liberty, implies that the church regards religion simply as a form of worship, an empty ceremony, and *not* a vital principle, requiring active benevolence, justice, love and good will towards man. It esteems sacrifices above mercy; psalm-singing above right doing; solemn meetings above practical righteousness. A worship that can be conducted by persons who refuse to give shelter to the houseless, to give bread to the hungry, clothing to the naked, and who enjoin obedience to a law forbidding these acts of mercy, is a curse, not a blessing to mankind.

But the church of this country is not only indifferent to the wrongs of the slave, it actually takes sides with the oppressors. It has made itself the bulwark of American slavery, and the shield of American slave-hunters. Many of its most eloquent Divines, those who stand as the very lights of the church, have, shamelessly, given the sanction of religion, and the bible, to the whole slave system.—They have taught that man may, properly, be a slave; that the relation of master and slave is ordained of God; that to send back an escaped bondman to his master is clearly the duty of all the followers of the Lord Jesus Christ; and this horrible blasphemy is palmed off upon the world for christianity.

For my part, I would say, welcome infidelity! welcome atheism! welcome anything! in preference to the gospel, *as preached by those Divines.* These ministers make religion a cold and flinty-hearted thing, having neither principles of right action, nor bowels of compassion. They strip the love of God of its beauty and leave the throne of religion a huge, horrible, repulsive form. It is a religion for oppressors, tyrants, man-stealers, and *thugs.*

The American church is guilty, when viewed in connection with what it is doing to uphold slavery; but it is superlatively guilty when viewed in connection with its ability to abolish slavery. The sin of which it is guilty is one of omission as well as of commission.

Let the religious press, the pulpit, the Sunday school, the conference meeting, the great ecclesiastical, missionary, bible and the tract associations of the land array their immense powers against slavery, slaveholding; and the whole system of crime and blood would be scattered to the winds, and that they do not do this involves them in the most awful responsibility of which the mind can conceive.

Americans! your republican politics, not less than your republican religion, is flagrantly inconsistent. You boast of your love of liberty, your superior civilization, and your pure christianity, while the whole political power of the nation, as embodied in the two great political parties, is solemnly pledged to support and perpetuate the enslavement of three millions of your countrymen. You hurl your anathemas at the crowned headed tyrants of Russia and Austria, and pride yourselves on your Democratic institutions, while you yourselves consent to be the mere *tools* and *body-guards* of the tyrants of Virginia and Carolina. You invite to your shores fugitives of oppression from abroad, honor them with banquets, greet them with ovations, cheer them, toast them, salute them, protect them, and pour out your money to them like water; but the fugitives from your own land, you advertise, hunt, arrest shoot and kill. You glory in your refinement, and your universal education; yet you maintain a system as barbarous and dreadful, as ever stained the character of a nation—a system begun in avarice, supported in pride, and perpetuated in cruelty. You shed tears over fallen Hungary, and make the sad story of her wrongs the theme of your poets, statesmen, and orators, till your gallant sons are ready to fly to arms, to vindicate her cause against her oppressors; but, in regard to the ten thousand wrongs of the American slave, you would enforce the strictest silence, and would hail him as an enemy of the nation who dares to make those wrongs the subject of public discourse! You are all on fire at the mention of liberty for France or for Ireland; but are as cold as an iceberg at the thought of liberty for the enslaved of America.—You discourse eloquently on the dignity of labor; yet, you sustain a system which, in its very essence, casts a stigma upon labor. You can bear your bosom to the storm of British artillery, to throw off a threepenny tax on tea; and yet wring the last hard earned farthing from the grasp of the black laborers of your country.

Fellow-citizens! I will not enlarge further on your national inconsistencies. The existence of slavery in this country brands your republicanism as a sham, your humanity as a base pretence, and your christianity as a lie. It destroys your moral power abroad; it corrupts your politicians at home. It saps the foundation of religion; it makes your name a hissing, and a byeword to a mocking earth. It is the antagonistic force in your government, the only thing that seriously disturbs and endangers your *Union*. It fetters your progress; it is the enemy of improvement, the deadly foe of education; it fosters pride, it breeds insolence, it promotes vice; it shelters crime; it is a curse to the earth that supports it; and yet, you cling to it; as if it were the sheet anchor of all your hopes. Oh! be warned! be warned! a horrible reptile is coiled up in your nation's bosom, the venomous creature is nursing at the tender breast of your youthful republic; *for the love of God, tear away,* and fling from you the hideous monster, and *let the weight of twenty millions, crush and destroy it for ever!*

But it is answered in reply to all this, that precisely what I have now denounced is, in fact, guaranteed and sanctioned by the Constitution of the United States; that, the right to hold, and to hunt slaves, is a part of that Constitution framed by the illustrious Fathers of their Republic. *Then,* I affirm, notwithstanding all I have said before, your Fathers stooped, basely stooped.

"To palter with us in a double sense
And keep the word of promise to the ear,
But break it to the heart."

And, instead of being the honest men I have before declared them to be, they were the veriest imposters that ever practised on mankind. *This* is the inevitable conclusion, and from it there is no escape; but I differ from those who charge this baseness on the framers of the Constitution of the United States. *It is a slander upon their memory,* at least, so I believe.

Fellow-citizens! there is no matter in respect to which the people of the North have allowed themselves to be so ruinously imposed upon as that of the pro-slavery character of the Constitution. In *that* instrument I hold there is neither warrant, license, nor sanction of the hateful thing; but interpreted, as it *ought* to be interpreted, the Constitution is a GLORIOUS LIBERTY DOCUMENT. Read its preamble, consider its purposes. Is slavery among them? Is it at the gateway? or is it in the temple? it is neither. While I do not intend to argue this question on the *present* occasion, let me ask, if it be not somewhat singular that, if the Constitution were intended to be, by its framers and adopters, a slaveholding instrument, why neither *slavery, slaveholding,* nor *slave* can anywhere be found in it. What would be thought of an instrument, drawn up, *legally* drawn up, for the purpose of entitling the city of Rochester to a track of land, in which no mention of land was made.

Now, take the constitution according to its plain reading, and I defy the presentation of a single pro-slavery clause in it. On the other hand, it will be found to contain principles and purposes, entirely hostile to the existence of slavery.

I have detained my audience entirely too long already. At some future period I will gladly avail myself of an opportunity to give this subject a full and fair discussion. Allow me to say, in conclusion, notwithstanding the dark picture I have this day presented, of the state of the nation, I do not despair of this country. There are forces in operation, which must, inevitably, work the downfall of slavery. "*The arm of the Lord is not shortened,*" and the doom of slavery is certain. I, therefore, leave off where I began, with *hope*.

Source

"The Celebration at Corinthian Hall," *Frederick Douglass' Paper*, July 9, 1852.

MEN OF COLOR, TO ARMS!

One of the biggest controversies of the American Civil War concerned the role that African Americans should play in the conflict. From the war's beginning in 1861, Frederick Douglass and other abolitionists pushed President Abraham Lincoln to allow black troops to fight for the Union and to make abolition a war aim. Lincoln hesitated initially because of the deep-seated racial prejudice that permeated the northern states. One fear was that white soldiers would refuse to fight alongside African Americans. Another was the widespread belief that blacks were too cowardly or too servile to act as soldiers. Following the announcement of the Emancipation Proclamation in September, 1862, however, Lincoln authorized the formation of black regiments. The first blacks to take up arms for the Union were units organized in Louisiana and South Carolina. In January 1863, with the Emancipation Proclamation officially freeing slaves in the areas still under rebellion, northern units began to form. Among the first was the 54th Massachusetts Volunteer Infantry, authorized by Governor John A. Andrew. Douglass acted as a recruiter for the regiment, and among the first enlistments were his sons Charles and Lewis. Because Massachusetts had a small African American population, he issued this call to reach potential recruits in neighboring states.

When first the rebel cannon shattered the walls of Sumter, and drove away its starving garrison, I predicted that the war, then and there inaugurated would not be fought but entirely by white men. Every month's experience during these two dreary years, has confirmed that opinion. A war undertaken and brazenly carried on for the perpetual enslavement of colored men, calls logically and loudly upon colored men to help to suppress it. Only a moderate share of sagacity was needed to see that the arm of the slave was the best defence against the arm of the slaveholder. Hence with every reverse to the National arms, with every exulting shout of victory raised by the slaveholding rebels, I have implored the imperrilled nation to unchain against her foes her powerful black hand. Slowly and reluctantly that appeal is beginning to be heeded. Stop not now to complain that it was not heeded sooner. It may, or it may not have been best that it should not. This is not the time to discuss that question. Leave it to the future. When the war is over, the country is saved, peace is established, and the black man's rights are secured, as they will be, history with an impartial hand, will dispose of that and sundry other questions. Action! action! not criticism, is the plain duty of this hour. Words are now useful only as they stimulate to blows. The office of speech now is only to point out when, [w]here and how, to strike to the best advantage. There is no time for delay. The tide is at its flood that leads on to fortune. From East to West, from North to South, the sky is written all over "NOW OR NEVER." Liberty won by white men would lose half its lustre. Who would be free themselves must strike the blow. Better even to die free, than to live slaves. This is the sentiment of every brave colored man amongst us. There are weak and cowardly men in all nations. We have them amongst us. They tell you that this is the "white man's war";—that you will be no "better off after, than before the war"; that the getting of you into the army is to "sacrifice you on the first opportunity." Believe them not—cowards themselves, they do not wish to have their cowardice shamed by your brave example. Leave them to their timidity, or to whatever motive may hold them back.

I have not thought lightly of the words I am now addressing to you. The counsel I give comes of close observations of the great struggle now in progress—and of the deep conviction that this is your hour, and mine.

In good earnest then, and after the best deliberation, I now for the first time during this war feel at liberty to call and counsel you to arms. By every consideration which binds you to your enslaved fellow country-men, and the peace and welfare of your country; by every aspiration which you cherish for the freedom and equality of yourselves and your children; by all the ties of blood and identity which make us one with the brave black men, now fighting our battles in Louisana, in South Carolina, I urge you to fly to arms, and smite with death the power that would bury the Government and your Liberty in the same hopeless grave. I wish I could tell you that the State of New York calls you to this high honor. For the moment her constituted authorities are silent of the subject. They will speak by and by, and doubtless on the right side; but we are not compelled to wait for her. We can [get] at the throat of treason and slavery, through the State of Massachusetts.

She was first in the war of Independence; first to break the chains of her slaves; first to make the black man equal before the law; first to admit colored children to her common schools, and she was first to answer with her blood the alarm cry of the nation—when its capital was menaced by rebels. You know her patriotic Governor, and you know Charles Sumner—I need not add more.

Massachusetts now welcomes you to arms as her soldiers. She has but a small colored population from which to recruit. She has full leave of the General Government to send one regiment to the war, and she has undertaken to do it. Go quickly and help fill up this first colored regiment from the north. I am authorized to assure you that you will receive the same wages, the same rations, the same equipments, the same protection, the same treatment and the same bounty secured to white soldiers. You will be led by able and skillful officers—men who will take especial pride in your efficiency and success. They will be quick to accord to you all the honor you shall merit by your valor—and see that your rights and feelings are respected by other soldiers. I have assured myself on these points—and can speak with authority. More than twenty years unswerving devotion to our common cause, may give me some humble claim to be trusted at this momentous crisis.

I will not argue. To do so implies hesitation and doubt, and you do not hesitate. You do not doubt. The day dawns—the morning star is bright upon the horizon! The iron gate of our prison stands half open. One gallant rush from the North will fling it wide-open, while four millions of our brothers and sisters, shall march out into Liberty! The Chance is now given you to end in a day the bondage of centuries, and to rise in one bound from social degradation to the plane of common equality with all other varieties of men. Remember Denmark Vesey of Charleston.—Remember Nathaniel Turner of South Hampton, remember Shields Green, and Cope and who followed noble John Brown, and fell as glorious martyrs for the cause of the slave.—Remember that in a contest with oppression the Almighty has no attribute which can take sides with oppressors. The case is before you. This is our golden opportunity—let us accept it—and forever wipe but the dark reproaches unsparingly hurled against us by our enemies. Win for ourselves the gratitude of our Country—and the best blessings of our posterity through all time. The nucleus of this first regiment is now in camp at Readville, a short distance from Boston. I will undertake to forward to Boston all persons adjudged fit to be mustered into the regiment, who shall apply to me at any time within the next two weeks.

FREDERICK DOUGLASS.

Rochester, March 2d, 1863.

SOURCE

"Men of Color, To Arms!" *Douglass' Monthly*, March 1863.

FREDERICK DOUGLASS TO ABRAHAM LINCOLN, AUGUST 29, 1864

During the Civil War, Frederick Douglass met twice with President Lincoln to discuss the role of African Americans in the conflict. At the first meeting in 1863, Douglass pressed the issue of unequal treatment accorded black troops. In August 1864, Lincoln requested a second meeting to discuss a potential new strategy for the conflict. In the third year of the war, a series of lackluster Union victories and high casualties had further diminished public support for the conflict. Facing reelection in the fall, Lincoln told Douglass he was considering ending the war with slavery intact. As a last ditch effort, he sought Douglass's advice on a plan to surreptitiously spread the word of emancipation across the South and draw slaves behind Union lines. This letter outlines how such a scheme might be implemented. A turn in the war to favor the Union following the battles of the Wilderness and Cold Harbor made the plan unnecessary.

———————

Rochester, New York, August 29, 1864

Hon. Abraham Lincoln
President of the United States

Sir:

Since the interview with which your Excellency was pleased to honor me a few days ago, I have freely conversed with several trustworthy and Patriotic Colored men concerning your suggestion that something should be speedily done to inform the slaves in the Rebel states of the true state of affairs in relation to them, and to warn them as to what will be their probable condition should peace be concluded while they remain within the Rebel lines. And more especially to urge upon them the necessity of making their escape. All with whom I have thus far spoken on the subject, concur in the wisdom and benevolence of the Idea, and some of them think it practicable.

That every slave who escapes from the Rebel states is a loss to the Rebellion and a gain to the Loyal Cause I need not stop here to argue. The proposition is self evident. The Negro is the stomach of the Rebellion, I will therefore briefly submit at once to your Excellency—the ways and means by which many such persons may be wrested from the enemy and brought within our lines:

1st. Let a general agent be appointed by your Excellency charged with the duty of giving effect to your Idea as indicated above. Let him have the means and power to employ twenty or twenty-five good men, having the cause at heart, to act as his agents.

2d. Let these agents which shall be selected by him, have permission to visit such points at the front as are most accessable to large bodies of Slaves in the Rebel States. Let each of the said agents have power to appoint one Sub agent or more in the locality where he may be required to operate—the said sub agent shall be thoroughly acquainted with the country—and well instructed as to the representations he is to make to the slaves and conduct such squads of slaves as he may be able to collect within the Loyal lines: Let the sub agents for this service be paid a sum not exceeding two dollars per day while upon active duty.

3dly. In order that these agents shall not be arrested or impeded in their work—let them be properly ordered to report to the Generals Commanding the several departments they may visit, and receive from them permission to pursue their vocation unmolested.

4th. Let provision be made that the Slaves or Freedmen thus brought within our lines shall receive subsistence until such of them as are fit shall enter the service of the country or be otherwise employed and provided for.

5th. Let each agent appointed by the General Agent be required to keep a strict account of all his transactions of all monies received and paid out, of the number and the names of slaves or freedmen brought into our lines under his auspices, of the plantations visited, and of everything properly connected with the prosecution of his work, and let him be required to make full reports of his proceedings at least once a fortnight to the general agent.

6th. Also let the General Agent be required as regained to keep a strict account of all his transactions with his agents, and report to your Excellency or an officer designated by you to receive such reports.

7th. Let the General Agent be paid a salary sufficient to enable him to employ a competant clerk, and let him be stationed at Washington or at some other point where he can more readily receive communications from, and send communications to his agents. The General Agent should also have a kind of roving Commission within our lines so that he may have a more direct and effective oversight of the whole work, and thus ensure the activity and faithfulness on the part of his agents.

Your Obedient Servant,
Frederick Douglass

SOURCE

Frederick Douglass to Abraham Lincoln, August 29, 1864, Frederick Douglass Papers, Library of Congress, Washington, D.C.

ORATION IN MEMORY OF ABRAHAM LINCOLN, APRIL 14, 1876

The nation mourned the assassination of President Abraham Lincoln in 1865, and one of the first memorials to his legacy was initiated by former slaves. Commemorating the president's Emancipation Proclamation and subsequent support for the total abolition of slavery, once the Civil War ended freed men and women began a fundraising campaign to erect a monument to Lincoln. The Freedmen's Monument, designed by Thomas Ball, was dedicated in 1876 as the nation neared the end of Reconstruction. It depicts Lincoln freeing a male slave, who is crouched at the president's feet. Situated in a square of Washington that was long used as a dumping site for garbage, during the Civil War the park where the monument stands was the location of Lincoln Hospital. Congress designated it as Lincoln Square in 1867; it subsequently became known as Lincoln Park. As one of the nation's most influential African Americans, Frederick Douglass was invited to give the keynote address at the monument's dedication.

April 14, 1876
Delivered at the Unveiling of The Freedmen's Monument in Memory of Abraham Lincoln
Lincoln Park, Washington, D.C.

Friends and Fellow-Citizens:
I warmly congratulate you upon the highly interesting object which has caused you to assemble in such numbers and spirit as you have today.

We stand today at the national center to perform something like a national act—an act which is to go into history; and we are here where every pulsation of the national heart can be heard, felt, and reciprocated. A thousand wires, fed with thought and winged with lightning, put us in instantaneous communication with the loyal and true men all over the country.

Friends and fellow-citizens, the story of our presence here is soon and easily told. We are here in the District of Columbia, here in the city of Washington, the most luminous point of American territory; a city recently transformed and made beautiful in its body and in its spirit; we are here in the place where the ablest and best men of the country are sent to devise the policy, enact the laws, and shape the destiny of the Republic; we are here, with the stately pillars and majestic dome of the Capitol of the nation looking down upon us; we are here, with the broad earth freshly adorned with the foliage and flowers of spring for our church, and all races, colors, and conditions of men for our congregation—in a word, we are here to express, as best we may, by appropriate forms and ceremonies, our grateful sense of the vast, high, and preeminent services rendered to ourselves, to our race, to our country, and to the whole world by Abraham Lincoln.

For the first time in the history of our people, and in the history of the whole American people, we join in this high worship, and march conspicuously in the line of this time-honored custom. First things are always interesting, and this is one of our first things. It is the first time that, in this form and manner, we have sought to do honor to an American great man, however deserving and illustrious. I commend the fact to notice; let it be told in every part of the Republic; let men of all parties and opinions hear it; let those who despise us, not less than those who respect us, know that now and here, in the spirit of liberty, loyalty, and gratitude, let it be known everywhere, and by everybody who takes an interest in human progress and in the amelioration of the condition of mankind, that, in the presence and with the approval of the members of the American House of Representatives, reflecting the general sentiment of the country; that in the presence of that august body, the American Senate, representing the highest intelligence and the calmest judgment of the country; in the presence of the Supreme Court and Chief-Justice of the United States, to whose decisions we all patriotically bow; in the presence and under the steady eye of the honored and trusted Cabinet, we, the colored people, newly emancipated and rejoicing in our blood-bought freedom, near the close of the first century in the life of this Republic, have now and here unveiled, set apart, and dedicated a figure of which the men of this generation may read, and those of after-coming generations may read, something of the exalted character and great works of Abraham Lincoln, the first martyr President of the United States.

Fellow-citizens, in what we have said and done today, and in what we may say and do hereafter, we disclaim everything like arrogance and assumption. We claim for ourselves no superior devotion to the character, history, and memory of the illustrious name whose monument we have here dedicated today. We fully comprehend the relation of Abraham Lincoln both to ourselves and to the white people of the United States. Truth is proper and beautiful at all times and in all places, and it is never more proper and beautiful in any case than when speaking of a great public man whose example is likely to be commended for honor and imitation long after his departure to the solemn shades, the silent continents of eternity. It must be admitted, truth compels me to admit, even here in the presence of the monument we have erected to his memory, Abraham Lincoln was not, in the fullest sense of the word, either our man or our model. In his interests, in his associations, in his habits of thought, and in his prejudices, he was a white man.

He was preeminently the white man's President, entirely devoted to the welfare of white men. He was ready and willing at any time during the first years of his administration to deny, postpone, and sacrifice the rights of humanity in the colored people to promote the welfare of the white people of this country. In all his education and feeling he was an American of the Americans. He came into the Presidential chair upon one principle alone, namely, opposition to the extension of slavery. His arguments in furtherance of this policy had their motive and mainspring in his patriotic devotion to the interests of his own race. To protect, defend, and perpetuate slavery in the states where it existed Abraham Lincoln was not less ready than any other President to draw the sword of the nation. He was ready to execute all the supposed guarantees of the United States Constitution in favor of the slave system anywhere inside the slave states. He was willing to pursue, recapture, and send back the fugitive slave to his master, and to suppress a slave rising for liberty, though his guilty master were already in arms against the Government. The race to which we belong were not the special objects of his consideration. Knowing this, I concede to you, my white fellow-citizens, a pre-eminence in this worship at once full and supreme. First, midst, and last, you and yours were the objects of his deepest affection and his most earnest solicitude. You are the children of Abraham Lincoln. We are at best only his step-children; children by adoption, children by forces of circumstances and necessity. To you it especially belongs to sound his praises, to preserve and perpetuate his memory, to multiply his statues, to hang his pictures high upon your walls, and commend his example, for to you he was a great and glorious friend and benefactor. Instead of supplanting you at his altar, we would exhort you to build high his monuments; let them be of the most costly material, of the most cunning workmanship; let their forms be symmetrical, beautiful, and perfect, let their bases be upon solid rocks, and their summits lean against the unchanging blue, overhanging sky, and let them endure forever! But while in the abundance of your wealth, and in the fullness of your just and patriotic devotion, you do all this, we entreat you to despise not the humble offering we this day unveil to view; for while Abraham Lincoln saved for you a country, he delivered us from a bondage, according to Jefferson, one hour of which was worse than ages of the oppression your fathers rose in rebellion to oppose.

Fellow-citizens, ours is no new-born zeal and devotion—merely a thing of this moment. The name of Abraham Lincoln was near and dear to our hearts in the darkest and most perilous hours of the Republic. We were no more ashamed of him when shrouded in clouds of darkness, of doubt, and defeat than when we saw him crowned with victory, honor, and glory. Our faith in him was often taxed and strained to the uttermost, but it never failed. When he tarried long in the mountain; when he strangely told us that we were the cause of the war; when he still more strangely told us that we were to leave the land in which we were born; when he refused to employ our arms in defense of the Union; when, after accepting our services as colored soldiers, he refused to retaliate our murder and torture as colored prisoners; when he told us he would save the Union if he could with slavery; when he revoked the Proclamation of Emancipation of General Fremont; when he refused to remove the popular commander of the Army of the Potomac, in the days of its inaction and defeat, who was more zealous in his efforts to protect slavery than to suppress rebellion; when we saw all this, and more, we were at times grieved, stunned, and greatly bewildered; but our hearts believed while they ached and bled. Nor was this, even at that time, a blind and unreasoning superstition. Despite the mist and haze that surrounded him; despite the tumult, the hurry, and confusion of the hour, we were able to take a comprehensive view of Abraham Lincoln, and to make reasonable allowance for the circumstances of his position. We saw him, measured him, and estimated him; not by stray utterances to injudicious and tedious delegations, who often tried his patience; not by isolated facts torn from their connection; not by any partial and imperfect glimpses, caught at inopportune moments; but by a broad survey, in the light of the stern logic of great events, and in view of that divinity which shapes our ends, rough hew them how we will, we came to the conclusion that the hour and the man of our redemption had somehow met in the person of Abraham Lincoln. It mattered little to us what language he might employ on special occasions; it mattered little to us, when we fully knew him, whether he was swift or slow in his movements; it was enough for us that Abraham Lincoln was at the head of a great movement, and was in living and earnest sympathy with that movement, which, in the nature of things, must go on until slavery should be utterly and forever abolished in the United States.

When, therefore, it shall be asked what we have to do with the memory of Abraham Lincoln, or what Abraham Lincoln had to do with us, the answer is ready, full, and complete. Though he loved Caesar less than Rome, though the Union was more to him than our freedom or our future, under his wise and beneficent rule we saw ourselves gradually lifted from the depths of slavery to the heights of liberty and manhood; under his wise and beneficent rule, and by measures approved and vigorously pressed by him, we saw that the handwriting of ages, in the form of prejudice and proscription, was rapidly fading away from the face of our whole country; under his rule, and in due time, about as soon after all as the country could tolerate the strange spectacle, we saw our brave sons and brothers laying off the rags of bondage, and being clothed all over in the blue uniforms of the soldiers of the United States; under his rule we saw two hundred thousand of our dark and dusky people responding to the call of Abraham Lincoln, and with muskets on their shoulders, and eagles on their buttons, timing their high footsteps to liberty and union under the national flag; under his rule we saw the independence of the black republic of Haiti, the special object of slave-holding aversion and horror, fully recognized, and her minister, a colored gentleman, duly received here in the city of Washington; under his rule we saw the internal slave-trade, which so long disgraced the nation, abolished, and slavery abolished in the District of Columbia; under his rule we saw for the first time the law enforced against the foreign slave trade, and the first slave-trader hanged like any other pirate or murderer; under his rule, assisted by the greatest captain of our age, and his inspiration, we saw the Confederate States, based upon the idea that our race must be slaves, and slaves forever, battered to pieces and scattered to the four winds; under his rule, and in the fullness of time, we saw Abraham Lincoln, after giving the slave-holders three months' grace in which to save their hateful slave system, penning the immortal paper, which, though special in its language, was general in its principles and effect, making slavery forever impossible in the United States. Though we waited long, we saw all this and more.

Can any colored man, or any white man friendly to the freedom of all men, ever forget the night which followed the first day of January, 1863, when the world was to see if Abraham Lincoln would prove to be as good as his word? I shall never forget that memorable night, when in a distant city I waited and watched at a public meeting, with three thousand others not less anxious than myself, for the word of deliverance which we have heard read today. Nor shall I ever forget the outburst of joy and thanksgiving that rent the air when the lightning brought to us the emancipation proclamation. In that happy hour we forgot all delay, and forgot all tardiness, forgot that the President had bribed the rebels to lay down their arms by a promise to withhold the bolt which would smite the slave-system with destruction; and we were thenceforward willing to allow the President all the latitude of time, phraseology, and every honorable device that statesmanship might require for the achievement of a great and beneficent measure of liberty and progress.

Fellow-citizens, there is little necessity on this occasion to speak at length and critically of this great and good man, and of his high mission in the world. That ground has been fully occupied and completely covered both here and elsewhere. The whole field of fact and fancy has been gleaned and garnered. Any man can say things that are true of Abraham Lincoln, but no man can say anything that is new of Abraham Lincoln. His personal traits and public acts are better known to the American people than are those of any other man of his age. He was a mystery to no man who saw him and heard him. Though high in position, the humblest could approach him and feel at home in his presence. Though deep, he was transparent; though strong, he was gentle; though decided and pronounced in his convictions, he was tolerant towards those who differed from him, and patient under reproaches. Even those who only knew him through his public utterances obtained a tolerably clear idea of his character and personality. The image of the man went out with his words, and those who read them knew him.

I have said that President Lincoln was a white man, and shared the prejudices common to his countrymen towards the colored race. Looking back to his times and to the condition of his country, we are compelled to admit that this unfriendly feeling on his part may be safely set down as one element of his wonderful success in organizing the loyal American people for the tremendous conflict before them, and bringing them safely through that conflict. His great mission was to accomplish two things: first, to save his country from dismemberment and ruin; and, second, to free his country from the great crime of slavery. To do one or the other, or both, he must have the earnest sympathy and the powerful cooperation of his loyal fellow-countrymen. Without this primary and essential condition to success his efforts must have been vain and utterly fruitless. Had he put the abolition of slavery before the salvation of the Union, he would have inevitably driven from him a powerful class of the American people and rendered resistance to rebellion impossible. Viewed from the genuine abolition ground, Mr. Lincoln seemed tardy, cold, dull, and indifferent; but measuring him by the sentiment of his country, a sentiment he was bound as a statesman to consult, he was swift, zealous, radical, and determined.

Though Mr. Lincoln shared the prejudices of his white fellow-countrymen against the Negro, it is hardly necessary to say that in his heart of hearts he loathed and hated slavery. The man who could say, "Fondly do we hope, fervently do we pray, that this mighty scourge of war shall soon pass away, yet if God wills it continue till all the wealth piled by two hundred years of bondage shall have been wasted, and each drop of blood drawn by the lash shall have been paid for by one drawn by the sword, the judgments of the Lord are true and righteous altogether," gives all needed proof of his feeling on the subject of slavery. He was willing, while the South was loyal, that it should have its pound of flesh, because he thought that it was so nominated in the bond; but farther than this no earthly power could make him go.

Fellow-citizens, whatever else in this world may be partial, unjust, and uncertain, time, time! is impartial, just, and certain in its action. In the realm of mind, as well as in the realm of matter, it is a great worker, and often works wonders. The honest and comprehensive statesman, clearly discerning the needs of his country, and earnestly endeavoring to do his whole duty, though covered and blistered with reproaches, may safely leave his course to the silent judgment of time. Few great public men have ever been the victims of fiercer denunciation than Abraham Lincoln was during his administration. He was often wounded in the house of his friends. Reproaches came thick and fast upon him from within and from without, and from opposite quarters. He was assailed by Abolitionists; he was assailed by slave-holders; he was assailed by the men who were for peace at any price; he was assailed by those who were for a more vigorous prosecution of the war; he was assailed for not making the war an abolition war; and he was bitterly assailed for making the war an abolition war.

Upon his inauguration as President of the United States, an office, even when assumed under the most favorable condition, fitted to tax and strain the largest abilities, Abraham Lincoln was met by a tremendous crisis. He was called upon not merely to administer the Government, but to decide, in the face of terrible odds, the fate of the Republic.

A formidable rebellion rose in his path before him; the Union was already practically dissolved; his country was torn and rent asunder at the center. Hostile armies were already organized against the Republic, armed with the munitions of war which the Republic had provided for its own defense. The tremendous question for him to decide was whether his country should survive the crisis and flourish, or be dismembered and perish. His predecessor in office had already decided the question in favor of national dismemberment, by denying to it the right of self-defense and self-preservation—a right which belongs to the meanest insect.

Happily for the country, happily for you and for me, the judgment of James Buchanan, the patrician, was not the judgment of Abraham Lincoln, the plebeian. He brought his strong common sense, sharpened in the school of adversity, to bear upon the question. He did not hesitate, he did not doubt, he did not falter; but at once resolved that at whatever peril, at whatever cost, the union of the States should be preserved. A patriot himself, his faith was strong and unwavering in the patriotism of his countrymen. Timid men said before Mr. Lincoln's inauguration, that we have seen the last President of the United States. A voice in influential quarters said, "Let the Union slide." Some said that a Union maintained by the sword was worthless. Others said a rebellion of 8,000,000 cannot be suppressed; but in the midst of all this tumult and timidity, and against all this, Abraham Lincoln was clear in his duty, and had an oath in heaven. He calmly and bravely heard the voice of doubt and fear all around him; but he had an oath in heaven, and there was not power enough on earth to make this honest boatman, backwoodsman, and broad-handed splitter of rails evade or violate that sacred oath. He had not been schooled in the ethics of slavery; his plain life had favored his love of truth. He had not been taught that treason and perjury were the proof of honor and honesty. His moral training was against his saying one thing when he meant another. The trust that Abraham Lincoln had in himself and in the people was surprising and grand, but it was also enlightened and well founded. He knew the American people better than they knew themselves, and his truth was based upon this knowledge.

Fellow-citizens, the fourteenth day of April, 1865, of which this is the eleventh anniversary, is now and will ever remain a memorable day in the annals of this Republic. It was on the evening of this day, while a fierce and sanguinary rebellion was in the last stages of its desolating power; while its armies were broken and scattered before the invincible armies of Grant and Sherman; while a great nation, torn and rent by war, was already beginning to raise to the skies loud anthems of joy at the dawn of peace, it was startled, amazed, and overwhelmed by the crowning crime of slavery—the assassination of Abraham Lincoln. It was a new crime, a pure act of malice. No purpose of the rebellion was to be served by it. It was the simple gratification of a hell-black spirit of revenge. But it has done good after all. It has filled the country with a deeper abhorrence of slavery and a deeper love for the great liberator.

Had Abraham Lincoln died from any of the numerous ills to which flesh is heir; had he reached that good old age of which his vigorous constitution and his temperate habits gave promise; had he been permitted to see the end of his great work; had the solemn curtain of death come down but gradually—we should still have been smitten with a heavy grief, and treasured his name lovingly. But dying as he did die, by the red hand of violence, killed, assassinated, taken off without warning, not because of personal hate—for no man who knew Abraham Lincoln could hate him— but because of his fidelity to union and liberty, he is doubly dear to us, and his memory will be precious forever.

Fellow-citizens, I end, as I began, with congratulations. We have done a good work for our race today. In doing honor to the memory of our friend and liberator, we have been doing highest honors to ourselves and those who come after us; we have been fastening ourselves to a name and fame imperishable and immortal; we have also been defending ourselves from a blighting scandal. When now it shall be said that the colored man is soulless, that he has no appreciation of benefits or benefactors; when the foul reproach of ingratitude is hurled at us, and it is attempted to scourge us beyond the range of human brotherhood, we may calmly point to the monument we have this day erected to the memory of Abraham Lincoln.

SOURCE

Frederick Douglass, *Oration by Frederick Douglass, delivered on the occasion of the unveiling of the freedmen's monument in memory of Abraham Lincoln, in Lincoln Park, Washington, D. C., April 14th, 1876.: With an appendix.* African American Perspectives: Pamphlets from the Daniel A.P. Murray Collection, 1818–1907, Library of Congress, American Memory, http://memory.loc.gov/cgi-bin/query/r?ammem/murray:@field(DOCID+@ lit(lcrbmrpt0c12div0)) (accessed February 10, 2012).

FREDERICK DOUGLASS ON WOMEN

Throughout his life, Frederick Douglass strongly supported women's rights, and enjoyed close personal friendships with a number of women activists. As an abolitionist, he worked side by side with many female reformers including Lucretia Mott, Elizabeth Cady Stanton, and his long-time friend Susan B. Anthony. In July 1848 he attended the Seneca Falls Convention on women's rights, where he was the lone male delegate to speak out in favor of the suffrage resolution in the meeting's Declaration of Sentiments. Douglass angered many of his female friends when in 1870 he abandoned their cause in the fight to gain the right to vote for black men. Believing the Fifteenth Amendment would fail if women were included, he temporarily shoved their needs aside. Making amends in later years, he often lectured on behalf of women's rights. He attended a meeting of the National Council of Women on February 20, 1895, and was escorted into the hall by Susan B. Anthony. He died at home later that day while preparing to offer an address in support of woman suffrage.

It is also due to myself, to make some more emphatic mention than I have yet done, of the honorable women, who have not only assisted me, but who according to their opportunity and ability, have generously contributed to the abolition of slavery and the recognition of the equal manhood of the colored race. When the true history of the anti-slavery cause shall be written, woman will occupy a large space in its pages; for the cause of the slave has been peculiarly woman's cause. Her heart and her conscience have supplied in large degree its motive and mainspring. Her skill, industry, patience, and perseverance have been wonderfully manifest in every trial hour. Not only did her feet run on "willing errands," and her fingers do the work which in large degree supplied the sinews of war, but her deep moral convictions, and her tender human sensibilities, found convincing and persuasive expression by her pen and her voice. Foremost among these notable American women, who in point of clearness of vision, breadth of understanding, fullness of knowledge, catholicity of spirit, weight of character, and widespread influence, was Lucretia Mott of Philadelphia. Great as this woman was in speech, and persuasive as she was in her writings, she was incomparably greater in her presence. She spoke to the world through every line of her countenance. In her there was no lack of symmetry—no contradiction between her thought and act. Seated in an anti-slavery meeting, looking benignantly around upon the assembly, her silent presence made others eloquent, and carried the argument home to the heart of the audience.

The known approval of such a woman of any cause, went far to commend it.

I shall never forget the first time I ever saw and heard Lucretia Mott. It was in the town of Lynn, Massachusetts. It was not in a magnificent hall, where such as she seemed to belong, but in a little hall over Jonathan Buffum's store, the only place then open, even in that so-called radical anti-slavery town, for an anti-slavery meeting on Sunday. But in this day of small things, the smallness of the place was no matter of complaint or murmuring. It was a cause of rejoicing that any kind of place could be had for such a purpose. But Jonathan Buffum's courage was equal to this and more.

The speaker was attired in the usual Quaker dress, free from startling colors, plain, rich, elegant, and without superfluity—the very sight of her a sermon. In a few moments after she began to speak, I saw before me no more a woman, but a glorified presence, bearing a message of light and love from the Infinite to a benighted and strangely wandering world, straying away from the paths of truth and justice into the wilderness of pride and selfishness, where peace is lost and true happiness is sought in vain. I heard Mrs. Mott thus, when she was comparatively young. I have often heard her since, sometimes in the solemn temple, and, sometimes under the open sky, but whenever and wherever I have listened to her, my heart was always made better, and my spirit raised by her words; and in speaking thus for myself I am sure I am expressing the experience of thousands.

Kindred in spirit with Mrs. Mott was Lydia Maria Child. They both exerted an influence with a class of the American people which neither Garrison, Phillips, nor Gerrit Smith could reach. Sympathetic in her nature, it was easy for her to "remember those in bonds as bound with them;" and her "appeal for that class of Americans called Africans," issued, as it was, at an early stage in the anti-slavery conflict, was one of the most effective agencies in arousing attention to the cruelty and injustice of slavery. When with her husband, David Lee Child, she edited the *National Anti-Slavery Standard*, that paper was made attractive to a broad circle of readers, from the circumstance that each issue contained a "Letter from New York," written by her on some passing subject of the day, in which she always managed to infuse a spirit of brotherly love and good will, with an abhorrence of all that was unjust, selfish, and mean, and in this way won many hearts to anti-slavery who else would have remained cold and indifferent.

Of Sarah and Angelina Grimke I knew but little personally. These brave sisters from Charleston, South Carolina, had inherited slaves, but in their conversion from Episcopacy to Quakerism, in 1828, became convinced that they had no right to such inheritance. They emancipated their slaves and came North and entered at once upon pioneer work in advancing the education of woman, though they saw then in their course only their duty to the slave. They had "fought the good fight" before I came into the ranks, but by their unflinching testimony and unwavering courage, they had opened the way and made it possible, if not easy, for other women to follow their example.

It is memorable of them that their public advocacy of anti-slavery was made the occasion of the issuing of a papal bull in the form of a "Pastoral letter," by the Evangelical clergy of Boston, in which the churches and all God-fearing people were warned against their influence.

For solid, persistent, indefatigable work for the slave, Abby Kelley was without rival. In the "History of Woman Suffrage," just published by Mrs. Stanton, Miss Anthony, and Mrs. Goslin Gage, there is this fitting tribute to her: "Abby Kelley was the most untiring and most persecuted of all the women who labored throughout the anti-slavery struggle. She traveled up and down, alike in winter's cold and summer's heat, with scorn, ridicule, violence, and mobs accompanying her, suffering all kinds of persecutions, still speaking whenever and wherever she gained an audience,—in the open air, in school-house, barn, depot, church, or public hall, on weekday or Sunday, as she found opportunity." And, incredible as it will soon seem, if it does not appear so already, "for listening to her on Sunday many men and women were expelled from their churches."

When the abolitionists of Rhode Island were seeking to defeat the restricted constitution of the Dorr party, already referred to in this volume, Abby Kelley was more than once mobbed in the old Town Hall in the city of Providence, and pelted with bad eggs.

And what can be said of the gifted authoress of "Uncle Tom's Cabin," Harriet Beecher Stowe? Happy woman must she be, that to her was given the power, in such unstinted measure, to touch and move the popular heart! More than to reason or religion are we indebted to the influence which this wonderful delineation of American chattel slavery produced on the public mind.

Nor must I omit to name the daughter of the excellent Myron Holley, who in her youth and beauty espoused the cause of the slave; nor of Lucy Stone, and Antoinette Brown; for when the slave had few friends and advocates they were noble enough to speak their best word in his behalf.

Observing woman's agency, devotion, and efficiency in pleading the cause of the slave, gratitude for this high service early moved me to give favorable attention to the subject of what is called "Woman's Rights," and caused me to be denominated a woman's-rights-man. I am glad to say I have never been ashamed to be thus designated. Recognizing not sex, nor physical strength, but moral intelligence and the ability to discern right from wrong, good from evil, and the power to choose between them, as the true basis of Republican government, to which all are alike subject, and bound alike to obey, I was not long in reaching the conclusion that there was no foundation in reason or justice for woman's exclusion from the right of choice in the selection of the persons who should frame the laws, and thus shape the destiny of all the people, irrespective of sex.

In a conversation with Mrs. Elizabeth Cady Stanton, when she was yet a young lady, and an earnest abolitionist, she was at the pains of setting before me, in a very strong light, the wrong and injustice of this exclusion. I could not meet her arguments except with the shallow plea of "custom," "natural division of duties," "indelicacy of woman's taking part in politics," the common talk of "woman's sphere," and the like, all of which that able woman, who was then no less logical than now, brushed away by those arguments which she has so often and effectively used since, and which no man has yet successfully refuted. If intelligence is the only true and rational basis of government, it follows that that is the best government which draws its life and power from the largest sources of wisdom, energy, and goodness at its command. The force of this reasoning would be easily comprehended and readily assented to in any case involving the employment of physical strength. We should all see the folly and madness of attempting to accomplish with a part what could only be done with the united strength of the whole. Though this folly may be less apparent, it is just as real, when one half of the moral and intellectual power of the world is excluded from any voice or vote in civil government. In this denial of the right to participate in government, not merely the degradation of woman and the perpetuation of a great injustice happens, but the maiming and repudiation of one-half of the moral and intellectual power for the government of the world. Thus far all human governments have been failures, for none have secured, except in a partial degree, the ends for which governments are instituted.

War, slavery, injustice, and oppression, and the idea that might makes right, have been uppermost in all such governments; and the weak, for whose protection governments are ostensibly created, have had practically no rights which the strong have felt bound to respect. The slayers of thousands have been exalted into heroes, and the worship of mere physical force has been considered glorious. Nations have been and still are but armed camps, expending their wealth and strength and ingenuity in forging weapons of destruction against each other; and while it may not be contended that the introduction of the feminine element in government would entirely cure this tendency to exalt might over right, many reasons can be given to show that woman's influence would greatly tend to check and modify this barbarous and destructive tendency. At any rate, seeing that the male governments of the world have failed, it can do no harm to try the experiment of a government by man and woman united. But it is not my purpose to argue the question here, but simply to state, in a brief way, the ground of my espousal of the cause of woman's suffrage. I believed that the exclusion of my race from participation in government was not only a wrong, but a great mistake, because it took from that race motives for high thought and endeavor, and degraded them in the eyes of the world around them. Man derives a sense of his consequence in the world not merely subjectively, but objectively. If from the cradle through life the outside world brands a class as unfit for this or that work, the character of the class will come to resemble and conform to the character described. To find valuable qualities in our fellows, such qualities must be presumed and expected. I would give woman a vote, give her a motive to qualify herself to vote, precisely as I insisted upon giving the colored man the right to vote, in order that he should have the same motives for making himself a useful citizen as those in force in the case of other citizens. In a word, I have never yet been able to find one consideration, one argument, or suggestion in favor of man's right to participate in civil government which did not equally apply to the right of woman.

SOURCE

Frederick Douglass, *Life and Times of Frederick Douglass* (Boston: De Wolfe & Fiske, Co., 1892), 569–576. Documenting the American South, http://docsouth.unc.edu/neh/dougl92/menu.html (accessed April 22, 2012).

LESSONS OF THE HOUR

In the last decade of Frederick Douglass's life, he watched as the civil rights gains he and other African Americans struggled for slowly eroded. At the end of Reconstruction in 1877, conservative political forces began to gain control of the southern states. Soon after, the Supreme Court nullified the citizenship clause of the Fourteenth Amendment and declared the 1875 Civil Rights Act unconstitutional. As the twentieth century approached, many wondered what to do about the so-called "Negro problem." Delivered for the first time in Detroit in 1893, then before a large audience at Washington's Metropolitan AME Church in 1894, this address was published and widely distributed as a pamphlet. Although written in his mid-seventies, Douglass's reflection on the impending nadir of race relations remains one of his most powerful orations.

———————

Friends and Fellow Citizens:—

No man should come before an audience like the one by whose presence I am now honored, without a noble object and a fixed and earnest purpose. I think that, in whatever else I may be deficient, I have the qualifications indicated, to speak to you this evening. I am here to speak for, and to defend, so far as I can do so within the bounds of truth, a long-suffering people, and one just now subject to much misrepresentation and persecution. Charges are at this time preferred against them, more damaging and distressing than any which they have been called upon to meet since their emancipation.

I propose to give you a colored man's view of the unhappy relations at present existing between the white and colored people of the Southern

States of our union. We have had the Southern white man's view of the subject. It has been presented with abundant repetition and with startling emphasis, colored by his peculiar environments. We have also had the Northern white man's view tempered by time, distance from the scene, and his higher civilization.

This kind of evidence may be considered by some as all-sufficient upon which to found an intelligent judgment of the whole matter in controversy, and that therefore my testimony is not needed. But experience has taught us that it is sometimes wise and necessary to have more than the testimony of two witnesses to bring out the whole truth, especially is this the case where one of the witnesses has a powerful motive for concealing or distorting the facts in any given case. You must not, therefore, be surprised if my version of the Southern question shall widely differ from both the North and the South, and yet I shall fearlessly submit my testimony to the candid judgment of all who hear me. I shall do so in the firm belief that my testimony is true.

There is one thing, however, in which I think we shall all agree at the start. It is that the so-called, but mis-called, negro problem is one of the most important and urgent subjects that can now engage public attention. It is worthy of the most earnest consideration of every patriotic American citizen. Its solution involves the honor or dishonor, glory or shame, happiness or misery of the whole American people. It involves more. It touches deeply not only the good name and fame of the Republic, but its highest moral welfare and its permanent safety. Plainly enough the peril it involves is great, obvious and increasing, and should be removed without delay.

The presence of eight millions of people in any section of this country constituting an aggrieved class, smarting under terrible wrongs, denied the exercise of the commonest rights of humanity, and regarded by the ruling class in that section, as outside of the government, outside of the law, and outside of society; having nothing in common with the people with whom they live, the sport of mob violence and murder is not only a disgrace and scandal to that particular section but a menace to the peace and security of the people of the whole country.

I have waited patiently but anxiously to see the end of the epidemic of mob law and persecution and prevailing at the South. But the indications are not hopeful, great and terrible as have been its ravages in the past, it now seems to be increasing not only in the number of its victims, but in its frantic rage and savage extravagance. Lawless vengeance is beginning to be visited upon white men as well as black. Our newspapers are daily disfigured by its ghastly horrors.

Not a breeze comes to us now from the late rebellious States that is not tainted and freighted with negro blood. In its thirst for blood and its rage for vengeance, the mob has blindly, boldly and defiantly supplanted sheriffs, constables and police. It has assumed all the functions of civil authority. It laughs at legal processes, courts and juries, and its red-handed murderers range abroad unchecked and unchallenged by law or by public opinion. Prison walls and iron bars are no protection to the innocent or guilty, if the mob is in pursuit of negroes accused of crime. Jail doors are battered down in the presence of unresisting jailers, and the accused, awaiting trial in the courts of law are dragged out and hanged, shot, stabbed or burned to death as the blind and irresponsible mob may elect.

We claim to be a Christian country and a highly civilized nation, yet, I fearlessly affirm that there is nothing in the history of savages to surpass the blood chilling horrors and fiendish excesses perpetrated against the colored people by the so-called enlightened and Christian people of the South. It is commonly thought that only the lowest and most disgusting birds and beasts, such as buzzards, vultures and hyenas, will gloat over and prey dead bodies, but the Southern mob in its rage feeds its vengeance by shooting, stabbing and burning when their victims are dead.

Now the special charge against the negro by which this ferocity is justi-fied, and by which mob law is defended by good men North and South, is alleged to be assaults by negroes upon white women. This charge once fairly started, no matter by whom or in what manner, whether well or ill-founded, whether true or false, is certain to subject the accused to imme-diate death. It is nothing, that in the case there may be a mistake as to identity. It is nothing that the victim pleads "not guilty." It is nothing that he only asks for time to establish his innocence. It is nothing that the accused is of fair reputation and his accuser is of an abandoned character. It is nothing that the majesty of the law is defied and insulted; no time is allowed for defence or explanation; he is bound with cords, hurried off amid the frantic yells and cursing of the mob to the scaffold and under its shadow he is tortured till by pain or promises, he is made to think he can possibly gain time or save his life by confession, and then whether inno-cent or guilty, he is shot, hanged, stabbed or burned to death amid the wild shouts of the mob. When the will of the mob has been accomplished, when its thirst for blood has been quenched, when its victim is speechless, silent and dead; his mobocratic accusers and murderers of course have the ear of the world all to themselves, and the world generally approves their verdict.

Such then is the state of Southern civilization in its relation to the col-ored citizens of that section and though the picture is dark and terrible I venture to affirm that no man North or South can deny the essential truth of the picture.

In an open letter addressed to me by ex-Governor Chamberlain, of South Carolina, and published in the "Charleston News and Courier," a letter which I have but lately seen, in reply to an article of mine on the subject published in the "North American Review," the ex-Governor says: "Your denunciation of the South on this point is directed exclusively, or nearly so, against the application of lynch law for the punishment of one crime, or one sort of crime, the existence, I suppose, I might say the prevalence of this crime at the South is undeniable. But I read your (my) article in vain for any special denunciation of the crime itself. As you say your people are lynched, tortured and burned for assault on white women. As you value your own good fame and safety as a race, stamp out the infamous crime." He further says, the way to stop lynching is to stamp out the crime.

And now comes the sweet voice of a Northern woman, of Southern principles, in the same tone and the same accusation, the good Miss Frances Willard, of the W.C.T.U. She says in a letter now before me, "I pity the Southerner. The problem on their hands is immeasurable. The colored race," she says, "multiplies like the locusts of Egypt. The safety of woman, of childhood, of the home, is menaced in a thousand localities at this moment, so that men dare not go beyond the sight of their own roof tree." Such then is the crushing indictment drawn up against the Southern negroes, drawn up, too, by persons who are perhaps the fairest and most humane of the negro's accusers. But even they paint him as a moral monster ferociously invading the sacred rights of women and endangering the homes of the whites.

The crime they allege against the negro, is the most revolting which men can commit. It is a crime that awakens the intensest abhorrence and invites mankind to kill the criminal on sight.

I do not pretend that negroes are saints or angels. I do not deny that they are capable of committing the crime imputed to them, but I utterly deny that they are any more addicted to the commission of that crime than is true of any other variety of the human family. In entering upon my argument, I may be allowed to say, that I appear here this evening not as the defender of any man guilty of this atrocious crime, but as the defender of the colored people as a class.

In answer to the terrible indictment, thus read, and speaking for the colored people as a class, I, in their stead, here and now plead not guilty and shall submit my case with confidence of acquittal by good men and women North and South.

I can and will show that there are sound reasons for doubting and denying this horrible and hell-black charge of rape as the peculiar crime of the colored people of the South. My doubt and denial are based upon two fundamental and invincible grounds.

The first is, the well established and well tested character of the negro on the very point upon which he is now violently and persistently accused. The second ground for my doubt and denial is based upon what I know of the character and antecedents of the men and women who bring this charge against him. I undertake to say that the strength of this position will become more manifest as I proceed with my argument.

I rest my conclusion not merely upon general principles, but upon well known facts. I reject the charge brought against the negro as a class, because all through the late war, while the slave masters of the South were absent from their homes in the field of rebellion, with bullets in their pockets, treason in their hearts, broad blades in their blood stained hands, seeking the life of the nation, with the vile purpose of perpetuating the enslavement of the negro, their wives, their daughters, their sisters and their mothers were left in the absolute custody of these same negroes, and during all those long four years of terrible conflict, when the negro had every opportunity to commit the abominable crime now alleged against him, there was never a single instance of such crime reported or charged against him. He was never accused of assault, insult, or an attempt to commit an assault upon any white woman in the whole South. A fact like this, although negative, speaks volumes and ought to have some weight with the American people.

Again, I do not believe it and utterly deny it, because those who bring the charge do not, and dare not, give the negro a chance to be heard in his own defence. He is not allowed to explain any part of his alleged offense. He is not allowed to vindicate his own character or to criminate the character and motives of his accusers.

Again, I do not believe it, and deny it because if the evidence were deemed sufficient to bring the accused to the scaffold through the action of an impartial jury, there could be, and would be, no objection to having the alleged offender tried in conformity to due process of law.

Again, I do not believe it, and deny it, because the charge is not so much against the crime itself, as against the color of the man alleged to be guilty of it. Slavery itself, you will remember, was a system of legalized outrage upon the black women of the South, and no white man was ever shot, burned, or hanged for availing himself of all the power that slavery gave him at this point.

Upon these grounds then,—grounds which I believe to be solid and immovable—I dare here and now in the capital of the nation and in the presence of Congress to reject it, and ask you and all just men to reject this horrible charge so frequently made and construed against the negro as a class.

I know I shall be charged with apologizing for criminals. But, what I contend for, and what every honest man, black or white should contend for, is that when any man is accused of this or any other crime, of whatever name, nature, or extent, he shall have the benefit of a legal investigation; that he shall be confronted by his accusers; and that he shall through proper counsel, be able to question his accusers in open court and in open daylight so that his guilt or his innocence may be duly proved and established.

I come now to the question of negro suffrage. It has come to be fashionable of late to ascribe much of the trouble at the South to ignorant negro suffrage. The great measure according suffrage to the negro recommended by General Grant and adopted by the loyal nation is now denounced as a blunder and a failure. They would, therefore, in some way abridge and limit this right by imposing upon it an educational or some other qualification. Among those who take this view are Mr. John J. Ingalls, and Mr. John M. Langston. They are both eloquent, both able, and both wrong.

I, therefore, cannot follow these gentlemen in their proposition to limit suffrage to the educated alone. I would not make suffrage more exclusive, but more inclusive. I would not have it embrace merely the elite, but would include the lowly. I would not only include the men, I would gladly include the women, and make our government in reality as in name a government of the people and of the whole people.

Much thoughtless speech is heard about the ignorance of the negro in the South. But plainly enough it is not the ignorance of the negro, but the malevolence of his accusers, which is the real cause of Southern disorder. The illiteracy of the negro has no part or lot in the disturbances there. They who contend for disfranchisement on this ground know, and know very well, that there is no truth whatever in their contention. To make out their case they must show that some oppressive and hurtful measure has been imposed upon the country by negro voters. But they cannot show any such thing.

The proposition to disfranchise the colored voter of the South in order to solve the race problem I hereby denounce as a mean and cowardly proposition, utterly unworthy of an honest, truthful and grateful nation. Do not ask me what will be the final result of the so-called negro problem. I cannot tell you. I have sometimes thought that the American people are too great to be small, too just and magnanimous to oppress the weak, too brave to yield up the right to the strong, and too grateful for public services ever to forget them or fail to reward them. I have fondly hoped that this estimate of American character would soon cease to be contradicted or put in doubt. But the favor with which this cowardly proposition of disfranchisement has been received by public men, white and black, by Republicans as well as Democrats, has shaken my faith in the nobility of the nation. I hope and trust all will come out right in the end, but the immediate future looks dark and troubled. I cannot shut my eyes to the ugly facts before me.

Strange things have happened of late and are still happening. Some of these tend to dim the lustre of the American name, and chill the hopes once entertained for the cause of American liberty. He is a wiser man than I am, who can tell how low the moral sentiment of this republic may yet fall. When the moral sense of a nation begins to decline and the wheel of progress to roll backward, there is no telling how low the one will fall or where the other may stop. The downward tendency already manifest has swept away some of the most important safeguards. The Supreme Court has surrendered. State sovereignty is restored. It has destroyed the civil rights Bill, and converted the Republican party into a party of money rather than a party of morals, a party of things rather than a party of humanity and justice. We may well ask what next?

The pit of hell is said to be bottomless. Principles which we all thought to have been firmly and permanently settled by the late war, have been boldly assaulted and overthrown by the defeated party. Rebel rule is now nearly complete in many States and it is gradually capturing the nation's Congress. The cause lost in the war, is the cause regained in peace, and the cause gained in war, is the cause lost in peace.

But I come now to another proposition held up just now as a solution of the race problem, and this I consider equally unworthy with the one just disposed of. The two belong to the same low-bred family of ideas.

This proposition is to colonize the colored people of America in Africa, or somewhere else. Happily this scheme will be defeated, both by its impolicy and its impracticability. It is all nonsense to talk about the removal of eight millions of the American people from their homes in America to Africa. The expense and hardships to say nothing of the cruelty of such a measure, would make success to such a measure impossible. The American people are wicked, but they are not fools, they will hardly be disposed to incur the expense, to say nothing of the injustice which this measure demands. Nevertheless, this colonizing scheme, unworthy as it is, of American statesmanship and American honor, and though full of mischief to the colored people, seems to have a strong hold on the public mind and at times has shown much life and vigor.

The bad thing about it is that it has now begun to be advocated by colored men of acknowledged ability and learning, and every little while some white statesman becomes its advocate. Those gentlemen will doubtless have their opinion of me; I certainly have mine of them. My opinion of them is that if they are sensible, they are insincere, and if they are sincere they are not sensible. They know, or they ought to know, that it would take more money than the cost of the late war, to transport even one-half of the colored people of the United States to Africa. Whether intentionally or not they are, as I think, simply trifling with an afflicted people. They urge them to look for relief, where they ought to know that relief is impossible. The only excuse they can make is that there is no hope for the negro here and that the colored people in America owe something to Africa.

This last sentimental idea makes colonization very fascinating to dreamers of both colors. But there is really for it no foundation.

They tell us that we owe something to our native land. But when the fact is brought to view, which should never be forgotten, that a man can only have one native land, and that is the land in which he was born, the bottom falls entirely out of this sentimental argument.

But the worse thing, perhaps, about this colonization nonsense is, that it tends to throw over the negro a mantle of despair. It leads him to doubt the possibility of his progress as an American citizen. It also encourages popular prejudice with the hope that by persecution or persuasion the negro can finally be driven from his natural home, while in the nature of the case, he must stay here, and will stay here and cannot well get away.

Colonization is no solution of the race problem.

When these false reasoners assert that the condition of the emancipated is wretched and deplorable, they tell in part the truth, and I agree with them. I even concur with them that the negro is in some respects, and in some localities, in a worse condition to-day than in the time of slavery, but I part with these gentlemen when they ascribe this condition to emancipation.

To my mind, the blame for this condition does not rest upon emancipation, but upon slavery. It is not the result of emancipation, but the defeat of emancipation. It is not the work of the spirit of liberty, but the work of the spirit of bondage, and of the determination of slavery to perpetuate itself, if not under one form, then under another. It is due to the folly of endeavoring to retain the new wine of liberty in the old bottles of slavery. I concede the evil but deny the alleged cause.

I now come to the so-called, but mis-called "Negro Problem," as a characterization of the relations existing in the Southern States.

The South has always known how to have a dog hanged by giving him a bad name. When it prefixed "negro" to the national problem, it knew that the device would awaken and increase a deep-seated prejudice at once, and that it would repel fair and candid investigation. As it stands, it implies that the negro is the cause of whatever trouble there is in the South. In old slave times, when a little white child lost his temper, he was given a little whip and told to go and whip "Jim" or "Sal" and thus regained his temper. The same is true, to-day on a larger scale.

I repeat, and my contention is, that this negro problem formula lays the fault at the door of the negro, and removes it from the door of the white man, shields the guilty, and blames the innocent. Makes the negro responsible and not the nation.

Now the real problem is, and ought to be regarded by the American people, a great national problem. It involves the question, whether, after all, with our Declaration of Independence, with our glorious free constitution, whether with our sublime Christianity, there is enough of national virtue in this great nation to solve this problem, in accordance with wisdom and justice.

The marvel is that this old trick of misnaming things, so often played by Southern politicians, should have worked so well for the bad cause in which it is now employed,—for the Northern people have fallen in with it. It is still more surprising that the colored press of the country, and some of the colored orators of the country, insist upon calling it a "negro problem," or a Race problem, for by it they mean the negro Race. Now—there is nothing the matter with the negro. He is all right. Learned or ignorant, he is all right. He is neither a Lyncher, a Mobocrat, or an Anarchist. He is now, what he has ever been, a loyal, law-abiding, hard working, and peaceable man; so much so, that men have thought him cowardly and spiritless. They say that any other people would have found some violent way in which to resent their wrongs. If this problem depended upon his character and conduct, there would be no problem to solve; there would be no menace to the peace and good order of Southern society. He makes no unlawful fight between labor and capital. That problem which often makes the American people thoughtful, is not of his bringing—though he may some day be compelled to talk, and on this tremendous problem.

He has as little to do with the cause of Southern trouble as he has with its cure. There is no reason, therefore, in the world, why he should give a name to this problem, and this lie, like all other lies, must eventually come to naught. A lie is worth nothing when it has lost its ability to deceive, and if it at all in my power, this lie shall lose its power to deceive.

But call this problem what you may, or will, the all important question is: How can it be solved? How can the peace and tranquility of the South, and of the country, be secured and established?

I will tell you how it can *not* be solved. It cannot be solved by keeping the negro poor, degraded, ignorant, and half-starved, as I have shown is now being done in the Southern States.

It cannot be solved by keeping the wages of the laborer back by fraud, as is now being done by the landlords of the South.

It cannot be done by ballot-box stuffing, by falsifying election returns, or by confusing the negro voter by cunning devices.

It cannot be done by repealing all federal laws enacted to secure honest elections.

It can, however, be done, and very easily done, for where there's a will, there's a way!

Let the white people of the North and South conquer their prejudices.

Let the great Northern press and pulpit proclaim the gospel of truth and justice against war now being made upon the negro.

Let the American people cultivate kindness and humanity.

Let the South abandon the system of "mortgage" labor, and cease to make the negro a pauper, by paying him scrip for his labor.

Let them give up the idea that they can be free, while making the negro a slave.

Let them give up the idea that to degrade the colored man, is to elevate the white man.

Let them cease putting new wine into old bottles, and mending old garments with new cloth.

They are not required to do much. They are only required to undo the evil that they have done, in order to solve this problem.

In old times when it was asked, "How can we abolish slavery?" the answer was "Quit stealing."

The same is the solution of the Race problem to-day. The whole thing can be done by simply no longer violating the amendments of the Constitution of the United States, and no longer evading the claims of justice. If this were done, there would be no negro problem to vex the South, or to vex the nation.

Apply these sublime and glorious truths to the situation now before you. Put away your race prejudice. Banish the idea that one class must rule over another. Recognize the fact that the rights of the humblest citizen are as worthy of protection as are those of the highest, and your problem will be solved; and, whatever may be in store for it in the future, whether prosperity, or adversity; whether it shall have foes without, or foes within, whether there shall be peace, or war; based upon the eternal principles of truth, justice and humanity, and with no class having any cause of complaint or grievance, your Republic will stand and flourish forever.

SOURCE

Frederick Douglass, *Lessons of the Hour* (Baltimore: Press of Thomas & Evans, 1894).

NOTES

INTRODUCTION

1. "Death of Fred Douglass," *New York Times*, February 21, 1895.
2. Raymond W. Smock, *Booker T. Washington: Black Leadership in the Age of Jim Crow* (Chicago: Ivan R. Dee, 2009), 104–105.
3. In the first four decades of the twentieth century, the best scholarship on Douglass appeared in Carter G. Woodson's *Journal of Negro History*. From the journal's inception in 1916 through 1945, Douglass is referenced 184 times in published articles and reviews.
4. Robert Allen Rutland, ed., *Clio's Favorites: Leading Historians of the United States, 1945–2000* (Columbia: University of Missouri Press, 2000), 57.
5. John Stauffer, foreword, in *In the Words of Frederick Douglass: Quotations from Liberty's Champion*, eds. John R. McKivigan and Heather L. Kaufman (Ithaca, N.Y.: Cornell University Press, 2012), xi.
6. Gregory Stephens, *On Racial Frontiers: The New Culture of Frederick Douglass, Ralph Ellison, and Bob Marley* (Cambridge: Cambridge University Press, 1999), 54–55.
7. Smock, *Washington*, 6.
8. "The Top 100," *Atlantic Monthly*, December 2006: 61–78.
9. Barack Obama, *The Audacity of Hope: Thoughts on Reclaiming the American Dream* (New York: Random House, 2006), 97.
10. See McKivigan and Kaufman, *In the Words of Frederick Douglass*.
11. L. Diane Barnes, "Frederick Douglass: From Slavery to Freedom and Beyond," Oxford African American Studies Center, http://www.oxfordaasc.com/public/features/archive/0107/index.jsp (accessed February 4, 2012).

CHAPTER 1

1. Dickson J. Preston, *Young Frederick Douglass: The Maryland Years* (Baltimore, Md.: Johns Hopkins University Press, 1980), 31–34.
2. Frederick Douglass, *Narrative of the Life of Frederick Douglass* (1845; New Haven, Conn.: Yale University Press, 2001), 13.
3. Ibid., 14.
4. Preston, *Young Frederick Douglass*, 219.

5. John Blassingame et al., eds., *The Frederick Douglass Papers, Series Two: Autobiographical Writings, Volume 2: My Bondage and My Freedom* (New Haven, Conn.: Yale University Press, 2003), 28–29; Preston, *Young Frederick Douglass*, 37–39.

6. Blassingame, *Bondage and Freedom*, 30.

7. Douglass, *Narrative*, 15–19.

8. Ibid., 29.

9. Blassingame, *Bondage and Freedom*, 80.

10. Ibid., 83.

11. Preston, *Young Frederick Douglass*, 87–91; Douglass, *Narrative*, 103–104n.

12. Blassingame, *Bondage and Freedom*, 91.

13. Preston, *Young Frederick Douglass*, 103–105.

14. Paraphrase of Luke 12:47, Douglass, *Narrative*, 44.

15. Douglass, *Narrative*, 43, 45 (quotation).

16. Ibid., 113–114n. In his writings, Douglass mistakenly listed 1833 as the year he spent with Covey.

17. Ibid., 46–47; Preston, *Young Frederick Douglass*, 118–119.

18. Douglass, *Narrative*, 54; Nathan Irvin Huggins, *Slave and Citizen: The Life of Frederick Douglass* (Boston: Little, Brown and Company, 1980), 9.

19. Blassingame, *Bondage and Freedom*, 155.

20. Douglass, *Narrative*, 60.

21. Blassingame, *Bondage and Freedom*, 159–169; William S. McFeely, *Frederick Douglass* (New York: W.W. Norton, 1991), 51–55.

22. Douglass, *Narrative*, 98n.

23. Ibid., 69.

24. Preston, *Young Frederick Douglass*, 146.

25. Blassingame, *Bondage and Freedom*, 182.

26. Ibid., 188–189; Preston, *Young Frederick Douglass*, 152–153.

27. Blassingame, *Bondage and Freedom*, 190.

CHAPTER 2

1. Frederick Douglass, *Narrative of the Life of Frederick Douglass* (1845; New Haven, Conn.: Yale University Press, 2001), 102; William S. McFeely, *Frederick Douglass* (New York: W.W. Norton, 1991), 70.

2. Frederick Douglass, *Life and Times of Frederick Douglass* (1892; New York: Collier Books, 1962), 203–204 (quotation); John Blassingame et al., eds., *The Frederick Douglass Papers, Series Two: Autobiographical Writings, Volume 2: My Bondage and My Freedom* (New Haven, Conn.: Yale University Press, 2003), 194–195.

3. Graham Russell Gao Hodges, *David Ruggles: A Radical Black Abolitionist and the Underground Railroad in New York City* (Chapel Hill: University of North Carolina Press, 2010), 1–2.

4. Blassingame, *Bondage and Freedom*, 196–197; Douglass, *Narrative*, 122; Kathryn Grover, *The Fugitive's Gibraltar: Escaping Slaves and Abolitionism in New Bedford, Massachusetts* (Amherst, Mass.: University of Massachusetts Press, 2001), 144–145.

5. Douglass, *Life and Times*, 207.

6. Blassingame, *Bondage and Freedom*, 199.

7. Douglass, *Life and Times*, 211.

8. Grover, *Fugitive's Gibraltar*, 123–124; Blassingame, *Bondage and Freedom*, 204 (quotation).

9. "Great Anti-Colonization Meeting in New Bedford," *Liberator*, March 29, 1839.

10. Douglass, *Life and Times*, 214.

11. Douglass, *Narrative*, 81.

12. Blassingame, *Bondage and Freedom*, 202.

13. Ibid.
14. Ibid., 203.
15. Ibid., 374; David W. Blight, *Frederick Douglass' Civil War: Keeping Faith in Jubilee* (Baton Rouge: Louisiana State University Press, 1989), 6–7.
16. William L. Andrews, "Frederick Douglass, Preacher," *American Literature* 54 (1982): 592–597.
17. Grover, *Fugitive's Gibraltar*, 148–149.
18. "Great Anti-Colonization Meeting in New Bedford," *Liberator*, March 29, 1839; Grover, *Fugitive's Gibraltar*, 134, 139–141.
19. Douglass, *Life and Times*, 467–468; Blassingame, *Bondage and Freedom*, 205 (quotation).
20. Rosetta Douglass Sprague, "Anna Murray Douglass—My Mother as I Recall Her," *Journal of Negro History* 8 (1923): 95; McFeely, *Frederick Douglass*, 82.
21. McFeely, *Frederick Douglass*, 84.
22. Douglass, *Life and Times*, 215; Blassingame, *Bondage and Freedom*, 375.
23. John R. McKivigan, *The War against Proslavery Religion: Abolitionism and the Northern Churches, 1830–1865* (Ithaca, N.Y.: Cornell University Press, 1984), 66–69.
24. "Antislavery Convention," *Liberator*, August 20, 1841.
25. Blassingame, *Bondage and Freedom*, 203.
26. "Antislavery Convention," *Liberator*, August 20, 1841.
27. Douglass, *Life and Times*, 215.
28. Ibid., 216; "Antislavery Convention," *Liberator*, August 20, 1841.

Chapter 3

1. "Meeting of Massachusetts A.S. Society," *Liberator*, August 27, 1841; John Blassingame et al., eds., *The Frederick Douglass Papers, Series Two: Autobiographical Writings, Volume 2: My Bondage and My Freedom* (New Haven, Conn.: Yale University Press, 2003), 207 (quotation).
2. For the most recent biography of Garrison see Henry Mayer, *All on Fire: William Lloyd Garrison and the Abolition of Slavery* (New York: St. Martin's Press, 1998).
3. Blassingame, *Bondage and Freedom*, 207.
4. John Blassingame et al., eds., *The Frederick Douglass Papers, Series One: Speeches, Debates, and Interviews*, 5 vols. (New Haven, Conn.: Yale University Press, 1979–1991), 1: 5 (hereafter *FDP*).
5. "American Prejudice and Southern Religion," in Blassingame, *FDP*, 1: 9–13.
6. "To the Public," *Liberator*, November 12, 1841.
7. Blassingame, *Bondage and Freedom*, 230.
8. Ibid., 230; James Oliver Horton and Lois E. Horton, *Black Bostonians: Family Life and Community Struggle in the Antebellum North* (New York: Holmes & Meier, 1979), 69–70.
9. John R. McKivigan et al., eds., *The Frederick Douglass Papers, Series Three: Correspondence, Volume 1, 1842–1852* (New Haven, Conn.: Yale University Press, 2009), 125–126n; William S. McFeely, *Frederick Douglass* (New York: W.W. Norton, 1991), 103.
10. Rosetta Douglass Sprague, "Anna Murray Douglass—My Mother as I Recall Her," *Journal of Negro History* 8 (1923): 95.
11. Douglass to Maria Weston Chapman, September 10, 1843, McKivigan, *Correspondence*, 13.
12. McKivigan, *Correspondence*, 17n.
13. "From the Congregational Observer," *Liberator*, June 17, 1842.
14. Blassingame, *FDP*, 1: lxxxix–xc; "Disgraceful Scenes in New-Bedford and Nantucket," *Liberator*, August 19, 1842.
15. McKivigan, *Correspondence*, 6.
16. Douglass to William Lloyd Garrison, November 8, 1842, McKivigan, *Correspondence*, 5.

17. McKivigan, *Correspondence*, 6–7; "Great Mass Meeting of Colored Citizens of Boston," *Liberator*, December 23, 1842; Horton and Horton, *Black Bostonians*, 99; Blassingame, *FDP*, 1: 230.
18. Unfortunately, several years later Latimer apparently turned to a life of crime. In 1854 Latimer was arrested and confessed to picking the pocket of a wealthy man in Boston. Douglass reported the incident in his paper, noting, "The prisoner has for a longtime borne a bad reputation." "George Latimer," *Frederick Douglass' Paper*, February 24, 1854.
19. Douglass to Chapman, September 10, 1843, McKivigan, *Correspondence*, 12.
20. Frederick Douglass, *Life and Times of Frederick Douglass* (1892; New York: Collier Books, 1962), 228.
21. "Letter from Charles Lenox Remond," *Liberator*, September 1, 1843.
22. "The Colored Convention," *Liberator*, September 8, 1843.
23. Waldo E. Martin, *The Mind of Frederick Douglass* (Chapel Hill: University of North Carolina Press, 1984), 56–57; Howard H. Bell, "National Negro Conventions of the Middle 1840's: Moral Suasion vs. Political Action," *Journal of Negro History* 42 (1957): 253.
24. "Minutes of the National Convention of Colored Citizens: Held at Buffalo, 16–19 August, 1843," in *Minutes of the Proceedings of the National Negro Conventions, 1830–1864*, ed. Howard Holman Bell (New York: Arno Press, 1969), 11. By the time of the next National Negro Convention in October 1847, Douglass was well underway with plans to begin publishing his own newspaper.
25. Douglass continued to espouse the Garrisonian position on the U.S. Constitution as a proslavery document even after initiating the *North Star*. See his editorial comment in *North Star*, March 9, 1849. On the conflict between Douglass and other prominent black reformers, see Joel Schor, "The Rivalry Between Frederick Douglass and Henry Highland Garnet," *Journal of Negro History* 64 (1979): 30–38.
26. Douglass, *Life and Times*, 230.
27. "Letter from William A. White," *Liberator*, October 13, 1843.
28. Douglass, *Life and Times*, 230–231.
29. A. Brook to Maria Weston Chapman, October 5, 1843, quoted in McFeely, *Frederick Douglass*, 112.
30. McFeely, *Frederick Douglass*, 113–114.
31. Douglass to Wendell Phillips, February 10, 1844, McKivigan, *Correspondence*, 16.
32. Douglass, *Life and Times*, 218.
33. Charles T. Davis and Henry Louis Gates, Jr., eds., *The Slave's Narrative* (Oxford: Oxford University Press, 1985), xvi.
34. James Matlack, "The Autobiographies of Frederick Douglass," *Phylon* 40 (1979): 17–18.
35. Stephen Butterfield, *Black Autobiography in America* (Amherst: University of Massachusetts Press, 1974), 1–2.
36. Blassingame, *Bondage and Freedom*, 209.

CHAPTER 4

1. R.J.M. Blackett, *Building an Antislavery Wall: Black Americans in the Atlantic Movement, 1830–1860* (Baton Rouge: Louisiana State University Press, 1983), 17–18, 79–80.
2. John Blassingame et al. eds., *The Frederick Douglass Papers, Series Two: Autobiographical Writings, Volume 2: My Bondage and My Freedom* (New Haven, Conn.: Yale University Press, 2003), 210.
3. Alasdair Pettinger, "Send Back the Money: Douglass and the Free Church of Scotland," in *Liberating Sojourn: Frederick Douglass and Transatlantic Reform*, eds. Alan J. Rice and Martin Crawford (Athens: University of Georgia Press, 1999), 46–47.
4. Blassingame, *Bondage and Freedom*, 211.

5. "Frederick Douglass," *Liberator*, October 3, 1845.
6. John Blassingame et al., eds., *The Frederick Douglass Papers, Series One: Speeches, Debates, and Interviews*, 5 vols. (New Haven, Conn.: Yale University Press, 1979–1991), 1: 64–65 (hereafter *FDP*).
7. Ibid., 1: xcvi.
8. Frederick Douglass, *Life and Times of Frederick Douglass* (1892; New York: Collier Books, 1962), 560.
9. William S. McFeely, *Frederick Douglass* (New York: W.W. Norton, 1991), 120–121.
10. Alan J. Rice and Martin Crawford, "Triumphant Exile: Frederick Douglass in Britain, 1845–1847," in Rice and Crawford, *Liberating Sojourn*, 6–8; Blackett, *Building an Antislavery Wall*, 79–80.
11. John R. McKivigan et al., eds., *The Frederick Douglass Papers, Series Three: Correspondence, Volume 1, 1842–1852* (New Haven, Conn.: Yale University Press, 2009), 78–79. In his letters, Douglass often referred to Isabel Jennings as "My Dear Isa."
12. Webb to Chapman, quoted in Rice and Crawford, "Triumphant Exile," 8.
13. Rice and Crawford, "Triumphant Exile," 7–8.
14. Blackett, *Building an Antislavery Wall*, 80–82.
15. Pettinger, "Send Back the Money," 31–36.
16. Ibid., 32–34; Blassingame, *FDP*, 1: 118 (quotation), 179–180.
17. Blassingame, *FDP*, 1: 118; Blackett, *Building an Antislavery Wall*, 85; Blassingame, *Bondage and Freedom*, 222–223.
18. Blassingame, *FDP*, 1: 316–317.
19. Blackett, *Building an Antislavery Wall*, 104.
20. Blassingame, *FDP*, 1: 340.
21. C. Duncan Rice, *The Scots Abolitionists, 1833–1861* (Baton Rouge: Louisiana State University Press, 1981), 133.
22. Douglass to the editor, *Protestant Journal*, reprinted in *Liberator*, August 28, 1846.
23. In U.S. dollars, $711.66 (contemporary dollars).
24. Wright to Douglass, December 12, 1846, McKivigan, *Correspondence*, 181.
25. Webb to Douglass, quoted in Blackett, *Building an Antislavery Wall*, 112–113.
26. Douglass to Wright, December 22, 1846, McKivigan, *Correspondence*, 184.
27. Blassingame, *Bondage and Freedom*, 381; Douglass, *Life and Times*, 255–258.
28. Blackett, *Building an Antislavery Wall*, 111–113.
29. "Minutes of the National Convention of Colored Citizens: Held at Buffalo, 16–19 August, 1843," in *Minutes of the Proceedings of the National Negro Conventions, 1830–1864*, ed. Howard Holman Bell (New York: Arno Press, 1969), 11.
30. Douglass to Jonathan D. Carr, November 1, 1847, McKivigan, *Correspondence*, 266–268.
31. McKivigan, *Correspondence*, 268.
32. McKivigan, *Correspondence*, 262–263; Maria Diedrich, *Love Across Color Lines: Ottilie Assing and Frederick Douglass* (New York: Hill & Wang, 1999), 179–182.
33. Douglass to John Thadeus Delane, April 3, 1847, McKivigan, *Correspondence*, 201–202; Douglass to William Lloyd Garrison, April 21, 1847, McKivigan, *Correspondence*, 203–205; Blassingame, *Bondage and Freedom*, 224–225, 392–393.
34. Douglass to John Thadeus Delane, April 3, 1847, McKivigan, *Correspondence*, 201–202.
35. Samuel Cunard, quoted in McKivigan, *Correspondence*, 202; Blassingame, *Bondage and Freedom*, 225.

CHAPTER 5

1. John Blassingame et al. eds., *The Frederick Douglass Papers, Series One: Speeches, Debates, and Interviews*, 5 vols. (New Haven, Conn.: Yale University Press, 1979–1991), 2: 19–20, 51 (hereafter *FDP*); "From the London Morning Advertiser," *Liberator*, April 30, 1847.

2. Douglass to William and Robert Smeal, April 29, 1847, John R. McKivigan et al., eds., *The Frederick Douglass Papers, Series Three: Correspondence, Volume 1, 1842–1852* (New Haven, Conn.: Yale University Press, 2009), 206–207.

3. Douglass to Anna Richardson, April 29, 1847, McKivigan, *Correspondence*, 208–210.

4. Douglass to William and Robert Smeal, April 29, 1847, McKivigan, *Correspondence*, 206–207.

5. "To the Editors of the Leeds Mercury," *Liberator*, May 14, 1847.

6. Douglass to Anna Richardson, April 29, 1847, McKivigan, *Correspondence*, 209.

7. Henry Mayer, *All on Fire: William Lloyd Garrison and the Abolition of Slavery* (New York: St. Martin's Press, 1998), 373–374.

8. "British Philanthropy," *Liberator*, June 26, 1847; "The Press for Douglass," *Liberator*, July 9, 1847 (quotation).

9. "From the *Chronotype*," *Liberator*, July 9, 1847; "Frederick Douglass and his Printing Press," *Liberator*, July 16, 1847 (quotation).

10. Douglass to Garrison, July 18, 1847, McKivigan, *Correspondence*, 222–223.

11. Douglass to Sydney H. Gay, August 8, 1847, McKivigan, *Correspondence*, 224 (first quotation); Douglass to Readers of the *Ram's Horn*, August 13 or 14, 1847, McKivigan, *Correspondence*, 229 (second quotation).

12. Douglass to Gay, August 13, 1847, McKivigan, *Correspondence*, 227–228.

13. Douglass to Gay, September 26, 1847, McKivigan, *Correspondence*, 252.

14. Douglass to Jonathan D. Carr, November 1, 1847, McKivigan, *Correspondence*, 267.

15. Douglass to Post, October 28, 1847, McKivigan, *Correspondence*, 266.

16. "The North Star," *North Star*, December 3, 1847.

17. Nancy A. Hewitt, *Women's Activism and Social Change: Rochester, New York, 1822–1872* (Ithaca, N.Y.: Cornell University Press, 1984), 116–117, 142–143.

18. May to Douglass, December 9, 1847, McKivigan, *Correspondence*, 278–279; Donald Yacavone, *Samuel Joseph May and the Dilemmas of the Liberal Persuasion, 1797–1871* (Philadelphia: Temple University Press, 1991), 159.

19. John R. McKivigan, "The Frederick Douglass—Gerrit Smith Friendship and Political Abolitionism in the 1850s," in *Frederick Douglass: New Literary and Historical Essays*, ed. Eric J. Sundquist (New York: Cambridge University Press, 1990), 205.

20. Smith to Douglass, December 8, 1847, McKivigan, *Correspondence*, 276–277.

21. McKivigan, "Frederick Douglass—Gerrit Smith Friendship," 209–211; John Stauffer, *The Black Hearts of Men: Radical Abolitionists and the Transformation of Race* (Cambridge, Mass.: Harvard University Press, 2001), 127–129.

22. Nathan Irvin Huggins, *Slave and Citizen: The Life of Frederick Douglass* (Boston: Little, Brown and Company, 1980), 50.

23. See Nikki Taylor, *Frontiers of Freedom: Cincinnati's Black Community, 1802–1868* (Athens: Ohio University Press, 2005).

24. "The Colored Convention," *Liberator*, September 8, 1843; Waldo E. Martin, *The Mind of Frederick Douglass* (Chapel Hill: University of North Carolina Press, 1984), 56–57; Howard H. Bell, "National Negro Conventions of the Middle 1840's: Moral Suasion vs. Political Action," *Journal of Negro History* 42 (1957): 253.

25. "The Colored Convention," *North Star*, 3 Dec. 1847.

26. Douglass attended all six National Negro Conventions held 1843, 1847, 1848, 1853, 1855, and 1864. Martin, *Mind of Frederick Douglass*, 56–57.

27. "Proceedings of the National Convention of Colored People and Their Friends, 6–9 October 1847," in *Minutes of the Proceedings of the National Negro Conventions, 1830–1864*, ed. Howard Holman Bell (New York: Arno Press, 1969), 6–7.
28. "Our Paper and Its Prospects," *North Star*, December 3, 1847.
29. Baron George Gordon Byron, *Childe Harold* (London: Oxford University Press, 1885), 102.
30. Criticism of Douglass's position on assimilation is discussed in William S. McFeely, "Visible Man: Frederick Douglass for the 1990s," in *Liberating Sojourn: Frederick Douglass and Transatlantic Reform*, eds. Alan J. Rice and Martin Crawford (Athens: University of Georgia Press, 1999), 15–27.
31. "What are the Colored People Doing for Themselves?" *North Star*, July 14, 1848.
32. "Colored National Convention at Cleveland," *North Star*, September 15, 1848.
33. "An Address to the Colored People of the United States," *North Star*, September 22, 1848; "Report of the Proceedings of the Colored National Convention, Held at Cleveland, Ohio, 6 September 1848," in Bell, *Proceedings*, 17–20.
34. Ruggles to Douglass, January 1, 1848, McKivigan, *Correspondence*, 281.
35. Wagoner to Douglass, January 27, 1848, McKivigan, *Correspondence*, 286.
36. McKivigan, *Correspondence*, 288.
37. "Colored Newspapers," *North Star*, January 7, 1848; Whipper to Douglass, January 23, 1848, McKivigan, *Correspondence*, 284–285 (quotations).
38. William McFeely, *Frederick Douglass* (New York: W.W. Norton, 1991), 154–155; Rosetta Douglass Sprague, "Anna Murray Douglass—My Mother As I Recall Her," *Journal of Negro History* 8 (1923): 97.
39. McKivigan, *Correspondence*, 262–263; Maria Diedrich, *Love Across Color Lines: Ottilie Assing and Frederick Douglass* (New York: Hill & Wang, 1999), 181.
40. Hewitt, *Women's Activism and Social Change*, 150; Martin, *Mind of Frederick Douglass*, 40–41.
41. Quoted in Martin, *Mind of Frederick Douglass*, 41.
42. Ibid., 42–43.
43. Douglass to Porter, January 12, 1852, McKivigan, *Correspondence*, 512–513.
44. Martin, *Mind of Frederick Douglass*, 43–44; McKivigan, *Correspondence*, 262–263.
45. "The Rights of Women," *North Star*, July 28, 1848.
46. "Woman's Rights Convention," *North Star*, August 11, 1848.
47. "The Anti-Slavery Bugle," *North Star*, March 9, 1849.
48. John Blassingame et al. eds., *The Frederick Douglass Papers, Series Two: Autobiographical Writings, Volume 2, My Bondage and My Freedom* (New Haven, Conn.: Yale University Press, 2003), 228.

Chapter 6

1. Frederick Douglass, *Life and Times of Frederick Douglass* (1892; New York: Collier Books, 1962), 278–279.
2. John R. McKivigan et al., eds., *The Frederick Douglass Papers, Series Three: Correspondence, Volume 1, 1842–1852* (New Haven, Conn.: Yale University Press, 2009), 493.
3. Douglass, *Life and Times*, 281–282; William Parker, "The Freedman's Story," *Atlantic Monthly* 17 (March 1866): 281–288.
4. "The Syracuse Fugitive Case," *Frederick Douglass' Paper*, October 9, 1851; "Judge Conkling's Decision," *Frederick Douglass' Paper*, October 30, 1851; John Stauffer, *The Black Hearts of Men: Radical Abolitionists and the Transformation of Race* (Cambridge, Mass.: Harvard University Press, 2001), 174–175.
5. "The National Free Soil Convention," *Frederick Douglass' Paper*, August 20, 1852.
6. "The Annual Meeting of the American A.S. Society," *Liberator*, May 16, 1851.

7. "Change of Opinion Announced," *Liberator*, May 23, 1851.

8. Douglass to Charles Sumner, September 2, 1852, in *The Life and Writings of Frederick Douglass*, 5 vols., ed. Philip S. Foner (New York: International Publishers, 1950), 2: 210 (quotation); Waldo E. Martin, *The Mind of Frederick Douglass* (Chapel Hill: University of North Carolina Press, 1984), 45–47.

9. Henry Mayer, *All on Fire: William Lloyd Garrison and the Abolition of Slavery* (New York: St. Martin's Press, 1998), 428–429.

10. John R. McKivigan, "The Frederick Douglass—Gerrit Smith Friendship and Political Abolitionism in the 1850s," in *Frederick Douglass: New Literary and Historical Essays*, ed. Eric J. Sundquist (New York: Cambridge University Press, 1990), 214–216.

11. "To the Liberty Party," *Frederick Douglass' Paper*, May 20, 1852.

12. McKivigan, "Frederick Douglass—Gerrit Smith Friendship," 217–219. Congressional records show Smith as a member of the Free Soil Party, but this is probably a misconstruction, considering his staunch abolitionist stance.

13. Martin, *Mind of Frederick Douglass*, 47.

14. John Stauffer, ed., *The Works of James McCune Smith: Black Intellectual and Abolitionist* (New York: Oxford University Press, 2006), xiii–xv.

15. McCune Smith to Douglass, October 8, 1851, McKivigan, *Correspondence*, 490–491.

16. Douglass, *Life and Times*, 273.

17. John Blassingame et al, eds., *The Frederick Douglass Papers, Series One: Speeches, Debates, and Interviews*, 5 vols. (New Haven, Conn.: Yale University Press, 1982), 2: 371 (hereafter *FDP*).

18. John Blassingame et al, eds., *The Frederick Douglass Papers, Series Two: Autobiographical Writings, Volume 2: My Bondage and My Freedom* (New Haven, Conn.: Yale University Press, 2003), xiii–xvii, xxix, xxx–xxxi.

19. Maria Diedrich, *Love Across Color Lines: Ottilie Assing and Frederick Douglass* (New York: Hill & Wang, 1999), xvi–xvii.

20. Ibid., 184–185.

21. Rosetta Douglass Sprague, "Anna Murray Douglass—My Mother as I Recall Her," *Journal of Negro History* 8 (1923): 99 (quotations); Douglass, *Life and Times*, 266–267.

22. "Our Plan for Making Kansas a Free State," *Frederick Douglass' Paper*, September 15, 1854.

23. David W. Blight, *Frederick Douglass' Civil War: Keeping Faith in Jubilee* (Baton Rouge: Louisiana State University Press, 1989), 48–49.

24. "Great Anti-Slavery Convention," *Frederick Douglass' Paper*, July 6, 1855; Stauffer, *Black Hearts of Men*, 8–9; Blight, *Frederick Douglass' Civil War*, 50–51.

25. "John Brown of Ossawatomie, Kansas," *Frederick Douglass' Paper*, June 27, 1856; Stauffer, *Black Hearts of Men*, 196–197.

26. Quoted in McKivigan, "Frederick Douglass—Gerrit Smith Friendship," 221.

27. Martin, *Mind of Frederick Douglass*, 34–35.

28. Blassingame, *FDP*, 3: 167.

29. Ibid., 3: 170.

30. Douglass, *Life and Times*, 302–303, 275.

31. Ibid., 275.

32. Ibid., 309.

33. Ibid., 320.

34. Quoted in ibid., 311.

35. McKivigan, "Frederick Douglass—Gerrit Smith Friendship," 222.

36. Blight, *Frederick Douglass' Civil War*, 96–97.

37. Blassingame, *FDP*, 3: 312–322.

38. William S. McFeely, *Frederick Douglass* (New York: W.W. Norton, 1991), 207–208.

39. "To My British Anti-Slavery Friends," *Douglass' Monthly*, June 1860.

40. "The Chicago Nominations," *Douglass' Monthly*, June 1860.

41. McKivigan, "Frederick Douglass—Gerrit Smith Friendship," 223.
42. "Equal Suffrage Defeated," *Douglass' Monthly*, December 1860.
43. "The Late Election," *Douglass' Monthly*, December 1860.

CHAPTER 7

1. "The Inaugural Address," *Douglass' Monthly*, April 1861.
2. "A Trip to Hayti," *Douglass' Monthly*, May 1861.
3. Henry Mayer, *All On Fire: William Lloyd Garrison and the Abolition of Slavery* (New York: St. Martin's Press, 1998), 518–520.
4. Quoted in James Brewer Stewart, *Wendell Phillips: Liberty's Hero* (Baton Rouge: Louisiana State University Press, 1986), 220–221; David W. Blight, *Frederick Douglass' Civil War: Keeping Faith in Jubilee* (Baton Rouge: Louisiana State University Press, 1989), 81–82.
5. John Blassingame et al. eds., *The Frederick Douglass Papers, Series One: Speeches, Debates, and Interviews*, 5 vols. (New Haven, Conn.: Yale University Press, 1979–1991), 3: 435–442 (hereafter *FDP*).
6. "General Fremont's Proclamation," *Douglass' Monthly*, October 1861.
7. Blight, *Frederick Douglass' Civil War*, 85–86; Benjamin Quarles, *The Negro in the Civil War* (Boston: Little, Brown and Company, 1953), 69 (quotation).
8. Blassingame, *FDP*, 3: 478, 483.
9. "The Situation of the War," *Douglass' Monthly*, March 1862 (quotation); Frederick Douglass, *Life and Times of Frederick Douglass* (1892; New York: Collier Books, 1962), 335–337.
10. "Emancipation," *Douglass' Monthly*, October 1862.
11. *The War of the Rebellion: A Compilation of the Official Records of the Union and Confederate Armies* (Washington, D.C.: GPO, 1880–1901), ser. 3, 2: 281.
12. Edwin S. Redkey, "Brave Black Volunteers: A Profile of the Fifty-fourth Massachusetts Regiment," in *Hope and Glory: Essays on the Legacy of the 54th Massachusetts Regiment*, eds. Martin H. Blatt, Thomas J. Brown, and Donald Yacovone (Amherst: University of Massachusetts Press, 2001), 22–23; William S. McFeely, *Frederick Douglass* (New York: W.W. Norton, 1991), 217–225.
13. Douglass to Gerrit Smith, June 19, 1863, Gerrit Smith Papers, George Arents Research Library, Syracuse University, Syracuse, N.Y.
14. "The Mob in New York," *New York Times*, July 14, 1863.
15. "The 54th Massachusetts at Fort Wagner," *Douglass' Monthly*, August 1863.
16. *Douglass' Monthly*, July 1863.
17. Blight, *Frederick Douglass' Civil War*, 160–163.
18. James M. McPherson, *The Negro's Civil War* (New York: Pantheon Books, 1965), 173–175; Douglass to G.L. Stearns, *Douglass' Monthly*, August 1863.
19. "The Commander-in-Chief and His Black Soldiers," *Douglass' Monthly*, August 1863.
20. Blight, *Frederick Douglass' Civil War*, 166.
21. Douglass to G.L. Stearns, *Douglass' Monthly*, August 1863.
22. Douglass to George Luther Stearns, August 12, 1863, Abraham Barker Papers, Historical Society of Pennsylvania, Philadelphia; Stearns endorsement, August 13, 1863, Frederick Douglass Papers, Library of Congress, Washington, D.C. (hereafter DLC); Douglass, *Life and Times*, 347–350; James Oakes, *The Radical and the Republican: Frederick Douglass, Abraham Lincoln, and the Triumph of Antislavery Politics* (New York: W.W. Norton, 2007), 210–213; Blight, *Frederick Douglass' Civil War*, 167–169.
23. Quoted in Oakes, *Radical and Republican*, 212.
24. Douglass, *Life and Times*, 347.
25. Ibid., 347; Oakes, *Radical and Republican*, 212–213.
26. Douglass to Stearns, August 12, 1863.

27. Douglass, *Life and Times*, 348–349.
28. Douglass to Stearns, August 12, 1863.
29. Douglass, *Life and Times*, 350.
30. C.W. Foster to Douglass, August 13, 1863, DLC; J.P. Usher to whom it may concern, August 1863, Douglass Papers, DLC.
31. C.W. Foster to Douglass, August 21, 1863, DLC.
32. Blight, *Frederick Douglass' Civil War*, 171–172; McFeely, *Frederick Douglass*, 230–231.
33. Douglass to the *Anglo African*, July 27, 1863, in *Black Abolitionist Papers, 1830–1865*, eds. George E. Carter and C. Peter Ripley (Sanford, N.C.: Microfilming Corporation of America, 1981), reel 14: 986.
34. Blight, *Frederick Douglass' Civil War*, 172–173.
35. Julia Griffiths Crofts to Douglass, December 10, 1863, DLC.
36. Blassingame, *FDP*, 4: 3, 11–12.
37. Douglass to E. Gilbert, May 23, 1864, in *The Life and Writings of Frederick Douglass*, 5 vols., ed. Philip Foner (New York: International Publishers, 1952), 3: 403.
38. Nathan Irvin Huggins, *Slave and Citizen: The Life of Frederick Douglass* (Boston: Little, Brown and Company, 1980), 98–99; Blight, *Frederick Douglass' Civil War*, 182–183.
39. Douglass, *Life and Times*, 358–359; Blight, *Frederick Douglass' Civil War*, 183–184.
40. Douglass to Lincoln, August 29, 1864, in Foner, *Life and Writings*, 3: 405–406.
41. Oakes, *Radical and Republican*, 238–238.
42. Douglass to Tilton, October 15, 1864, in Foner, *Life and Writings*, 3: 424.
43. Douglass to Garrison, September 17, 1864, ibid., 3: 407.
44. Blight, *Frederick Douglass' Civil War*, 184–185.
45. Blassingame, *FDP*, 4: 31, 38.
46. McFeely, *Frederick Douglass*, 234–237, 248.
47. Douglass, *Life and Times*, 363.
48. Ibid., 363–366; Oakes, *Radical and Republican*, 241–243.
49. Blassingame, *FDP*, 4: 74–79.

CHAPTER 8

1. "Annual Meeting of the American A. S. Society," *Liberator*, May 12, 1865; James Brewer Stewart, *Wendell Phillips: Liberty's Hero* (Baton Rouge: Louisiana State University Press, 1986), 264.
2. "Thirty Second Anniversary of the American Anti-Slavery Society," *Liberator*, May 19, 1865.
3. Stewart, *Wendell Phillips*, 264–265.
4. John Blassingame, et al. eds., *The Frederick Douglass Papers, Series One: Speeches, Debates, and Interviews*, 5 vols. (New Haven, Conn.: Yale University Press, 1979–1991), 4: xv–xvi, 186 (quote 86) (hereafter *FDP*) ; Frederick Douglass, *Life and Times of Frederick Douglass* (1892; New York: Collier, 1962), 374–376.
5. Philip S. Foner, ed., *The Life and Writings of Frederick Douglass*, 5 vols. (New York: International Publishers, 1955), 4: 182–191 (quotes 85, 189); David Blight, *Frederick Douglass' Civil War: Keeping Faith in Jubilee* (Baton Rouge: Louisiana State University Press, 1989), 190–191.
6. Douglass to Josephine Sophie White Griffing, September 27, 1868, in Foner, *Life and Writings*, 4: 212–213; Nathan Irvin Huggins, *Slave and Citizen: The Life of Frederick Douglass* (Boston: Little, Brown and Company, 1980), 120–121.
7. Douglass, *Life and Times*, 387–389 (quote 389).
8. Blassingame, *FDP*, 4: 123–133 (quote 132).

9. Maria Diedrich, *Love Across Color Lines: Ottilie Assing and Frederick Douglass* (New York: Hill & Wang, 1999), 272–273.
10. Charles Douglass to Frederick Douglass, August 16, 1867, Frederick Douglas Papers, Library of Congress, Washington, D.C. (hereafter DLC).
11. Douglass to Theodore Tilton, September 1867, in Foner, *Life and Writings*, 4: 205–206; Blight, *Frederick Douglass' Civil War*, 196–197; Dickson J. Preston, *Young Frederick Douglass: The Maryland Years* (Baltimore: Johns Hopkins University Press, 1980), 175–177; Receipt, DLC.
12. William Slade to Douglass, July 29, August 18, 1867, DLC; Douglass to Slade, August 12, 1867, DLC; Charles Douglass to Douglass, August 22, September 21, 1867, DLC; William S. McFeely, *Frederick Douglass* (New York: W.W. Norton, 1991), 259–261.
13. Douglass to J. Sella Martin, April 5, 1869, in Foner, *Life and Writings*, 4: 213–14; Huggins, *Slave and Citizen*, 129.
14. Blight, *Frederick Douglass' Civil War*, 203.
15. Douglass to Hamilton Fish, April 3, 1871, DLC.
16. Douglass, *Life and Times*, 410–411; Blight, *Frederick Douglass' Civil War*, 210.
17. Douglass, *Life and Times*, 412.
18. "Letter from the Editor," June 13, 1872, in Foner, *Life and Writings*, 4: 294–296.
19. Quoted in McFeely, *Frederick Douglass*, 276.
20. Douglass to Gerrit Smith, August 15 and September 11, 1872, in Foner, *Life and Writings*, 4: 297.
21. Ronald M. Labbé and Jonathan Lurie, *The Slaughterhouse Cases: Regulation, Reconstruction, and the Fourteenth Amendment* (Lawrence: University Press of Kansas, 2004), esp. 164–178.
22. Blight, *Frederick Douglass' Civil War*, 210–213; Douglass, *Life and Times*, 416–417.
23. McFeely, *Frederick Douglass*, 280–285; Douglass to S.L. Harris, March 30, 1874, in Foner, *Life and Writings*, 4: 305.
24. Douglass, *Life and Times*, 400.
25. She was no relation to Nathan Sprague.
26. Blassingame, *FDP*, 4: 440–443 (quotation p. 442).
27. Hayes, quoted in Foner, *Life and Writings*, 4: 101.
28. *New York Age*, January 12, 1889.
29. Blight, *Frederick Douglass' Civil War*, 218.
30. Douglass, *Life and Times*, 426.
31. "Marshal Douglass' Lecture," *New York Times*, May 11, 1877; Douglass, *Life and Times*, 426–427.
32. Douglass, *Life and Times*, 440.
33. Ibid., 442; Blassingame, *FDP*, 4: 477–478.
34. McFeely, *Frederick Douglass*, 296–297.
35. Ibid., 297–298.
36. Douglass, *Life and Times*, 428.

CHAPTER 9

1. Nathan Irvin Huggins, *Slave and Citizen: The Life of Frederick Douglass* (Boston: Little, Brown and Company, 1980), 149. The provisions of the 1875 Act remained in the federal statutes, and would reemerge in the 1960s and 1970s as a tool for furthering civil rights.
2. Subject File, Recorder of Deeds, 1881–1886, Frederick Douglass Papers, Library of Congress, Washington, D.C. (hereafter DLC).
3. Frederick Douglass, *Life and Times of Frederick Douglass* (1892; New York: Collier Books, 1962), 475–478.

4. Ottilie Assing to Douglass, November 18, 1878, DLC.

5. Ibid. (quotations); William S. McFeely, *Frederick Douglass* (New York: W.W. Norton, 1991), 297–298; Maria Diedrich, *Love Across Color Lines: Ottilie Assing and Frederick Douglass* (New York: Hill & Wang, 1999), 327–330.

6. Sylvester M. Betts to Douglass, October 8, 1881, DLC.

7. John Blassingame et al., eds., *The Frederick Douglass Papers, Series One: Speeches, Debates, and Interviews*, 5 vols. (New Haven, Conn.: Yale University Press, 1979–1992), 4: 510 (hereafter *FDP*).

8. Frederick Douglass, "The Negro Exodus from the Gulf States," *Journal of Social Science* 11 (1880): 1–21; "Reasons For and Against the Negro Exodus," *New York Times*, September 13, 1879.

9. Douglass, *Life and Times*, 428.

10. Douglass to the Citizens of Easton, Maryland, June 22, 1867, DLC; Douglass, *Life and Times*, 451.

11. McFeely, *Frederick Douglass*, 312–313.

12. Quoted in Frederic May Holland, *Frederick Douglass: The Colored Orator* (New York: Funk & Wagnalls Company, 1891), 351.

13. Blassingame, *FDP*, 5: 80–84.

14. Ibid., 5: 110–112; Douglass, *Life and Times*, 541 (quote); Huggins, *Slave and Citizen*, 151–152.

15. Leigh Fought, "Douglass, Helen Pitts," Oxford African American Studies Center, http://www.oxfordaasc.com/article/opr/t0009/e0008 (accessed December 30, 2011).

16. Douglass, *Life and Times*, 534.

17. Fought, "Douglass, Helen Pitts."

18. Diedrich, *Love Across Color Lines*, 363–375 (quote p. 375); Kelly Boyer Sagert, "Assing, Ottilie," Oxford African American Studies Center, http://www.oxfordaasc.com/article/opr/t0009/e0002 (accessed December 31, 2011).

19. Douglass to Elizabeth Cady Stanton, May 30, 1884, in *The Life and Writings of Frederick Douglass*, 5 vols., ed. Philip Foner (New York: International Publishers, 1955), 4: 410–411.

20. Credit accounting, August 10, 1886, Recorder of Deeds, Subject File, 1881–1886, DLC.

21. Frederick Douglass Diary, September 13, 1886, Diaries, DLC.

22. Douglass, *Life and Times*, 586.

23. Diary, May 10, 1887, DLC; Douglass, *Life and Times*, 588–589.

24. McFeely, *Frederick Douglass*, 332–333.

25. Blassingame, *FDP*, 5: xxii, 278.

26. Ibid., 5: xxii–xxiii; Holland, *Frederick Douglass*, 365–367.

27. Blassingame, *FDP*, 5: 390.

28. "All Waiting on Chicago," *New York Times*, June 20, 1888.

29. "Duty of To-day," *New York Times*, October 23, 1888.

30. McFeely, *Frederick Douglass*, 335–334; Myra Himelhoch, "Frederick Douglass and Haiti's Môle St. Nicolas," *Journal of Negro History* 56 (1971): 164–165, 169–170; "Starting for Hayti," *New York Times*, August 26, 1889.

31. Himelhoch, "Frederick Douglass and Haiti's Môle St. Nicolas," 161–168.

32. Huggins, *Slave and Citizen*, 162–163.

33. "The Only Hope for Hayti," *New York Times*, October 24, 1889.

34. "Off on the Cruise To-day," *New York Times*, December 3, 1889.

35. Quoted in Himelhoch, "Frederick Douglass and Haiti's Môle St. Nicolas," 170.

36. Ibid., 173–174.

37. Ibid., 174.

38. Douglass to James G. Blaine, April 23, 1891, in *A Black Diplomat in Haiti: The Diplomatic Correspondence of U.S. Minister Frederick Douglass from Haiti, 1889–1891*, 2 vols., ed. Norma Brown (Salisbury, N.C.: Documentary Publications, 1977), 2: 106.

39. "Haiti's Broken Promise," *New York Times*, March 25, 1891.
40. Blassingame, *FDP*, 5: 458–458.
41. "The Only Hope for Hayti," *New York Times*, October 24, 1889; Huggins, *Slave and Citizen*, 166–167.
42. "Frederick Douglass," *Plaindealer*, February 10, 1893.
43. Huggins, *Slave and Citizen*, 168.
44. Ida B. Wells, ed., *The Reason Why the Colored American Is Not in the World's Columbian Exposition*, http://digital.library.upenn.edu/women/wells/exposition/exposition.html (accessed January 5, 2012); McFeely, *Frederick Douglass*, 366–367.
45. Blassingame, *FDP*, 5: 575–576.
46. Ibid., 607.
47. "Death of Fred Douglass," *New York Times*, February 21, 1895.
48. McFeely, *Frederick Douglass*, 381–383; "Death of Fred Douglass," *New York Times*, February 21, 1895.
49. James Oakes, *The Radical and the Republican: Frederick Douglass, Abraham Lincoln, and the Triumph of Antislavery Politics* (New York: W.W. Norton, 2007), 28–32.
50. Peter C. Myers, *Frederick Douglass: Race and the Rebirth of American Liberalism* (Lawrence: University Press of Kansas, 2008), 6–7.

BIBLIOGRAPHY

Primary Sources

Newspapers and Unpublished Sources

Abraham Barker Papers, Historical Society of Pennsylvania, Philadelphia, Penna.
Douglass' Monthly (Rochester, N.Y.).
Frederick Douglass' Paper (Rochester, N.Y.).
Frederick Douglass Papers, Library of Congress, Washington, D.C.
Gerrit Smith Papers, George Arents Research Library, Syracuse University, Syracuse, N.Y.
Liberator (Boston).
New York Times.
North Star (Rochester, N.Y.).
Plaindealer (Detroit).

Published Sources

Blassingame, John, et al., eds. *The Frederick Douglass Papers, Series One: Speeches, Debates, and Interviews.* 5 vols. New Haven, Conn.: Yale University Press, 1979–1991.

Blassingame, John, et al., eds. *The Frederick Douglass Papers, Series Two: Autobiographical Writings, Volume 2: My Bondage and My Freedom.* New Haven, Conn.: Yale University Press, 2003.

Brown, Norma, ed. *A Black Diplomat in Haiti: The Diplomatic Correspondence of U.S. Minister Frederick Douglass from Haiti, 1889–1891.* 2 vols. Salisbury, N.C.: Documentary Publications, 1977.

Carter, George E. and C. Peter Ripley, eds. *Black Abolitionist Papers, 1830–1865.* Sanford, N.C.: Microfilming Corporation of America, 1981.

Douglass, Frederick. *Life and Times of Frederick Douglass.* 1892; New York: Collier Books, 1962.
———. *Narrative of the Life of Frederick Douglass, An American Slave Written by Himself.* 1845; New Haven, Conn.: Yale University Press, 2001.
———. "The Negro Exodus from the Gulf States." *Journal of Social Science* 11 (1880): 1–21.

Foner, Philip, ed. *The Life and Writings of Frederick Douglass.* 5 vols. New York: International Publishers, 1950–1955.

Holland, Frederic May. *Frederick Douglass: The Colored Orator.* New York: Funk & Wagnalls Company, 1891.

McKivigan, John R., et al., eds. *The Frederick Douglass Papers, Series Three: Correspondence, Volume 1, 1842–1852.* New Haven, Conn.: Yale University Press, 2009.

Parker, William. "The Freedman's Story." *Atlantic Monthly* 17 (March 1866): 281–288.

Sprague, Rosetta Douglass. "Anna Murray Douglass—My Mother as I Recall Her." *Journal of Negro History* 8 (1923): 93–101.

Wells, Ida B., ed. *The Reason Why the Colored American Is Not in the World's Columbian Exposition,* http://digital.library.upenn.edu/women/wells/exposition/exposition.html. Accessed January 5, 2012.

SECONDARY SOURCES

Andrews, William L. "Frederick Douglass, Preacher." *American Literature* 54 (1982): 592–597.

Bell, Howard H. "National Negro Conventions of the Middle 1840's: Moral Suasion vs. Political Action." *Journal of Negro History* 42 (1957): 247–260.

Bell, Howard Holman, ed. *Minutes of the Proceedings of the National Negro Conventions, 1830–1864.* New York: Arno Press, 1969.

Blackett, R.J.M. *Building an Antislavery Wall: Black Americans in the Atlantic Movement, 1830–1860.* Baton Rouge: Louisiana State University Press, 1983.

Blight, David W. *Frederick Douglass' Civil War: Keeping Faith in Jubilee.* Baton Rouge: Louisiana State University Press, 1989.

Butterfield, Stephen. *Black Autobiography in America.* Amherst: University of Massachusetts Press, 1974.

Davis, Charles T. and Henry Louis Gates, Jr., eds. *The Slave's Narrative.* Oxford: Oxford University Press, 1985.

Diedrich, Maria. *Love Across Color Lines: Ottilie Assing and Frederick Douglass.* New York: Hill & Wang, 1999.

Grover, Kathryn. *The Fugitive's Gibraltar: Escaping Slaves and Abolitionism in New Bedford, Massachusetts.* Amherst, Mass.: University of Massachusetts Press, 2001.

Hewitt, Nancy A. *Women's Activism and Social Change: Rochester, New York, 1822–1872.* Ithaca, N.Y.: Cornell University Press, 1984.

Himelhoch, Myra. "Frederick Douglass and Haiti's Môle St. Nicolas." *Journal of Negro History* 56 (1971): 161–180.

Hodges, Graham Russell Gao. *David Ruggles: A Radical Black Abolitionist and the Underground Railroad in New York City.* Chapel Hill: University of North Carolina Press, 2010.

Horton, James Oliver and Lois E. Horton. *Black Bostonians: Family Life and Community Struggle in the Antebellum North.* New York: Holmes & Meier, 1979.

Huggins, Nathan Irvin. *Slave and Citizen: The Life of Frederick Douglass.* Boston: Little, Brown and Company, 1980.

Labbé, Ronald M. and Jonathan Lurie. *The Slaughterhouse Cases: Regulation, Reconstruction, and the Fourteenth Amendment.* Lawrence: University Press of Kansas, 2004.

Martin, Waldo E. *The Mind of Frederick Douglass.* Chapel Hill: University of North Carolina Press, 1984.

Matlack, James. "The Autobiographies of Frederick Douglass." *Phylon* 40 (1979): 15–28.

Mayer, Henry. *All on Fire: William Lloyd Garrison and the Abolition of Slavery.* New York: St. Martin's Press, 1998.

McFeely, William S. *Frederick Douglass.* New York: W.W. Norton, 1991.

———. "Visible Man: Frederick Douglass for the 1990s." In *Liberating Sojourn: Frederick Douglass and Transatlantic Reform.* Edited by Alan J. Rice and Martin Crawford. Athens: University of Georgia Press, 1999.

McKivigan, John R. "The Frederick Douglass—Gerrit Smith Friendship and Political Abolitionism in the 1850s." In *Frederick Douglass: New Literary and Historical Essays.* Edited by Eric J. Sundquist. New York: Cambridge University Press, 1990.

———. *The War against Proslavery Religion: Abolitionism and the Northern Churches, 1830–1865.* Ithaca, N.Y.: Cornell University Press, 1984.

——— and Heather L. Kaufman, eds. *In the Words of Frederick Douglass: Quotations from Liberty's Champion.* Ithaca, N.Y.: Cornell University Press, 2012.

McPherson, James M. *The Negro's Civil War.* New York: Pantheon Books, 1965.

Myers, Peter C. *Frederick Douglass: Race and the Rebirth of American Liberalism.* Lawrence: University Press of Kansas, 2008.

Oakes, James. *The Radical and the Republican: Frederick Douglass, Abraham Lincoln, and the Triumph of Antislavery Politics.* New York: W.W. Norton, 2007.

Obama, Barack. *The Audacity of Hope: Thoughts on Reclaiming the American Dream.* New York: Random House, 2006.

Pettinger, Alasdair, "Send Back the Money: Douglass and the Free Church of Scotland." In *Liberating Sojourn: Frederick Douglass and Transatlantic Reform.* Edited by Alan J. Rice and Martin Crawford. Athens: University of Georgia Press, 1999.

Preston, Dickson J. *Young Frederick Douglass: The Maryland Years.* Baltimore, Md.: Johns Hopkins University Press, 1980.

Quarles, Benjamin. *The Negro in the Civil War.* Boston: Little, Brown and Company, 1953.

Redkey, Edwin S. "Brave Black Volunteers: A Profile of the Fifty-fourth Massachusetts Regiment." In *Hope and Glory: Essays on the Legacy of the 54th Massachusetts Regiment.* Edited by Martin H. Blatt, Thomas J. Brown, and Donald Yacavone. Amherst: University of Massachusetts Press, 2001.

Rice, Alan J. and Martin Crawford, "Triumphant Exile: Frederick Douglass in Britain, 1845–1847." In *Liberating Sojourn: Frederick Douglass and Transatlantic Reform.* Edited by Alan J. Rice and Martin Crawford. Athens: University of Georgia Press, 1999.

Rice, C. Duncan. *The Scots Abolitionists, 1833–1861.* Baton Rouge: Louisiana State University Press, 1981.

Schor, Joel. "The Rivalry Between Frederick Douglass and Henry Highland Garnet." *Journal of Negro History* 64 (1979): 30–38.

Smock, Raymond W. *Booker T. Washington: Black Leadership in the Age of Jim Crow.* Chicago: Ivan R. Dee, 2009.

Stauffer, John. *The Black Hearts of Men: Radical Abolitionists and the Transformation of Race.* Cambridge, Mass.: Harvard University Press, 2001.

———, ed. *The Works of James McCune Smith: Black Intellectual and Abolitionist.* New York: Oxford University Press, 2006.

Stephens, Gregory. *On Racial Frontiers: The New Culture of Frederick Douglass, Ralph Ellison, and Bob Marley.* Cambridge: Cambridge University Press, 1999.

Stewart, James Brewer. *Wendell Phillips: Liberty's Hero.* Baton Rouge: Louisiana State University Press, 1986.

Yacavone, Donald. *Samuel Joseph May and the Dilemmas of the Liberal Persuasion, 1797–1871.* Philadelphia: Temple University Press, 1991.

INDEX